A Useable Past

~~~

Volume 1: Victorian Agitator,
George Jacob Holyoake (1817–1906):
Co-operation as 'This New Order of Life'

A Useable Past

A History of Association, Co-operation, and un-Statist
Socialism in 19th and early 20th century Britain.
In 3 volumes.

Volume 1: Victorian Agitator, George Jacob Holyoake (1817–1906): Co-operation as 'This New Order of Life'

Stephen Yeo

*Principal of Ruskin College, Oxford, 1989–97;
Chair of the Co-operative College and then the
Co-operative Heritage Trust, 1999–2015*

EER
EER Edward Everett Root, Publishers, Brighton, 2025

EER
Edward Everett Root, Publishers, Co. Ltd.
3rd Floor, 15 West Street, Brighton, Sussex, BN1 2RE, England

www.eerpublishing.com
edwardeverettroot@yahoo.co.uk

First published in Great Britain in 2017

© Stephen Yeo, 2017

This edition © Edward Everett Root Publishers 2025

ISBN 9781915115706 paperback
ISBN 9781911204572 hardback
ISBN 9871911204824 eBook

Stephen Yeo has asserted his right to be identified as the author of this Work in accordance with the Copyright, Designs and Patents Act 1988 as the owner of this Work.

All rights reserved. No part of this publication may be reproduced, stored in a retrieval system or transmitted in any form or by any means, electronic, mechanical, photocopying, recording or otherwise, without the prior permission of the copyright owner.

Design and typesetting by Pageset Ltd, High Wycombe, Buckinghamshire

The three volumes in this set are

Volume 1. *Victorian Agitator, George Jacob Holyoake (1817–1906): Co-operation as 'This New Order of Life'*

Volume 2. *A New Life, The Religion of Socialism in Britain 1883–1896: Alternatives to State Socialism*

Volume 3. *Class Conflict and Co-operation in 19th and 20th Century Britain. Education for Association: re-membering for a new moral world*

*For the trustees of the
Co-operative Heritage Trust, 2007–*

*and to celebrate Ian MacPherson 1939–2013,
and Andy Durr 1944–2014*

"Co-operation, as it is presented in these pages, is an attempt made by men (sic) profoundly convinced of the eternal reality of moral truth, to embody the high ideal of duty in institutions applying to the daily events of our ordinary lives." – Thomas Hughes and Edward Vansittart Neale, *Foundations: a study in the Ethics and Economics of the Co-operative Movement*, prepared at the request of the Co-operative Congress held at Gloucester in April 1879, revised in 1915 by A. Stoddart and W. Clayton (Manchester: The Co-operative Union, 1915), p.87.

"What extended comparative study of the varying characteristics of communities that embody networks of giving and receiving may teach us is how better to identify what relationships of the relevant kinds of giving and receiving already exist in our own local community and how perhaps to a greater extent than we have realised there is already a degree of shared recognition of the common good. About such communities we will need to bear in mind (that)… even when they are at their best, the exercise of shared deliberative rationality is always imperfect and what should impress us is not so much the mistakes made and the limitations upon its exercise at any particular stage as the ability through time and conflict to correct those mistakes and to move beyond those limitations. The exercise of practical relationships in communities always has a history and it is the direction of that history that is important." – Alasdair MacIntyre, *Dependent Rational Animals: Why Human Beings Need the Virtues* (1999) (London: Duckworth, 2009 edition), p.144.

"Co-operators should meet in stores or communities men of every sect, without hostility or dislike – since particular faiths are to be honoured as far as they make men into brethren, and are to be accepted by all who deem them true; while their special varieties are to be equally regarded as arising in geographical or chronological accidents, and not to be ascribed to sin.... Co-operators will never remain leal and true to their society unless a foundation which never gives way is laid in the understanding". G.J. Holyoake, *The History of Co-operation* (London: T. Fisher Unwin, 1908), pp.402–3.

"The breakthrough of the new political economy of the free market was also the breakdown of the old moral economy of provision. After the (Napoleonic) wars all that was left of it was charity – and Speenhamland. The moral economy of the crowd took longer to die: it is picked up by the early co-operative flour mills, by some Owenite socialists, and it lingered on for years somewhere in the bowels of the Co-operative Wholesale Society" – E.P. Thompson: 'The moral economy of the English crowd in the eighteenth century', in Customs in Common (London: Penguin books, 1993), p.258; originally in *Past and Present*, no. 50, 1971.

"Going to a distant town to mitigate some calamity there, will illustrate the principle of action prescribed by Secularism. One man will go on this errand from pure sympathy with the unfortunate; this is goodness. Another goes because his priest bids him; this is obedience. Another goes because the twenty-fifth chapter of Matthew tells him that all such persons will pass to the right hand of the Father; this is calculation. Another goes because he believes God commands him; this is piety. Another goes because he believes that the neglect of suffering will not answer; this is utilitarianism. But another goes on the errand of mercy, because it is an errand of mercy, because it is an immediate service to humanity; and he goes with a view to attempt material amelioration rather than spiritual consolation; this is Secularism, which teaches that goodness is sanctity, that Nature is guidance, that reason is authority, that service is duty, that Materialism is help". – G.J. Holyoake, *The Trial of Theism* (London: Holyoake and Co., 1858), p.175.

'It would be foolish... to underestimate the long and tenacious revolutionary tradition of the British commoner... It has expressed itself most naturally in the language of moral revolt'. – E. P. Thompson, 'Revolution', in *Out of Apathy* (London, Stevens and Sons, 1960), p.308.

Contents

Preface and Acknowledgements   1

PRELIMINARIES   7
Questions
Intentions
The run of the argument and its sources

Part I LIFE AND LEADING IDEAS   21
Work and family
Movements
'Publishing for Pioneers'
'Ideas are like seeds'
Character, Scale and Power
Sweet courtesy and consideration
Minds open to opposites
'…the working people want to do the same'

Part II A USEABLE PAST?   73
Introduction

IIa. An associational-socialist alternative to the Marxist revolutionary tradition of c.1848 to c.1959   80
A peaceful path?
Not only the political but also the social
A state within the state

IIb. Towards an autonomous, ethical or moral 'tradition'   105
'Tradition'
Traditions: some signs and symptoms

Language and contested meanings
Ways of telling
Codification, or cataloguing the virtues
Principles of organisation as the – contested – embodiment of values and beliefs

IIc. A religion of co-operation? 157
'Religion'
Co-operation, religion and Holyoake
Final questions

SELECT BIBLIOGRAPHY AND
INFORMATION FOR FURTHER WORK 187

Notes and references 201

Index 241

Illustrations

Inge Street in 1817, from E.O. Greening, *The Story of the Life of George Jacob Holyoake* (1917) 6

Holyoake, from National Co-operative Archive 14

A Tale of Millions, The present position of the Co-operative Wholesale Society, from the 37th *Annual Co-operative Congress Report*, Paisley 1905 43

Holyoake at Robert Owen's Memorial Newtown, 1902, from NCA 50

Holyoake House, Hanover St, Manchester, from E.O Greening, *The Story of the life of George Jacob Holyoake* (1917)	53
Plaque on Holyoake House, 1911, from NCA	56
Map of the City of Leeds and District from Holyoake's *Jubilee History of the Leeds Industrial Co-operative Society* (1897)	91
Self-Help Boots and Shoes, from the 37th *Annual Co-operative Congress Report*, Paisley 1905	97
Holyoake shoes, courtesy of the Co-operative Group archive, n.d.	98
Central Stores, Toad Lane, 1868, from Holyoake's *History of the Rochdale Pioneers*	102
A CWS postcard from the NCA (found by Mervyn Wilson)	112
The Doffers appear on the opening day of the Original Toad Lane Store in Rochdale, a drawing from Holyoake's *History of Co-operation*	121

Preface and Acknowledgements

It's very simple. I would not and could not have written this book without the people and the movements it has been written from and for. Not only for them, of course, because the history – the useable past and the present practice – of co-operation and co-operatives are of urgent contemporary relevance for twenty-first century society, politics and economics more generally. Co-operatives have been exceptionally close to the wider working-class movement in Britain. At least as much as the members of other types of labour and community movement, co-operators still identify themselves as a, or even as *the* social movement.

It was at a conference on 'Mainstreaming Co-operation' organized by Linda Shaw, Rachel Vorberg-Rugh and Tony Webster on behalf of the Co-operative College in 2012 – the United Nations Year of Co-operatives – that I began to think again about the nature of the mainstream we might be talking about. Co-operatives as successful businesses, yes; co-operation as constituting an 'economic', small p 'political' mainstream able to take the capital letter away from orthodox Party Politics, yes; but also co-operation as an ethic, a morality, able (perhaps) to redefine what a 'religious' mode of existence might mean. What did Co-operators – particularly in what George Jacob Holyoake called their 'pioneer', 'enthusiastic' and 'constructive' periods – mean by words they used so much: 'social', 'association' and 'associational'? Were they (are they still?) not only 'alternative' but also 'oppositional' in their nature, in a whole-society sense, with the potential to replace the powers that be: 'a state within the state'?

So I went back to Holyoake (1817–1906), a Birmingham-born radical, co-operator and secularist who was better known nationally and internationally in his own time than he is now, although he is still revered by mainstream co-operators. I had found his copious writings attractive while my first Doctoral student at Sussex, Robin Thornes, was working on the early history of co-operatives in Britain, and while Eileen Janes Yeo engaged with Holyoake, among other thinkers, during her work on the social history of Owenism which led to *The Contest for Social Science in Britain: Relations and Representations of Gender and Class in the Nineteenth and Twentieth Centuries* (London: Rivers Oram Press, 1996). A subsequent Doctoral student, Peter Gurney, also wrote in an innovative way about Holyoake in the collection of essays Sussex students and faculty presented to J.F.C Harrison in 1988, *New Views of Co-operation* (London: Routledge, 1988, and Routledge Revivals, 2016).

Many of Holyoake's papers are in the National Co-operative Archive (NCA) in Holyoake House in the middle of the Co-operative quarter in Manchester. This archive is a rich resource. Thanks to Holyoake it contains Robert Owen's correspondence. The papers of Edward Owen Greening are also there, alongside rich records pertaining to the Co-operative Wholesale Society (now the Co-operative Group) and the records of many other Societies and individual Co-operators. Holyoake House is also the home of the Co-operative

College, Co-ops UK (the apex body and trade association of the movement in Britain) and of the Co-operative Press (the publisher of *Co-operative News*, still going strong after almost one hundred and fifty years).

It is an understatement to say that Gillian Lonergan has helped me. As the head Librarian and Archivist of the NCA for many years, she has helped generations of Co-operators and Co-operative Societies with their day-to-day business, as well as with their historical enquiries. Gillian is more than a keeper of co-operative history – a resource that the movement needs more than ever. With Sophie Stewart she also discovers things nobody knows are there and selflessly produces, distributes and exchanges them with every enquirer. I am also very grateful for the expert index she made for this book, as a member of the Society of Indexers. Mervyn Wilson, the Principal of the Co-operative College from 1999 to 2015, has been my friend and ally for many years, before, during and after his time at the College. He recently retired after forty years work in the movement.

I worked with the College in a variety of roles as soon as I left Ruskin College in 1997. Co-operative History Workshops flourished during the 1980s. Then came teaching and learning for the International Co-operative Alliance's 1995 *Statement of Co-operative Identity, Values and Principles*, led from the top by Graham Melmoth, Chief Executive of the CWS as it became the Co-operative Group. We moved the College back to its roots in Manchester. Then we developed the Pioneers' Museum in Rochdale with the generous help of the Heritage Lottery Fund and the Co-operative Group, making these twenty years energizing for me, but also highly educational. I found that I needed to learn how a prophet like Holyoake thought and wrote, and why Co-operators at home and abroad valued him so much. What was it that he had which might still be needed? The Trustees of the Co-operative Heritage Trust which Mervyn and I catalyzed into being in 2007 and which I chaired until 2015, have all helped me in ways they know about, as well as in some they will not. Without the Archive in Holyoake House and the Pioneers' Museum in Rochdale everyone's work on the useable past of the movement would be much less enjoyable as well as more difficult, for parties of local school-children as well as for international co-operators and students visiting a mecca for the movement.

    Robin Murray, Pat Connaty, Andrew Bibby, Rob Colls, Gill Scott, Nick Matthews, Ed Mayo, Peter Couchman, Peter Gurney, Alun Burge, Tom Woodin, Gregory Claeys, Paddy Maguire, Timothy Ashplant, Graham Melmoth and Maurice Glasman (I apologise to anyone I have inadvertently left out) all took the trouble to read, relate to and criticize my text as it developed. Ursula Howard read drafts too many times to remember, with all her patient skill. John Spiers, founder (last year) of Edward Everett Root Publishers and long before that of the legendary Harvester Press, was my first tutorial student at Sussex University in 1967. The tutorial was on R. H. Tawney's *Religion and the Rise of Capitalism*, a text in Sussex's Introduction to History course. John's Weberian *Geist* – as in the spirit of capitalism – has enabled many hard-to-find texts and many diffident folk to make public what it is they have within them to say. Sussex was a wonderful university to work in while I was there from 1966 to 1989. Thank you to all friends and colleagues there, at Ruskin College during the following decade, and students and staff, past and present at the Co-op. College.

October 1st 2016

INGE STREET IN 1817.
(A restoration, partly conjectural, but chiefly from authentic sources.)
No. 1 (Holyoake's birthplace) is seen on the left. "At No. 2 (next door) Mrs. Massey lived . . . . who sold cakes and tarts, which lay enticingly in a low, broad bow-window."

Holyoake's birthplace, 'partly conjectural'

Preliminaries

[i] Questions.

George Jacob Holyoake was born at number 1 Inge Street, Birmingham in 1817, the second child and eldest son of a whitesmith and a horn button dealer, who had twelve other children. He was educated near his home, at a Dame School and at Carr's Lane, Wesleyan Sunday School where there was a 'sand class', at which writing was taught by tracing figures in the sand.[1]

Until he was seven or eight Holyoake worked at button-making in his mother's workshop until, attracted by the brightness of a neighbouring tinsmith's shop, he tried piecework, soldering on the handles of lanterns. He burnt his fingers, while earning up to 3/6d a week.[2] By the time he was seventeen, George Jacob 'had perceived that the problem of the age was the position of labour.'[3] He spent the rest of his long life following this commitment through in entrepreneurial as well as empirical ways: it was Holyoake, for example, who suggested that the British Diplomatic and Consular service should collect foreign Labour statistics and that the Government should publish their reports. 'Until then we had no official knowledge of the working classes of other countries'.⁴ At nineteen he began going to classes in rhetoric, grammar, geometry and trigonometry at Birmingham Mechanics' Institute. He grew up to become a prolific writer, speaker and social *animateur* on behalf of his class 'confessing to a certain wilfulness of opinion which might perplex and perturb his readers'. Holyoake died in 1906 at Eastern Lodge overlooking the sea in Brighton: by then he was known as the 'Grand Old Man of Co-operation', a title which deliberately echoed Gladstone's sobriquet: the G O M of the British political scene.⁵

My main question in this book is: could Holyoake's life and work help co-operative and associated movements to move forward in the modern world? Late in life, writing for co-operators in Derby, Holyoake wrote that 'with or without "signs and portents" heralding this new order of life, it is appearing.' In January 1906, shortly before he died, he observed 'the growth and trend', through his chosen movement, of nothing less than 'a new Order of Labour.' ⁶ In 2017 such hopefulness is in shorter supply. But could this idiosyncratic agitator, journalist and moralist be a resource for a journey of hope among today's co-operators or – to use a word not used by Holyoake – for 'co-operativism'?⁷

Throughout his life Holyoake wanted to make the co-operative movement more complete internally, as 'a state within the state'. But he also wanted to give the movement more of what he called an 'outside': not only one way of doing business co-existing with others, but also an entire outlook on the world, a distinct morality or ethic, 'a moral art as well as a new form of economy'.⁸ 'It is not the few who make the many, but the many who make the few… The Author has honour alone for those who have an *outside* nature, and this record is mainly of movements and men having this aim or passion.'⁹

Such passion survives today among active members of co-operatives. But, as it did in Holyoake's time, it extends well beyond a singular movement. In a recent paper written for Co-ops UK, the federal organisation which brings co-operatives and mutuals in Britain together (formerly known as the Co-operative Union), 'open co-operativism' is stated as the aim, leading to a worldwide 'solidarity economy'.[10] Synergy between a range of local (in the positive sense of *located*) movements and Societies, all with a common objective, remains an active project at a time when capitalist forms of market and state threaten to pull the roof of the world down on everyone's heads even more obviously than they did when they went to war not long after the end of Holyoake's life.[11]

> 'We are attempting to find the common ground and the overarching principles and practices that might unite the global movement for a moral and sustainable economy... We are promoting a new cooperativism that is linked to the growing demand for a social and economic morality that places the common good above private profit and situates our economic future in relation to the environmental requisites of a truly humane and sustainable culture. Hence the growing need for an explicit convergence between co-operativism, commons and sustainability'.[12]

Holyoake followed his 'many making the few' with another characteristic maxim – arguing within and tilting against other-wordly religion as he always did – 'those who by their own choice stand apart from humanity will have no claim to rise again in another world having been of no use to any one in this.'[13] Could his work help to give the modern co-operative movement a more powerful presence in the world, working with allies who share co-operators' objections to the adulteration of peaceful co-existence, the commons and the climate?

[ii] Intentions.

I began to think about Holyoake again during 2012, while celebrating the United Nations Year of Co-operatives in Manchester and Rochdale. Wishing to rise to the occasion of a UN Year in which Rochdale was declared the World Capital of Co-operation, I remembered his ambitious way of putting things: co-operation as 'this new order of life'. I was enjoying his notoriously untidy, 682-page *History of Co-operation* which he began writing in 1873 and of which a 'revised and completed' edition was published in 1908, when I realised that this book, like many of his others, is as much a series of essays in social ethics or morality – full of parable and fable – as it is a conventional history. As such, it is as useful for changing the future as for understanding the past. When it was sent to him as a present, Gladstone's response to the book was to invite Holyoake to breakfast. Like his associate Guiseppe Mazzini (1805–1872), who lived in exile in England for many years, Holyoake saw history as a body of knowledge facing forwards rather than backwards – or, as a recent President of the International Co-operative Alliance put it, history as 'a memory of the future'.[14] Read as evidence for what Holyoake thought *could* and should happen, as much as for what *had* happened, the *History* remains as entertaining as George Eliot found it while George Henry Lewes read it aloud to her during August 1875, 'every evening, much to our pleasure and profit. The light, firm touch and quiet epigrams would make the dullest subject readable; and this subject is <u>not</u> dull'.[15]

Charles Goss, the first Librarian of the Bishopsgate Institute and Holyoake's devoted bibliographer, also appreciated the *History*:

> 'the work supplies facts and expounds principles in a very pleasant manner, with constant touches of graphic description, of quiet, quaint humour, and of good-natured gentle satire, the whole being written with an easy gracefulness sometimes strictly narrative, sometimes biographical, sometimes sketchy, occasionally introducing touches of autobiography which give a pleasant sparkle and colour to its pages'.[16]

Holyoake makes reading a pleasure by his playful use of metaphor. J.T.W. Mitchell's face was 'as radiant as a jubilee'. Alexander Campbell's voice 'sounded like a truce'. There was a Leeds activist 'whose sonorous voice is itself an argument'.[17] One opponent came across in debate as a 'moral rhinoceros'. As for Prime Minister Palmerston, 'he became great simply by living long and keeping his eyes open'... 'His face was wrinkled with treaties. If pricked he would have bled despatches'.[18] It is easy to imagine the smiles on co-operators' faces when they remembered aphorisms like this:

> 'The middleman... is like the Australian rabbit, very well for cooking purposes; but when he multiplies, and is everywhere eating up every green thing growing in the fields of profit, he becomes a pest.' [19]

Or this:

> 'Many think that a government of the wise would be a good thing, but such government has this disadvantage – it prevents anyone else being wise'.[20]

At its best, Holyoake's writing style recalls Charles Dickens: sometimes epigrammatic, sometimes convoluted, and always full of wit, story, and memorable turns of phrase.[21] Soon after he died, J.C Gray of the Co-operative Union and Hebden Bridge Fustian Manufacturing Co-operative Society said of Holyoake that 'his command of the finest and choicest language made him the idol of us all'…. 'He has been one to make our movement known to all the world'.[22]

So I resolved to revisit Holyoake. I decided to be unafraid of the first person singular, not to shun his discursive way with words and sometimes wayward way with facts, and not to hide my own preoccupations. Holyoake is unusual. He was more than a spectator in two generative periods for radicalisms and socialisms in Britain – the 1830s to 1840s and the 1880s to 1890s. Seen in that way, he offers a prophetic critique of twentieth-century socialisms, as well as a contribution to defining a 'moral force' politics of the Left which, with his help, we might develop as 'associationism'.[23] 'Is it not true to say', asked T.W Mercer in 1920, 'that whereas members of the Labour Party are collectivists, co-operators are associationists?'[24] Towards the end of his life Holyoake described the 'lofty faith of co-operators' quite simply as 'wise association'. 'We propose progressive improvement, association, transformation of the corrupted medium in which we are now living.' [25] 'By good sense and wise association', 'society' could create 'that condition of social life in which it should be impossible for a man to be deprived or poor'.[26] 'Creating circumstances' was Holyoake's way of handling Owenite determinism, misunderstood (Holyoake thought) partly because of Owen's famous statement: 'man's character is formed for him and not by him'. For Holyoake this meant that, 'as a subject for judgement, man was regarded as the creature of anterior circumstances which gave him at birth his peculiar faculties, and those which subsequently surrounded him. But as a member of society man was an acting power, which every circumstance of reason, morality, art, order, and material influence instructed'.[27]

'it was the knowledge given to co-operators of the human burden of inherited capacity that imparted to them that great strength of patience and charity of judgement which enabled their societies to endure, while the retaliating and fiercer political and religious parties around them fought themselves out...Those who learn this know no more haste or apathy, foolish hatred or foolish despair.'[28]

On the penultimate page of his *History of the Rochdale Pioneers*, Holyoake quoted from a speech he made in Rochdale in 1892. The co-operative movement, he said, 'is intended to do what Mazzini told the Italian workmen co-operation could do -"Unite Capital and Labour in the same hands"... The remedy, is the association of labour'.[29]

Alongside his elevated earnestness, there was something stylish, Bohemian - even impish - about Holyoake. It is visible in his portraits. He liked to make himself hard to pin down, and he remains so. Joseph McCabe, author of the two-volume, Holyoake *Life and Letters*- seen by historians as unreliable because of McCabe's partisan take on the history of his own (and therefore Holyoake's) times - acknowledged the flexibility of his subject. On the one hand Holyoake was on 'the extreme left wing of the Liberal Party... for his far-reaching ideas of social reform'. On the other hand he was not quite one of us in Reform League circles, because of his leaning towards present compromise in the interest of

Holyoake: a studio portrait

ultimate advance and because of his advocacy, for example, of an intelligence franchise. But he was also critical of the League's 'virtual exclusion of women from the franchise'. McCabe's defence was that Holyoake's 'was the flexibility of principle: theirs the inflexibility of phrase'.[30] On the one hand he reassured his readers that Co-operators did not threaten existing property holders. However unjust their entitlements to property might be, there would be no all-at-once 'recasting of society'. 'If we undertook to settle all property on foundations of justice', he wrote in 1890, 'co-operation would be postponed to the next century'. On the other hand Co-operators worked to 'supersede competition'. Unquestionably 'reformist' in terms of socialist debates during the Second International period, the Co-operator 'has the encouragement of the Italian proverb that he who goes slowly goes far – providing he keeps moving'.[31]

In *Sixty Years of an Agitator's Life,* one of his two autobiographies, Holyoake quipped in a characteristically arch, self-deprecating way – seeking attention while also turning away from it:

> 'I admired Robespierre – not on account of principles ascribed to him, but because he used one sized paper, and wrote out himself all his speeches in a large and careful hand. No one can do that without detecting verbiage, irrelevance, and limpness of expression. But though I knew the plan to be good, I have never had time to follow it'.[32]

'A page of laughter', Holyoake wrote, 'is a better defence against a worthless adversary than a volume of anger'.[33] His studied irreverence – a kind of personal Jacobinism – has meant that he has not been celebrated as a weighty prophet within the co-operative movement, in the way that his mentor

Robert Owen (1771 - 1858) still is, or in the way that his French and German contemporaries Jean-Baptiste Godin (1817–1888) and Friedrich Wilhem Raiffeisen (1818–1888) are. Or, for that matter, in the way that the twentieth-century prophet of the Mondragon complex in Spain, Jose Maria Arizmendiarrieta (1915–1976), is today. 'I never set up as a chief. I never talked of loyalty to me, but of loyalty to principle alone'.[34] A modern 'Life and Times' is overdue, for which this book will, I hope, serve as a provocation.[35]

[iii] The run of the argument and its sources.

Starting life as a long essay, this book is divided into Parts I and II rather than into chapters.[36] There are subheadings in each Part, designed to allow the reader to breathe. In the course of the work I talked with many people who recognised Holyoake's name, but wondered whether he remains of more than scholarly interest. So in Part I (pages 21–72) I outline his LIFE AND LEADING IDEAS. Beginning with his *work and family* (p.21), I go on to the *movements* Holyoake joined (p.24), to his *publications* (p.28) and then to a phrase he used: *'ideas are like seeds'* (p.34). *'Character'* and *'power'* were also words he thought about a lot (p.37), as was what his friend E.O. Greening called Holyoake's *'sweet courtesy and consideration'* (p.48). He was also committed to *'minds open to opposites'* (p.59). Part I ends with a key phrase of Holyoake's, used in his lengthy correspondence with Gladstone, *'the working people want to do the same'* (p.67). This phrase is key because it unlocks more late nineteenth-century working-class radicalism than that of Holyoake. It was when working people had organized themselves – into large-scale, successful co-operatives, friendly societies, trade unions, clubs, building societies and educational associations which started to do better (for themselves) than capitalist (or state) retailers, insurers, employers, brewers, housing-loan providers and educators – that serious and seemingly-innocent counter-attacks began to be mounted against them. Whatever kind of a 'system' might emerge if 'working people' were allowed 'to do the same' as their masters?

Part II, A USEABLE PAST? (pages 73–185) is more tentative. I offer three possible ways to carry forward Holyoake's legacy. Co-operators, in particular, may find my suggestions here otiose – having, perhaps, no inclination to move in any of the directions suggested. But I hope to interest readers less dedicated to the co-operative movement than Holyoake, but who share his commitment to cognate radicalisms on behalf of the commons.

The subheadings in this part move from an *Introduction* to all of my suggestions (p.73), to an examinatiSon of each of them in turn. I call the first, *An associational-socialist alternative to the Marxist revolutionary tradition* (Part IIa p.80). This starts with *a peaceful path to social reform* (p.80), continues with *not only the social but also the political* (p. 86) and ends with *a state within a state* (p.99).

The title of my second suggestion (IIb) is *Towards an autonomous, ethical or moral 'tradition'* (p.105) This begins with a consideration of *traditions in general* (p.105) and continues with *some signs and symptoms* of a tradition in the particular sense of the word used here (p.113). The first of these signs and symptoms is headed *Language and contested meanings* (p.114); the second is *Ways of telling* (p.119); the third is *Codification, or cataloguing the virtues* (p.129), and the final sign or symptom of a 'tradition' in my sense is *Principles of organisation as the – contested – embodiment of values and beliefs* (p. 140).

I call the third suggestion *'a religion of co-operation'* (p.157). This starts with a consideration of the category *'religion'* (p.157) continues with *Co-operation, religion and Holyoake* (p.162) and ends with some *Final questions* (p.183).

Although I refer to Holyoake's speeches and articles, the book concentrates throughout on his finished books. These have been put down as 'readable but unreliable', in the same way that many historians have placed Holyoake as a man from the working class only interested in 'respectability'.[37] From the Left, Holyoake's liberalism has been seen as disappointingly tied to Liberal Party and other personages, including aristocrats and clerics belonging to the establishment.

Individual chapters in Holyoake's books often appeared first in the press, giving them the direct address of good journalism. Writing day by day and on the front line between co-operators' and secularists' beliefs and those of their patrons and enemies, Holyoake chose ways of expressing himself which were more decorative than utilitarian. Using his autobiographical and historical work as I have – rather than going through his periodical articles [38] – I have been more open to a collective *persona* he strove to project – for 'Labour', 'the people', 'the common people', 'the English character', etc.[39] – than to what he did in any single year or decade. I take comfort from a contemporary admirer's view that 'it is quite futile to attempt a full interpretation of the whole of Mr Holyoake's writings'. Among his 'giant contemporaries... few if any wrote so many separate books or pamphlets on such a variety of subjects'.[40]

I quote Holyoake at length throughout because he is one of the most compelling stylists and story-tellers the co-operative movement has produced. An anthology of his best writing would still be enjoyable as well as useful. To any social movement or embryonic tradition trying to put down roots, stories provide good compost, as do the commemorative objects which many co-operators still collect.[41] 'The story-teller' has had a generative function in the history of human culture, as Walter Benjamin knew, particularly when art is seen as 'an extension of our capacity for organisation' and when it is acknowledged that 'there are, essentially, no "ordinary" activities, if by "ordinary" we mean the absence of creative interpretation and effort'.[42]

I want to give enough space to the pitch and tone of co-operative radicalism to persuade modern readers that liberalism in Britain included much that in other places mostly waited for Marxism: this is one of these nations' peculiarities. Could liberalism be so capacious again? [43] J.M. Baernreither, a liberal and member of the Austrian parliament who visited and wrote about Britain in the 1880s, marvelled at the associational culture which was giving British society what he thought was a new and 'decisive stamp' during that time.[44] Seriously-radical, 'new' or *social* liberalism is unfamiliar in the twenty-first century, now that 'individualism' – the target of 'socialism' in Britain before 'capitalism' was described as such– has infected liberalism, along with negative ('freedom from') ideas of liberty, 'neo' liberalism and conservatism.

{ 1 }

Life and leading ideas

[i] Work and family.

'In those days', Holyoake wrote of his childhood, 'horn buttons were made in Birmingham'. It was the manner of their making in his mother's domestic workshop which stayed with him:

> 'My mother had a workshop attached to the house, in which she conducted a business herself, employing several hands. She had the business before her marriage. She received the orders; made the purchase of materials; superintended the making of the goods; made out the accounts; and received the money; besides taking care of her family'.[45]

Catherine Groves (1792–1867) 'a Puritan-minded woman', married George Holyoake (1790–1853), a man 'with an honest voice and an expression which told you he could be trusted'. They had thirteen children, of whom George Jacob was the second and the eldest son. Between the ages of nine and twenty-two George Jacob worked alongside his father as a whitesmith in a workplace very different from his mother's.

His description of its tyrannies is a classic of its kind, the polar opposite of a co-operative or mutual enterprise.[46]

Holyoake's main means of support from his early twenties onwards came from what the French still call *le mouvement social*.[47] A journal called *The Movement* (1843-5) was the first of many which he edited as more than a temporary stand-in. (He had already stood in for Charles Southwell on *The Oracle of Reason* while Southwell was locked up for his beliefs). It was Holyoake's manual skills, learned in the Eagle Foundry, which led to an opportunity for him to work as an assistant at the Birmingham Mechanics' Institute. Always an advocate of skilled self-activity, he had made his own, prize-winning set of compasses as part of his time as an apprentice whitesmith. These were shown at the Institute and much praised by Isaac Pitman when awarding prizes to students. The students in the senior class elected him as their secretary in November 1836, and when their teacher (Daniel Wright) died suddenly, they lobbied the directors of the Institute to appoint Holyoake as his successor. But advancement as a teacher within the Institute, which Holyoake appears to have wanted, proved to be as difficult for a convert to Owenism, which he was by then, as similar advancement was to become for a later generation of Communists in 1950s Britain.[48]

Fortunately Holyoake found employment in the movement, as many Co-operators were to do for the next one hundred and fifty years. In Holyoake's case paid work came from the Owenite Central Board. He was employed as a missionary, first in Worcester, then in Sheffield. He then taught and lectured among the Owenites in London, moving to Glasgow for a year in 1845. Thereafter, writing, editing, printing, promoting and campaigning with journals and newspapers became his trade. With his brother Austen, George Jacob established a printing firm which took over

James Watson's publishing business in 1853. The brothers worked together from 147 Fleet Street for almost ten years. Their output included items like *The Child's First Reading Book* (1853), a *First Word Book* (1854) and a *Second Letter Book*, subtitled *for reading and writing at once* in 1853. His *Practical Grammar* (1844) went through eight editions before 1870 and was full of stories and examples.[49] While Holyoake continued to have 'family responsibilities and social and intellectual aspirations beyond his limited means'[50], co-operative, secularist, liberal and labour ideas and organisations provided support – and he to them – in many different ways. When he was ill or in difficulties, Holyoake was also supported by subscription: testimonials on his behalf were raised from well-wishers. When Holyoake heard a rumour in 1881 that someone had lobbied Gladstone on his behalf for a pension, Holyoake impressed the great man by telling him he had no need of such a thing.[51]

George Jacob married Eleanor Williams, the daughter of a small farmer from Kingswinford in 1839. They had met at the Unitarian book store in Birmingham. She died in 1884 after forty-five years of marriage. Eleanor and George had five children. A daughter, Madeline, was born in 1840, followed by Eveline. They were joined by three brothers: Manfred, Malthus, and Maximilien Robespierre. Such names show Holyoake's defiant streak, recalling a Byronic hero who refused to repent having broken serious social taboos; a scarcity and population theorist unpopular among those who, like Holyoake, opposed the Poor Laws; and an 'extremist' inventor of a secular, state religion.[52] Writing about the years 1847-8, during the hard times when child 'Malthus' was an infant, Holyoake's first biographer, who first met Holyoake in the early 1890s, described the family situation in appropriately Malthusian terms: 'of weak constitution and constantly ailing, he (Holyoake) was faced with the dilemma of an increasing family and a small and stationary income'.[53]

Holyoake married again in 1886, the year in which he moved to Brighton. His second wife, Mary Jane Pearson, was the daughter of a clothier and a widow twenty-eight years younger than him. During the Brighton years, from his late sixties onwards while he was still a growing international presence in the co-operative movement, he nevertheless took an active interest in local affairs. In 1896 Holyoake was to be found contributing three articles to the Independent Labour Party paper, the *Labour Leader*, on 'the treatment of Musicians by the Bandmaster of the West Pier Brighton'. [54]

[ii] Movements.

George Jacob survived for sixty years after 1848. What did he leave that we might still use? At the very least, animating prose, written for and from the movements among which he made his way.

Like Dickens, Holyoake liked to gaze at the sea. 'Sitting at the windows of the Marina, St Leonards, watching the great ocean raging all alive with tumultuous and ungovernable motion, surging and roaring, I have thought how like it was to the industrial world....

> 'There is unfathomable cruelty in murderous waves. Vessels, laden with anxious emigrants, have been, by them, sucked down to death. As far as the eye can stretch the raging ocean covers all space, resembling some insane and boundless beast. Society heaves with the unrest of pitiless competition more devastating than that of the sea. Its remorseless billows wash away the fruits of humble labour. There is no bay or

cavern where property lies but is guarded by capitalist or trader, whose knives gleam if the indigent are seen to approach it. The co-operator is not one of them. He can create wealth for himself, and foresees that the rapacity and tumult of greed will be stilled, as the principle of equity in industry comes to prevail.' [55]

While doing my research, I learned that Holyoake's writing puts off many modern readers, even co-operators. His style certainly belongs more to the Victorian press, platform and pulpit than it does to the age of Google. It is interesting, perhaps, that during the last twenty years of his life 'his study walls at Brighton were a portrait gallery of Divines'.[56] Employed for a time as an Owenite 'Social Missionary', he was fond of communicating by means of parables and Bunyanesque dialogues between archetypes such as Tom Seekout and Jack Tellall. [57] He loved a good story – good in the sense that it could encourage progressive action. When he compared the 'enthusiastic' Owenite period in the history of co-operatives with the 'constructive', mid- to-late-nineteenth century period, Holyoake took the high ground and the long view:

> 'Free Government is yet in its infancy, and the line is not yet traced between State action and local life... Of one thing we are sure, that the world has been too much governed by persons whose talent has lain chiefly in taking care of themselves. There have always been too many people ready to regulate society in their own interests... Humanity has been too much sat upon by rulers – Heaven-born and Devil-born – the latter class chiefly prevailing'

But rather than going on about the errors and betrayals to the Left or Right of him and insisting on his own correctness,

Holyoake used his writing to engage people ('the people') in *making* progress for themselves, within and 'outside' their own Societies:

> 'the State – not a thing independent of the people, but a system under the control of the people – should have charge only of those general interests which from time to time may be committed to it... the welfare of the world lies in the direction of self-government...What we want in society is no leadership save that of thought – no authority save that of principles – no laws save those that increase honest freedom – no influence save that of service. The English working class, if not brilliant, have a steady, dogged, unsubduable instinct of self-sufficiency in them... They are alike impatient of military or spiritual mastery, or paternal coddling... They make it their business to take care of the State, and not to call upon the State to take care of them' [58]

Beyond his part in the Owenite socialist movement and then in the co-operative movement, Holyoake is best known as a pioneer of secularism – a term he invented; for his self-defence in 1842 in one of the last trials for blasphemy in Britain; and for what he called his 'deliberate' liberalism. [59] He liked to contrast his own political philosophy with what he called 'stationary' liberalism. His speech in his own defence at his 1842 trial in Cheltenham lasted for nine hours. It was rewarded by six months in prison.

The offence was characteristic. His lecture on May 24th 1842 'on the general principles of co-operation' was entitled 'Home colonization as a means of superseding poor laws and emigration'. Holyoake scrupulously avoided any reference to God in the lecture, but at the end a local preacher asked what place was assigned to God in a Socialist community? Holyoake replied that the people were too poor to have a God, unless, like the soldiers after the war against Napoleon, He (god) was put on half-pay. By this he meant to infer no more than that the incomes of the clergy could be cut. But the remark was the basis for the charge of blasphemy. It was alleged that Holyoake had spoken as follows, only the last sentence of which he disowned:

> 'Our national debt already hangs like a millstone round the poor man's neck, and our national Church and general religious institutions cost us about twenty million annually. Worship being thus expensive I appeal to your heads and your pockets whether we are not too poor to have a God. If poor men cost the State as much, they would be put like officers on half-pay, and while our distress lasts I think it would be wise to do the same with Deity... Morality I regard, but I do not believe there is such a thing as God.' [60]

Holyoake never cut and ran from any movement. He was a member of nearly every leading society for reform from the revived Birmingham Political Union in 1837 to the Reform League in 1867, including the last executive of the National Charter Association in 1852. He was something of a social movement collector, or *entrepreneur*. In outline, his life-journey ran as follows: from Owenite co-operative socialist, to politically-thoughtful, 'moral force' Chartist, to campaigner for free trade in knowledge and all other forms of communication, to secularist, to radical co-operative Liberal to radical liberal Co-operator. [61] He was President of Congress – a great honour in the co-operative movement – at the Carlisle Congress of 1887. When Congress came to Rochdale in 1892 Holyoake's speech at the tomb of William Cooper, the first cashier of the Pioneers Society, might have been about himself: 'he was always willing to go on to platforms, and speak or write, in defence of Liberalism, of Co-operation and of Labour'. [62] As soon as secularists looked like becoming as dogmatic in their atheism as believers were in their theism (as he thought Owen was in the 1830s and Bradlaugh in the 1870s), Holyoake turned his attention back to co-operation. This occupied much of the last twenty years of his life. His writing during those years can be read as part of late-nineteenth century *social* radicalism (different, and more radical than *social democracy*), as well as a source for the late flowering of early-nineteenth century Owenite, co-operative socialism.

Throughout a long life, Holyoake was energetic as author, publisher, journalist, debater, autobiographer, grammarian and on three occasions (1857, 1868 and 1884) as a Parliamentary candidate. On each of these occasions he withdrew before the poll, perhaps a sign of where his priorities lay, in the dissemination rather than the manufacture of 'opinion'. [63] His 1857 candidature has been seen by historians of Labour Representation as the first self-conscious attempt to represent Labour in Parliament, albeit in a Lib-Lab rather than an Independent Labour Party mould. Rather than recommending an independent Party – still less a Party machine – Holyoake would tell potential electors that 'legislation can do little more than enable the people to help themselves'. [64]

[iii] *Publishing for Pioneers.*

Holyoake's best-known book was his History of the Rochdale Pioneers. Its full title was *Self-Help By The People: the History of the Rochdale Pioneers.* It quickly became as iconic as its subjects. Everyone needs a parent even if they have to invent one. Sentences like 'the success of the parent society in Rochdale soon spread in the district, and before long societies were formed in...', became common in self-produced 'Jubilee Histories' of 'Our Society'. [65] As a little red book, Holyoake on the Pioneers has a rich history, indicating that, expressionist rather than realist though it was – all over the place, a conventional historian might say – 'this book has been useful... Not fewer than 500 or 600 copies were sold in Rochdale'. [66] Part 1 came out in 1857; ten editions followed before 1893. Part 2 was added in 1878. A revision of both Parts came out in 1893. This revision was reprinted three times before 1907.[67] I was able to use an Italian translation of the *History* at a celebration of the Pioneers by Legacoop, the major Italian consumer cooperative, in Genoa in 2014. Pirated, translated and variously titled, the book put the idea of what is now known as 'the Rochdale tradition' on the map, for co-operators across the world to celebrate, imitate and challenge. The Co-operative College in Manchester keeps a list of 'Rochdale Connections', describing the many Societies all over the world, by no means all of them consumer co-operatives, which use 'Rochdale' or 'The Pioneers' in their names.

Holyoake wrote other histories of local Societies, helping to bring into being the whole genre of 'Jubilee Histories'. These have continued to be part of the co-operative movement – and of the social history of public history – ever since his day. [68] He published on the Halifax Industrial Co-operative Society in 1867, having first read a paper on the subject to the Social Science Congress of 1864. [69] He celebrated the Leeds Industrial Co-operative Society in 1897, and the Derby Co-operative Provident Society in 1900. Amos Scotton, who 'for forty years served the Derby Society in every capacity, official and representative', co-wrote his Society's book – a satisfying artefact in itself, for members and subsequent enthusiasts to handle. Holyoake's aim as a people's historian was to address members and potential supporters of co-operatives. A copy of the Derby Jubilee History was presented to each of the 14,000 members of the Society, each of whom was also given a commemorative teapot. 'Already', he encouraged them in his final chapter, 'co-operation, like electricity, has become a new power in the commercial world, irradiating the paths which lead to the commonwealth of co-operative labour, the radiant land of Equity, where Justice is not blind, but seeing and protective'.[70]

Holyoake edited some of the beautifully produced, book-length Co-operative Congress Reports. These are models of pre-digital democratic connectivity. He was the proprietor or editor of no less than eighteen radical journals. The most enduring of these was *The Reasoner* (1846–1861).[71] He was also on the executive or its equivalent of twenty-two different progressive Leagues and Associations. [72] Like his contemporary Henry Mayhew (1812–1887), his work belongs to the history of journalism as critical construction rather than superficial comment.[73] He wrote regularly for many newspapers. J.A. Hobson chose two words with which to honour Holyoake at a memorial meeting held in South Place Institute in 1906: 'demagogue' and 'agitator'. 'These were two words, tarnished and degraded by the contempt and prejudice of the upper classes of this country, which more than anything else described his work. What finer title could any man claim than that?' Demagogue, Hobson explained, properly meant 'a leader of the people'; agitator 'one who generated energy of action'.[74] In keeping with his ethic, Holyoake preferred the word 'advocate'. 'Denunciation of persons we do not want, but denunciation of wrong we do want. Honest agitators are not demagogues, they are advocates; and advocates are very much wanted'.[75]

Perhaps the best way of seeing Holyoake in the round is as an epitome of Antonio Gramsci's idea of an 'organic intellectual'. That is to say as a thinker-writer-activist whose career was symbiotic with that of a class – or in Holyoake's case a specific alliance of classes – rather than devoted to his own advancement, about which Holyoake was often careless. He was as class conscious as any aristocrat. 'The populace are my choice – of them I am one, and like a recent premier, Earl Grey, am disposed "to stand by my order"'.[76] He was preoccupied with what would now be seen as the sociology of knowledge. And like Antonio Gramsci and Walter Benjamin, Holyoake connected the sites or provenance of knowledge with its content or direction. Whose? What for? Why not everyone's? These are the questions which underpin his work, alongside a kind of Nature-based Aristotelianism: 'every creature must be allowed to articulate after its kind, and would do better if it only knew how'.[77]

There was no reason why mathematics should be a 'mystery' to the many, or why 'the beauties and uses of Euclid' should be not be widely known among working people.[78] 'The highest truths of transcendental metaphysics will one day reach the populace... It was once said all could not learn to read, write and account...They will one day learn all things... But it will be accomplished piece-meal'.[79] Prejudice 'against extending the common and general benefits of education to the children of the poor' had existed, literally, for ages. Not to be confused with his *History* of the Pioneers, Holyoake's *Self Help a Hundred Years Ago* (1890) was written in part to recall people such as Thomas Bernard, Henry Brougham and W. E. Forster who, in his view, had chipped away against the opponents of education's common benefits. Holyoake acknowledged a long list of such patrons, including many *bien pensant* aristocrats and clerics. But there was still, he thought, a long way to go. Board Schools in London were an advance, 'it is something to have more persons than formerly who are willing to control education' 'But we still have many who, if they cannot control education are willing to destroy it.'[80]

'Ethical criticism has this further merit, that on the platform of discussion the miner, the weaver or farm labourer, are on the same level as the priest. A man goes to Heaven upon his own judgement: whereas, if his belief is based on the learning of others, he goes to Heaven second hand'.[81] If Holyoake was consistent about anything, it was about the fact and ideology of *class*, without always using the word. Before this is dismissed as out of date, it is important to understand what he meant by it. Class as a structure of feeling as well as thought, to use Raymond Williams's terms, points to *agency* or associated, self-made 'futurity'. It makes 'self-help' by working people ('the many') material rather than ideological, collective rather than individual, political rather than moralistic – as opposed to the use of 'class' as endless sociological classification.

Holyoake saw Owen, Bright, Hughes and other reforming 'friends of labour' with whom he worked, as fundamentally 'Tory'. They saw the world *de haut en bas*. The same, he wrote, was true of continental socialists like Lassalle and state 'socialists' like Bismarck. In an eloquent paragraph in a chapter of the *History of Co-operation* called 'The Song of State Socialism' Holyoake wrote of Lassalle, Marx, Disraeli, Comte and Napoleon in a single breath. 'They were all known by one sign – Paternal Despotism... If the expression is allowable to me, I should say – God preserve working men from the "Saviours of Society"'.[82]

Holyoake's steadiest friend in the co-operative movement, Edward Owen Greening, thought that Holyoake's 'career was one long conquest of self, in remarkable ways'.[83] Robert Green Ingersoll (1833–1899) an American Civil War hero, friend of Walt Whitman and champion of free thought, defended Holyoake in 1888 in an interesting register. Holyoake, he thought, had 'that happy mingling of gentleness and firmness found only in the highest type of moral heroes'. At that time, unnamed denigrators were saying that Holyoake was 'governed by a desire to please the rich and powerful', that he was 'afraid of public opinion and one who in the perilous hour denies or conceals his convictions'. Not so, wrote Ingersoll. 'He has lived his creed... He has the simplicity of childhood, the enthusiasm of youth and the wisdom of age. He is not abusive, but he is clear and conclusive. He is intense without violence, firm without anger. He has the strength of perfect kindness.'[84]

For Holyoake, 'policies of selfishness' were as much of an issue in social movements as they were in an individual's life. The first of his six 'Maxims of Association' set out in 1859 was: 'it is only by serving those beyond ourselves that we can secure for ourselves protection, sympathy or honour'. The fourth was that 'service and endurance are the chief personal duties of man'.[85] Thirty years later 'the principles of association' were couched in equally ethical terms.[86] 'The Cobden School' of Free Traders, the Independent Labour Party, and even the Women's Suffrage League all tended towards what he thought of as 'Ishmaelitism'. By this he meant exclusive preoccupation with a single interest or nostrum which entailed a divorce between means and ends. And 'the great French Revolution, which promised the emancipation of Europe, was destroyed by the determination of each party to obtain the ascendancy of its own theories, at the peril of the republic'.[87] Holyoake seldom apostasised 'the State'. Nor was he a 'communitarian' in the late twentieth-century use of the term which projects 'community' away from popular practice onto professional policy-making and inclines towards 'community' made from above, by 'the State'.[88] Late in life Holyoake let the word 'state' stand for the common good or 'public welfare'. States and towns could build schools, 'organise railway transit' and 'even acquire the land using the increment in its value for national expenditure as the public welfare may determine'. 'General interests' could be harmed, like 'the republic', by individualist interests. Holyoake wanted – indeed he witnessed among co-operators – a less factional, less interest-based, less structurally violent, more equitable and co-operative world. He thought that the practice of members of co-operatives in a large-scale movement was a precondition rather than an obstacle to its becoming a universal 'system', but it would need to be a system of a novel kind, for 'feudality is not out of the bones of people in England, even now'. 'The State' is to be understood not as 'a thing independent of the people, but a system under the control of the people'.[89]

[iv] *'Ideas are like seeds'.*

There is a coherence to Holyoake's work despite its lack of consistency or conventional literary and academic shape. There is something, he insists – always addressing readers as if he knew them personally – which is elevated and contagiously attractive, almost sacred, about the *idea* of co-operation, with its essential link to the practice of actually-existing Co-operative Societies joined, as they were, in a singular social movement. In an 1878 Preface to *The History of Co-operation* he wrote, 'the only useful history of a movement is a history of its ideas'. Elsewhere he wrote that 'ideas are like seeds'.[90] 'Freethought is of the nature of intellectual Republicanism... All are equal who think, and the only distinction is in the capacity of thinking. In freethought there is no leadership save the leadership of ideas'.[91] The best *idea* co-operators ever had, he insisted, was inseparable from their *practice* in co-operatives as new, associational forms. These forms were, quite simply, the instantiation of an idea to remake the world. For Holyoake, Co-operators and their Societies, individually and corporately, belong to a very ordinary but at the same time extraordinarily *social* movement. The word 'social' carried revolutionary weight among early co-operators, and meant more than terms like 'social co-operatives' used today, for example to describe the mutualisation of welfare in European, particularly Italian, co-operatives. 'Social science' began life as the Owenite term coined to describe the 'science of co-operation' as opposed to political economy, the science of competition. Holyoake liked to use the phrase a 'social society' to oppose the anti-social, competitive society which surrounded him.[92] For Holyoake, Owen was a pioneer 'social philosopher', 'the founder of Social Ideas among the people'.[93] In 1888 he proposed *Social Ideas a Hundred Years Ago* as a title for the book which was published as *Self-Help A Hundred Years Ago*. 'Social Ideas' was rejected because 'it was thought that the title might refer to "socialism"'.[94] A good social history of the word 'social' is urgently needed for the 21st century. Its neutering by social scientists, social workers, social democrats and people pleased with their social life away from work, is something which Owenites and early co-operators could help modern co-operators to become more conscious of.[95] Ian Macpherson had this in mind in his *Background Paper* (1996), designed to be used with the International Co-operative Alliance's 1995 *Statement of Co-operative Identity* of which he was the leading *animateur*. He explained how, in modern European co-operatives, 'by "social" is meant the meeting of social goals, such as the provision of health services or child care' rather than society itself.[96]

Co-operators, Holyoake thought, were developing their own moral tradition concerning matters of sociability which, since his time, have been treated in narrower (for example 'economic') ways: matters such as debt, equity ('equitable' was a characteristic Pioneers' word, built into the name of their Society), independence and union. 'Union' was not the same as 'unity', still less synonymous with sameness. It embraced differences in belief, affiliations outside co-operatives, and in (so far predominantly anti-social) circumstances. A new practice or ethic of association was abroad, in Societies up and down the land. The idea was that the co-operative movement had discovered ways of realising human potential which were uniquely adapted for transforming an industrial age in the interests of Labour rather than Capital.

The novelty of an industrial age or 'manufacturing system' organized in a particular way, generated the novelty of Robert Owen's *New View of Society* (1816) – a whole society to be constructed in a completely different way. With all their differences, Owen and his successors in the co-operative movement organized around the idea that, for the first time in human history, it had become materially possible, within the power of people – not 'utopian' – to end poverty. Looking back on the 1790s from the 1890s Holyoake recalled how 'in those days people in low circumstances believed that rich persons were always to exist and that the poor would never cease in the land'. 'Precariousness to be sometimes mitigated by benevolence' was all 'the people' expected 'until co-operation came and proved itself a new force of industry capable of delivering the people from poverty'.[97]

Holyoake was in the habit of capitalising the words Labour and Capital and also Co-operation, as opposed to Competition, perhaps to convey them as primary rather than incidental opposites which could, however, be united by this 'new force of industry'.

'Co-operation creates a new person, a new character, and a new policy, and the new knowledge required is as extensive and various as that which has perfected the science of antagonism which we call "civilization"'[98]

Holyoake's epochal terms aimed to encourage his readers to think in elevated ways. Down to earth, they encourage me to reconnect with Max Weber's work on *The Protestant Ethic and the Spirit of Capitalism* (1904, translated 1930).[99] Holyoake would surely have smiled on the idea of a latter-day Max Weber using some of the co-operative stories he told and the characters or ideal types he described to trace the emergence of what he, Holyoake, might even have had the *chutzpah* to call *The Co-operative Ethic and the Spirit of Associationism*. This is a book the movement hugely needs, rooted in 'the associative spirit' which Holyoake identified in his history of the Derby Society.[100] How will it be possible to escape what Weber famously described, on the final page of the *Protestant Ethic*, as the 'iron cage' of capitalistic rationality without some equivalent to the Protestant ethic and without the forms of association – the Protestant sects – which enabled that ethic to become the common sense of an epoch? The question for the next epoch is whether co-operative societies – better placed than sects in that they are themselves materially productive – could serve the spirit (or *Geist* in German, which also means 'mind') of associationism in the same way that Protestant sects served the spirit of capitalism?

[v] Character, Scale and Power.

Labour and capital are words Holyoake often used. He also favoured 'character', a word much used in Victorian England

– but not usually by the same people who saw labour and capital as poles in a field of force.[101] Samuel Smiles borrowed the term 'self-help' from Holyoake and he subtitled his best-seller *Self-Help* (1859): *'with illustrations of character and conduct'*. In 1871 Smiles published a whole book called *Character*, in which he wrote, 'all men can without difficulty become what some men are' – an instruction which cuts both ways. 'Capital', in Holyoake's view, 'is always aggressive', while 'character' need not be. He kept reminding his readers that the conflict or 'war' between labour and capital which is always disabling and sometimes violent, can be countered by harmonious forms of 'unity' – as in the Manchester Unity of Oddfellows.[102] For acolytes of Robert Owen, harmony was never the same as homogeneity. This could be why dancing was favoured at New Lanark, and why there was an affinity between late-nineteenth century Co-operative Societies and choirs. At the turn of the nineteenth and twentieth centuries, an advocate of the local Society's choir in the *Reading Co-operative Record* wanted it to be 'of the kind which shall have an ennobling influence on men's characters, which shall demonstrate to them "the harmony of Co-operative effort", and prepare them for the ideal of substituting a Co-operative commonwealth for the present competitive commercialism.'[103] 'Harmony', wrote Hughes and Neale, 'consists in many different sounds combined so that each, while preserving its individual distinctness, contributes to the all-embracing ideal unity'.[104]

There 'can be no unity save among equals', Holyoake explained in 1887. 'Unequal who is free?' as Milton put it in *Paradise Lost*. In a leaflet for the use of delegates to a conference of co-operators in London in 1884, Holyoake suggested that 'co-operation means social equality, and that equality of consideration to each will do much to beget and maintain equality of interest to all'.[105] If equality entailed mutual 'consideration' on a day-to-day basis, it was also open to individual differentiation (which was not the same as individualism). This was a necessary condition of fully mutual, or common, shared work among very large numbers of people. Differences and commonalities were being fused in new forms of working-class association. 'The problem of association' was the frame in which Holyoake set his own book on the Rochdale Pioneers from its opening page onwards. This was how working people in Rochdale had already taken 'their own affairs into their own hands and what is more to the purpose...kept them in their own hands'...'The working class are not considered to be very rich in the quality of self-trust, or mutual trust. The business habit is not thought to be their forte. The art of creating a large concern, and governing all its complications, is not usually supposed to belong to them.'[106]

The Manchester Unity of the Independent Order of Oddfellows ran a competition in 1846 to develop new learning materials for members, as initiatory rites of passage within the Order. At a time when he needed recognition as well as money, Holyoake won against seventy-nine other entrants. He used the money to start *The Reasoner.* His prize-winning lectures on Charity, Truth, Knowledge, Science and Progression were an exercise in applied, associational philosophy.[107] They were still being used sixty years later.[108] Learning by members marked their journeys through 'degrees' of membership, distinguished by the colours white, blue, scarlet, gold and purple. A distinctive moral philosophy was taught in which nothing less than knowledge itself was considered to be at stake, together with how human 'understanding' should relate to 'present conduct'. The culminating, or 'Purple' lecture suggested that while Progression was inscribed in Nature and, for that reason, available to humanity, 'its *certainty* depends upon the *amount* of wise action in the world'. While 'the *extensive* existence of right intention depends upon *every individual*... Our Order, by the delivery of these Lectures, seeks to increase it... We learn the invaluable lesson of *living now*... The *present* then is the moment of action, of use, of enjoyment, of advantage – teaching us that Progression is no idle dream but a *living principle* of practice'.[109] The lectures were designed to have a 'proper effect upon the minds of the hearers, as they are intended to inform the understanding, elevate the sentiments, and direct the daily conduct of our Brethren'. 'Philosophy' rather than 'vanity or caprice'...'originates the principle on which we associate', namely that 'whatever a man perceives that society will correct in its future practice he is bound to correct in his present conduct or he falls below the standard of right and wrong evident to his understanding'.[110]

The lecture on Charity, seen as 'the keystone of the moral virtues', dwelt on disagreement and dislike and how to deal with these within 'the charm and satisfaction of association'. This lecture argued for the mutualisation of charity, explaining the difference between 'almsgiving charity' and 'fraternal charity'. Holyoake was attempting to develop 'a taste for reasoning on morality apart from theology', believing that 'oddfellowship, like religion, can only sustain and commend itself by association with morality'.[111]

The Manchester Unity, like the Ancient Order of Foresters, was a giant federation of self-governing branches of working people independently taking care of their 'social' (meaning more than convivial) futures. By the end of the nineteenth century many members of co-operative societies in Britain were also members of Friendly Societies like the Unity, and perhaps also (in the case of men) of a local club in membership of the Club and Institute Union. The Rochdale Pioneers initially registered themselves as a Friendly Society, there being no separate 'Co-operative Society' category recognised at state level in 1844. The catalyst for the Hebden Bridge Fustian Manufacturing Co-operative Society, thirty years later (celebrated by Holyoake as 'the Nutclough Pioneers') was the immediate need for a friendly society to serve as a burial society for a deceased member.[112] It is worth noting also that branches of the Owenite 'National Association' Friendly Society, later the Rational Friendly Society, continued to flourish until the end of the twentieth century.

Scale was what working-class associational culture was partly about during Holyoake's lifetime: *size* signifying intention, present achievement as manifestly-possible future direction. The Co-operative Union's proud, six hundred and thirty-nine page *Report of The 37th Annual Co-operative Congress held in the G.A.Clark Town Hall, Paisley on June 12th, 13th and 14th 1905* invites proud handling and display as well as dedicated reading, as does the entire series of Congress Reports. If Congresses became known as 'annual parliaments' of the Movement,' 'the Cooperative Union was established as its ministry'. 'It soon became Holyoake's task to write descriptive narratives of each Congress annually in the columns of the *Co-operative News*'.[113] Finely-bound and embossed, full of delegates' names, Societies' statistics, verbatim reports of fringe meetings, 'conversazione', papers and lectures as well as Congress sessions, these annual volumes show a complex democracy at work. "Ah but ..." a modern, metropolitan networker might be tempted to sigh, alert to patriarchy, bureaucracy, English insularity, and implying that these were all sad reasons for the 'failure' of the movement. "Ah but..." a contemporary participant of either gender might have replied, "here We ARE. In your time, will you do any better?" Using Paisley in 1905 as an instance – the last full year of Holyoake's life – the 'we' in question included Womens' Co-operative

Guilds, the Garden City movement, Ruskin College, Lifeboat associations, the National Union of Teachers ... and a strong international alliance.[114]

A full-page advertisement for the Co-operative Wholesale Society, 'built up by the perseverance, industry and loyalty of British working people', tells its own tale. The 1905 Congress Report celebrated 1469 Distributive Societies; 2,078,178 members; £25,139,504 in share capital; 51,449 employees ; and a net profit, including 'Productive Societies', of £9,411,348... In the same year there were six million members in 27,000 independent Friendly Societies or Branches in Britain, with funds approaching £42 million. Multiply more than 50 times for today's values. There were nearly two million members of one thousand two hundred different Trade Unions, and one and a half thousand self-governing Clubs affiliated to the Working Mens' Club and Institute Union.

No wonder 'the Foreign Deputations' present at Congress in Paisley that year were impressed with such a combinatory culture. Marcel Mauss (Emile Durkheim's nephew and the author of one of the most influential, theoretical accounts of mutuality[115]), spoke to Congress (in English) as a representative of the Union of Socialist Co-operative Societies of France. In France, 'they were only beginning to enter into the question of federative organisation, and he was pleased to say that their hopes of success were as high as those of British co-operators. They longed to organise their societies on the model of the British Co-operative Union and Wholesale Societies, those wonders of the world'.[116] Six months before this (unusual) tribute from the French labour movement to the British, Holyoake had penned a 'Christmas Message' to the movement. *The Co-operative News* headlined it as 'from our G.O.M'.

A TALE OF MILLIONS.

THE PRESENT POSITION OF THE
Co-operative Wholesale Society.

Shareholders (1,150 Societies),	1½ Millions.
Capital - - nearly	4 Millions.
Reserve Funds, nearly	1 Million.
Land, Buildings, &c., nearly	3 Millions.
Depreciation - over	1¼ Millions.
Sales for Year, nearly	20 Millions.
Total Sales - over	275 Millions.
Total Profit - over	4 Millions.
Bank Turnover, over	90 Millions.
Direct Imports, nearly	6 Millions.
Own Manufactures -	3½ Millions.

.. Built up by the ..
Perseverance, Industry & Loyalty
... OF ...
British Working People.

'My contention is that the millennium, in fragments, is about... There are gleams of hopefulness, well visible to co-operative eyes... Over the whole field of industry no self-helping spot could formerly be described... Now, we behold a widely different scene. The stores have become fortresses of industry, and mostly stand on freehold ground...thousands of solid, self-helping, self-built stores have arisen – centres not only of local prosperity, but more or less of news, intelligence, and of much profitable enterprise, undreamed of by our forefathers – enterprises ever surprising, ever growing, the end of which none can foresee'.[117]

Twenty-first century radicals cannot be reminded enough of the 'great organisation(s) outside parliament' which working people bequeathed to them a century ago, and of the ethic or spirit which brought them into being. An office worker in a fustian mill, introduced to co-operation in the Nutclough Mill of the Hebden Bridge Fustian Manufacturing Co-operative Society became Assistant General Secretary of the Co-operative Union in 1884 and General Secretary in 1891. As Chairman of Co-operative Congress in 1906, he (J.C. Gray) called for the hundreds of independent Societies to combine more closely, creating one big Co-operative Society.

'Then we may go forward towards the realization of a true Co-operative State or Commonwealth, wherein justice and equity shall rule; where industry in all its forms shall receive its just reward; where homes shall be made healthy and happy; where all the comforts of life may be enjoyed by those who have earned them; and where the poor and oppressed may be uplifted and find rest, and misery and want be banished from our land'.[118]

Holyoake's vision of 'Co-operative Associations' [119] was that they constituted a practice, a way of living 'abroad and at home' which fostered distinct ways of behaving: reinforcing character on Labour's behalf – character as agency rather than complacency. Conceit was to be avoided, for 'a conceited associate has gas on the brain which inflates all his faculties and makes him think they are solid because they feel big'. And a bit more than self-interest was to be cultivated, for 'by mere business sense a man may be found in his place on dividend day (but) more than this will be wanted to make him a pleasant, ardent and continuous associate'.[120]

Holyoake retained enough of his early Owenism in later life to suggest that people could not be blamed for 'their capacity and manners' any more than they could for 'their stature and complexion'. It followed from this that 'indignation became in the co-operative mind a foolish futility'. If it could be avoided, co-operators would free their energy to act instead of railing against their own, individual condition. 'Half the time of ordinary-minded persons is taken up with anger, repugnance and resentment. Being free from these time-wasting sentiments, the co-operators have leisure to think, and peradventure to discover how best to live.' [121]

He had seen that co-operatives could work as consciously-created 'circumstances' capable of generating new manners and capacities, for example in the town of Rochdale. 'Human nature must be different in Rochdale from what it is elsewhere', Holyoake quipped in the first sentence of his history of the Pioneers. The fact was that the form of their Society, incomplete though it was, had proved itself to have staying power, in and against dominant forms of market and state. The common sense of today is to reduce co-operative *praxis* to 'skills', many aspects of a distinctive ethic of association having been lost to competitive, 'economic' individualism as opposed to any kind of social-ism. Holyoake insisted that co-operatives were unique in their insistence on financial rewards for members based upon *use*; in their democratic self-government detached from wealth; and in a no-more-than-equitable wage to be paid by labour for necessary capital. Ordinary, necessary things, made by people who need and use them – 'candles and treacle' – properly exchanged, properly produced by human beings seen from on high as a 'labouring class', carried 'world-making' potential. 'It was a great descent from the imperial attitude of world-making to selling long-sixteen candles and retailing treacle. Doubtless, if only we knew it, the beginning of civilized society was not less absurd'. The 'first co-operative society motto I have found', Holyoake wrote, was that of the Economical Society in London in 1821. It consisted of Milton's lines 'Our greatness will appear/ Then most conspicuous, when great things of small/ Useful of hurtful, prosperous of adverse/ We can create.' [122]

Holyoake suggests that Labour *already has* power: the power which belongs to making and doing. So the question is, how can Labour (we) help ourselves to articulate what is inherent in us in mutually rewarding ways. This is not only a theory of value of the kind political economists produce. For Holyoake, it is also a plain fact about human agency. You, Co-operators, he said again and again, do not need to take, capture, seize…still less vote others into power. You/We can build with that which belongs to us, is in our nature despite our current class position. We can 'arrange our powers', working in unity with what we already possess or lack, knowing through daily experience what it is that we need. We can use the capital we accumulate in Societies which share the rewards of work (labour) by means of associated co-operation rather than individualized competition.

Think what masters would do, Holyoake continued to ask,

if working people stopped producing. He liked to describe employers' impotence, deprived of labour.[123] Ways of seeing were, or should be, integral to ways of acting. So for the most part Holyoake ignored an emergent language of 'masses', much used to describe ordinary people as the objects rather than the subjects of politics and commerce from the 1840s onwards. (Gladstone liked to refer to 'the classes versus the masses' during the 1880s). Phrases like the working or labouring class, and words like independence, association, self-help, self-government, unity, character, morality, social, secular, equitable, Order (a Friendly Society word for a whole society) crop up regularly in his writing. 'Labour is the industrious man's capital', he told a meeting to name a new engine for the Nutclough Pioneers in 1887. So Labour 'should be respected like the rich man's capital'.[124] 'The capitalist', he told the members of the Derby Co-operative Society at the end of the nineteenth century, in the same register he had used fifty years before in his Owenite days:

> 'merely risks his money, and sleeps while it is doubled and tripled by the toil of others, while labour contributes all its power and its life...Without labour, the capitalist's money would go with him at last to where metal melts. At best, capital is no more than the half-brother of production and labour, the other brother, is entitled to at least half the profits of the joint undertaking'.[125]

'It may be a good thing, and it often has been, when capital hires labour', Holyoake told delegates to the Carlisle Co-operative Congress in 1887, but 'it is better when labour hires capital; pays it according to its risk, pays it even generously, but pays it only once – taking care that it does not come back a second time, filching the dividend of labour'.[126]

[vi] *'Sweet courtesy and consideration'*.

His friend Edward Owen Greening remembered how Holyoake 'treated all his opponents in debate with such sweet courtesy and consideration as are not easy to describe'.[127] Lectures and debates were communicative forms which had their own ethic, or 'terms, conditions and character' which were, in themselves, worth communicating.[128] Holyoake's book on the *Rudiments of public speaking and debate* went into thirteen editions between 1849 and 1906. It was important, he thought, to draw out people's objections to one's own position and to give them real space, to the extent of taking the trouble to state the objections oneself.

But although he spoke in public a great deal, Holyoake was no orator. His voice and stature were small, like John Stuart Mill's. (He claimed to have introduced Mill to his first rowdy public meeting.[129]) 'When mischief was intended to me personally it never came to much. My protection was often my voice. Had I been capable of speaking in striding and imperious tones, my opinions would have been counted highly objectionable'.... 'A striking gesture, a new tone, will sometimes make the fortune of a speech. But without resonance of voice, the tone which charms the ear may not occur. I had nothing to recommend me but the passion of persuasion and the aim of usefulness.'[130] When contributing half a guinea to an appeal to fund an assistant curate in the parish of St Bride's because of the Vicar's illness, he explained that he did this not because he was likely to need the curate's services, but his poorer neighbours in Temple Bar might. Besides, 'I am perhaps the only person extant who is not fully assured of his own infallibility.' [131]

Holyoake thought people, however 'other', were worth celebrating even when they went wrong, as in his view the

Rochdale Pioneers did with regard to 'the bonus to labour'. He liked to celebrate other people in the movement, giving orations or graveside addresses – a characteristic form among radicals – among others for Emma Martin, Henry Hetherington, William Cooper, John Smithies and Thomas Livesey. In Hetherington's case, Holyoake conducted the whole funeral service at Kensal Green cemetery. He was committed to equal citizenship and full property and other rights for women, which were achieved in Co-operative Societies before they existed elsewhere. His experience with Women's Co-operative Guilds taught him that,

> 'If a man accepts a principle and finds it takes trouble to put it into practice, he explains it away, and says he carries it out – when he does not – and his assurances satisfy the male mind. But you cannot fool a woman this way. She expects a right principle to be acted upon, and she will not, if she knows it, connive at its evasion.' [132]

An intended address for Robert Owen's funeral in 1858 had to wait until 1902 when the Newtown monument to Owen was completed. Priests resented graveside addresses by lay leaders of working-class social movements. However, when the local Rector prevented Holyoake's encomium to Owen at Newtown in 1858, anger mounted among the mourners that the great man was being buried in the context of a church service. Holyoake's emollient comment was typical: 'better ten popes officiated at his funeral than disturb it with a broil'.[133] At a Co-operative Congress in Derby some secularists criticized him for standing up while up while the Bishop of Southwell offered a prayer. At another Congress he insisted on standing in silence to honour the death of F.D. Maurice, the most profound theologian among the Christian Socialists.

Holyoake at Robert Owen's Newtown monument in 1902

Holyoake was committed to continual debate, humorous when possible and over many days when necessary. 'When debate is forbidden the charlatan is king'.[134] The question was how best to conduct such debate, without competitive 'annihilation', or 'thrashing' of opponents.[135] Instead of denunciation, 'the Co-operator does not rail at wrong, his business is to make it impossible':

> 'it was a doctrine of mine that anger was but the exhibition of ignorance taken by surprise: and that hatred was opposed to economy of time, as it enables persons whom you knew and detested, to occupy your thoughts with schemes of retaliation. There is a period in law when debts are no longer recoverable, and I have suggested to co-operative societies that associative animosities should be closed with the accounts, and not carried forward to the next quarter.'[136]

The term 'policy', in particular 'social policy', was not used by Holyoake in the way that experts and politicians now use it – as something one group of people does for or to another. He devoted a chapter of the *History of Co-operation* to the 'social policy of co-operative societies'.... 'If a man intends to live by industry and to get on by good sense, he adopts certain rules of probity and usefulness, and integrity and service constitute his policy.' There will be 'marauders'. 'No sooner is it discerned that Co-operation creates wealth than swarms of mercenaries swoop down upon it, to avail themselves of it as a means of gain, caring nothing for the social education and equality it was intended to promote'. But 'business watchfulness' and simple virtues like 'geniality' were important. Smiles of critical recognition among members attending Quarterly Meetings can be imagined as they reached the sting in the tail of passages like this:

'... a pleasantry of manner which never fails is a quality above all value in a co-operator in office. His smile is a public gift, the tone of his voice is an act of friendship. A hard man, with a sharp tongue and a short temper, is a local misfortune, diffusing discomfort wherever he treads. I know entire towns which never had a genial man in them – where every speech is an attack, every suggestion a suspicion, and every meeting a conflict. Co-operation in these places is always rheumatic and unhappy – labouring under a sort of suppressed gout.'[137]

Being in the 'business' of making wrong impossible is a very particular way of describing what Co-operative Societies do, by means of the production, distribution and exchange of 'candles and treacle'. *The Co-operative Movement Today*, in which the phrase appears, was first published in 1891 at about the same time as *News from Nowhere*. It is as if Holyoake was saying to socialists like William Morris that 'Somewhere', in most places in Britain in fact, a local Society was at work – a business consisting of manufactories and stores, reading rooms and meetings, just as material as William Morris and Co. – in which the 'habit of life' which Morris dreamed of 'growing on us' in Nowhere, was already being cultivated. If not 'easy', as Morris suggested it would be in *Nowhere*, it had at least become easier 'for us to live without robbing each other'. In 'The Policy of Abstention' (1887) Morris recommended 'a great organization outside parliament actively engaged in reconstructing society'. In a sense Holyoake was saying to revolutionary Socialists from a different class like Morris: 'here you are... here is your great organization'.

In 1885 J.C. Gray, with whose priorities Holyoake was for the most part aligned, wrote an article on 'Association in Production' in *Co-operative News*.[138] Gray, like Holyoake, had direct experience of how the 'greatest evils' of Competition fell

HOLYOAKE HOUSE, HANOVER STREET, MANCHESTER.
(Headquarters of the Co-operative Union, Limited.)

A tribute from seven hundred and ninety-four Societies, and the present home of the Co-operative College, Co-operatives UK, the National Co-operative Archive and the Co-operative News on the poorest of working people. In January and February of 1888 he read a paper on 'Co-operation versus Competition' at the conferences of the Calderdale and Huddersfield District Associations of the Co-operative Union. He characterised the ideal-type individual within competitive capitalism thus:

> 'You are an independent unit, existing without responsibility of any kind beyond your own personal desires or wishes – before you lies the world and society, make them your prey – so conduct and order your business life that it shall bring you wealth. The world is an orange, to be sucked – a sponge to be squeezed – squeeze it to the utmost of your power and if, in one direction, you do not succeed in your purpose, try another way; but in all your exertions have in view your own material benefit, no matter who sinks or swims in the struggle.'[139]

When Holyoake died in 1906, seven hundred and ninety-four Co-operative Societies from every District got together to subscribe to a fund to build Holyoake House in Manchester, which opened in 1911 as the headquarters of the Union. Holyoake had told the members of the Leeds Society in 1897:

> 'Co-operation does not make men perfect. There are few associations which do... (There) is the more practical aim of *inventing facilities which enable men to be good* (my italics). The faculty of being good, or of doing good, and the desire of it, and the pleasure in it, every man has, but there are millions without the facility or means of it. What they want is *a way of establishing conditions of daily life* (my italics) in which it shall be nearly impossible to be depraved or poor. It is this at which co-operation aims and which makes it a name of social inspiration'.[140]

Holyoake searched for ways of explaining to his readers, in this instance in Leeds, not *what* they should do or *why* they should do it but *how* to associate so that it becomes easier, not only for them but also for everyone else around them, to do right. Without concealing his own opinions, he preferred explanation to persuasion: 'My propaganda consisted in explaining things – never in persuading, since the responsibility of holding opinions belonged to those who accepted them. My own opinion was not concealed, for I always distrusted and often conceived contempt for the silent, whose philosophical impartiality ended in concealing their own thought'.[141] At the same time, this moralist was no moralizer. He could be quite sharp: 'Society does not recognise that morality has material conditions. Sacred motives have their place and power. Nevertheless, a philosopher or divine without a meal, will think more of his dinner than his principles. After a few days at sea, foodless in an open boat, a vegetarian will reconcile himself to devouring his grandmother.'[142]

> 'A man by good exertion can climb up the front of a house. It is better to use a ladder. A man may swim across a wide river, but it is better to take a boat. Why should not the poor man do it, if he can? ...The cant of self-help may be very brutal when it calls upon helpless men to do things impossible to them, and disregards the aid which the strong and wealthy use and can command at will'.[143]

Holyoake resisted masters and mastery with his whole being and had a nose for rhetoric among colleagues and opponents. For him, imperialism was a personal as well as a political and class issue. He claimed to have coined the term 'jingo'. He saw 'individual preeminence' as 'pernicious'.[144] This accounts for his resistance to what he called 'Imperial Chartism', on which

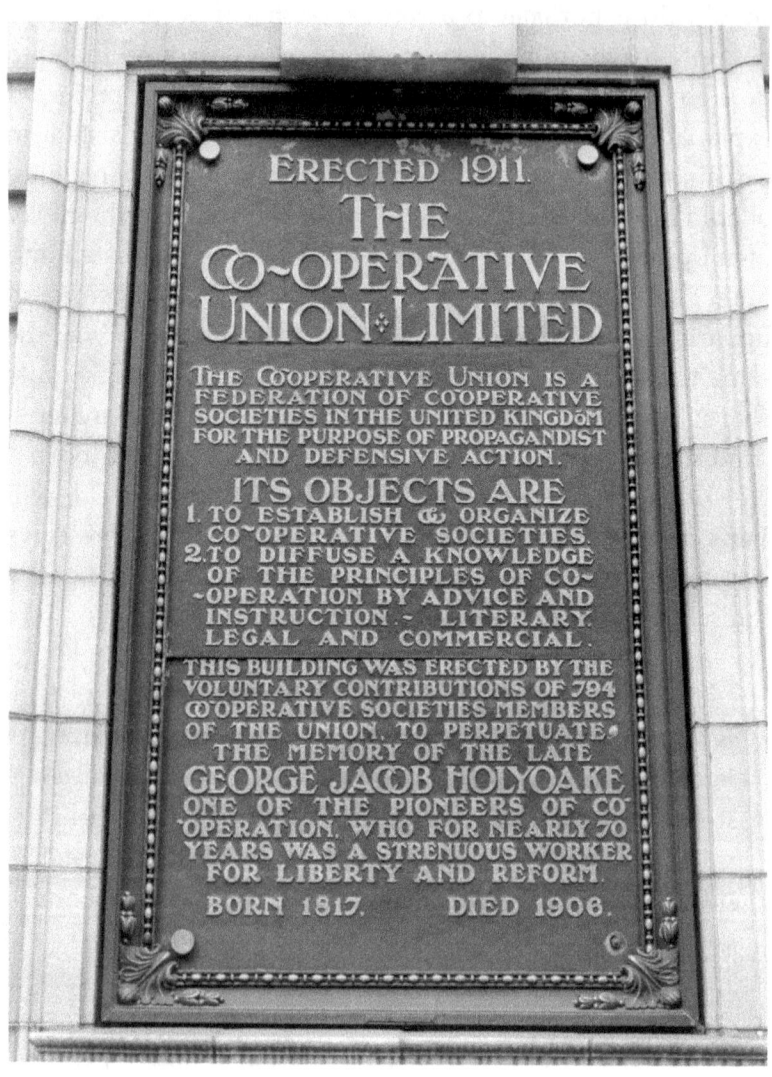

The 1911 commemorative plaque on Holyoake House

he gave a lecture which 'excited the suspicion of the *Northern Star*', the Chartist paper dominated by Fergus O'Connor, who was the leading 'Physical Force' Chartist. Holyoake offered,

> 'an argument against physical force reformation on the three-fold ground of Morality, Policy and Progress. In what respect do I differ from Mr O'Connor?... I will take this opportunity of repeating that personally I have great respect for Mr O'Connor. He has displayed more energy than all the Chartist politicians put together... yet I must be permitted to dissent from that incoherence and injustice of diatribe which is hurled at all who question his infallibility or differ from his opinions'.[145]

'Paramountcy' was the word Holyoake favoured to describe people he identified as possessing 'the ordinary governing mind', with its 'passion for ascendancy.' Such people worked through state and system rather than through solidarity and self-government.[146] Paramountcy is 'that dangerous war-engendering term of Imperialism which only the arrogant pronounce and only the subjected submit to'.[147] Holyoake's best writing on top-down 'social reformers' retains its power to rebuke modern social democrats among other social engineers. Anticipating twentieth-century authoritarian extremes, Right and Left, he insisted that those who 'propose to remake the world all at once, 'must remove the human race, since the past is in the bones of all who live, and a nihilistic removal of everybody would render the reconstruction of society difficult'.[148]

Holyoake saw divisions of labour within production as an individual as well as a social problem for co-operators, rather than as the economic opportunity which 'the division of labour' became in the work of political economists inspired by Adam

Smith's pin manufacturers. Committee members among the Rochdale Pioneers were expected to work with their hands. So it needed a Minute from the Committee in June 1854 to allow 'that Cooper, the cashier, be exempt from coffee grinding'.[149] And can this passage from a paper by Holyoake on *Moral errors which endanger the permanence of co-operative societies* – which was presented to the Political Economy section of the National Association for the Promotion of Social Science at their Guildhall Congress of 1862 and published by the Bury Co-operative Society – be dismissed as merely moralistic?

> The moral obstacles which constantly frustrated co-operative success, and dissipated it when achieved, were the difficultly of acting with, and tolerating, people one disliked, trusting those in whom one had no confidence, the difficulty of creating personal authority and prohibiting offensive imputations, as well as the difficulty of viewing with satisfaction, and personally promoting, the growing prosperity and influence of those considered to be unworthy.[150]

Holyoake was unwilling to allow the enemies of co-operatives to appropriate and enclose morality. The financial obstacles to the success of co-operatives were always being discussed, but what about the moral ones? Goss wrote of this paper: 'it is really an appeal to co-operators to agree to follow the advice of Robert Owen, to agree to consider the errors of mankind as proceeding more from defect of knowledge than defect of goodness'.[151] Another essay on 'The Store as an Institution' is in the same mode, mixing morality with management, good business with good manners, social analysis with methods of social advance.[152] He knew that private self-discipline would have to be part of the effective, public organisation of ideas.[153]

[vii] Minds open to opposites.

Although his relations with the early Pioneers were complicated, Holyoake saw 'our co-operatives of Rochdale' as having performed a 'moral miracle'. He records how it was Samuel Tweedale, 'considered the "talking man" of the store' who gave 'the first little lecture' they had at Toad Lane on a Sunday night. 'They have had the good sense to differ without disagreeing; to dissent from each other without separating; to hate at times, and yet always hold together'.[154] So their solidarity (a key Co-operative Value in the 1995 International Co-operative Alliance *Statement of Co-operative Identity*) was not based on similarity, still less on sameness. They had, he thought, discovered a dynamic form capable of turning difference into energy. The phrase 'moral miracle' in *Self-Help by the People* was quickly followed by a memorable portrait of the labour movement archetype which William Morris made famous in *News from Nowhere*: 'the Grumbler'. 'Some of the members grumbled', Holyoake wrote of the disputatious Leeds Society. 'No doubt they did'. So the issue became how not to 'convert discontent into dislike' and at the same time not to 'discourage expression of opinion'? Within Co-operative Societies as well as in public debates, 'the best rebuke is to state the case' (of a member with whom one disagrees) 'and answer it. That creates no irritation and makes no enemy'.[155] The task was 'to combat without contemning others'.[156]

In his late eighties Holyoake reflected that 'were I to edit a new journal again I would call it "Open Thought" '[157]. 'I love the picturesqueness of personal opinion' he wrote, arguing that minds closed to opposites were unhelpful in co-operatives.[158] Indeed one of the reasons why there were thousands of books in the Pioneers' library by the 1860s, together with Monthlies and Quarterlies of all persuasions, was that 'the Co-operators wisely set themselves against being made into half-minded men. They would not imitate those timid creatures who are afraid to know the other side of the question, and go squinting at truth all their days, never looking it squarely in the face, so that when they meet it plain in their way they do not know it'[159] and again: 'There are two sides to most questions and co-operators have less furrowed brows because they know this'.[160]

Holyoake admired the way in which the Rochdale Pioneer James Scowcroft, a Swedenborgian, would linger in the Store, not to convert others but to be open to their arguments.[161] During hard times in Victorian Britain when the centre might easily not have held, radical eccentricity was *there*, to be understood as symptom, as sad, sometimes grotesque theatre and even as apocalypse. But it was also to be admired – as Holyoake did, with a smile on his face – rather than pre-scripted as 'failure'. Times of discontinuous change, like the world's first industrial revolution, spawn oddities, of which the stories of the Ham Common Concordium and the life of Peter Baume in *The History of Co-operation* are two examples in which Holyoake invited his readers to take delight. 'As we all know, a nimble eccentricity always treads on the heels of change.'[162]

The 1843 Concordium and its prophet James Pierrepont Greaves deserve the study recently devoted to them by historians.[163] Holyoake was involved with them at the time. He also liked a good story, particularly when he could point to a moral. Their tale cannot be fully told here, though it is part of the pre-history of the Co-operative Wholesale Society. As a visitor and part-time participant Holyoake had it that the Concordium's 'inmates…repudiated even salt and tea, as stimulants, and thought most of those guests who ate their cabbage uncooked. They preached abstinence from marriage, and most things else... preferring damp sheets to dry ones'. 'Their cardinal doctrine was that happiness was wrong'. However, they were given to waiting for direct spiritual instructions and this, Holyoake thought, had its advantages. 'Mr. Greaves' disciples had the great merit of pausing before they did anything until they found out why they should do it, a doctrine which would put a stop to the mischievous activity of a great many people, if thoughtfully followed'.[164]

Pierre Henri Baume's life (1797–1875) would need a novel to do it justice. Holyoake provides the preliminaries:

> 'Some persons are deemed eccentric because they have some peculiarity, or because they differ from others in some conspicuous way. Whereas Mr Baume seemed to have every peculiarity and to differ from everybody in every way.'

A heady combination of prophet, impresario, promoter of 'public houses without drink' and paranoid conspirator, it is good to imagine what Dickens might have done with Baume's story, building on Holyoake's *History of Co-operation*. In 1857, Baume:

> 'settled in the Isle of Man, and purchased an estate there. At Douglas he fitted up an odd kind of residence, the entrance to which he made almost inaccessible, and admission to which could only be obtained by those whom he had initiated in a peculiar knock. In this little den he lived like a hermit, sleeping in a hammock slung from the roof, for the room was so crowded with dusty books that there was no space left for a bedstead, or even for a table on which to take his food. He resided in this place for several years, but his decease occurred at a tradesman's house in Duke St Douglas'.[165]

Holyoake could not stop himself admiring Baume's 'honest craze for social and educational projects…and…constant conviction, very honourable of its kind, that it was a man's duty to resist injustice and knavery, and he would really make great sacrifices to defeat it'. At the same time – and participants in community movements nowadays will recognise the type – 'there could not have been a greater calamity to any struggling movement than that Mr Baume should take an interest in it'.

This 'mechanical philanthropist' took Robert Owen's idea of universal as opposed to familial attachment to its limit.

> 'Mr Owen reasonably taught that the sympathies of ordinary people were too confined, and ought to be extended to their neighbours. Mr Baume brought sharp ridicule upon the wise sentiment by proposing that the mothers should suckle their children through an aperture in a metal plate, through which the mother was to place the nipple of her breast; the child was to suckle on the other side, thus concealing the child and parent from each other, lest filial and maternal ties should frustrate the universal sympathies which were to be cultivated.'[166]

Holyoake's writings are studded with intriguing references to Quakers, for and against, as if their quirky independence was of some consequence to him. Mr French, 'a little rosey-faced Quaker of bright unassuming ways' befriended him as a youth by letting him borrow books in the tyrannical workshop in Birmingham where Holyoake learned his trade.[167] Like Robert Owen, Holyoake admired the Quaker reformer, John Bellers, although he was more critical than Owen of Bellers' all-at-once, statist approach. Writing about Bellers' *Proposals for Raising a College of Industry* (1695), Holyoake upheld 'a sect derided and despised, and for whom the pillory was thought to be too good – men with whom the "respectable classes" of the day would not entrust their workmen'.[168] He praised Thomas Paine, 'a famous Quaker of Thetford'. 'The colonists of America' needed Paine's 'backbone', he thought, 'to stand up properly against George III'.[169] Holyoake's description of his 'tall and comely father' – forty years in the Eagle Foundry in Birmingham which George Jacob escaped from as soon as he could – is revealing in this context:

> What laws of etiquette he had were his own. When summoned by his employers he always walked up (unless into office or a private room) without uncovering his head, as was usual with others. His not doing so seemed natural to him. It was not disrespect, it was self-respect... Though entirely without self-assertion, he had a quiet implacable will.'[170]

In his history of the Derby Co-operative Provident Society, Holyoake singled out John Ellis, a Quaker and Chair of the Great Midland Railway Company which, by 1892, employed 10,000 people in Derby. The GMR was the first company to attach third-class carriages to every train, 'to bring the poor man to London in the same time as the gentleman'. Ellis presided at a meeting during the Leicester Co-operative Congress of 1877. Holyoake admired the way he 'used the wise language of instruction and encouragement, without patronage'. 'John Ellis gave expression to the opinion that not over-labour but luxury was the danger to the nation... His speech showed that the inner light of the Quakers, though sometimes narrow, was wiser than the outer light of many less attentive to the dictates of a cultivated conscience'. In the same book Holyoake told how Quakers had had difficulty establishing themselves in Derby, George Fox having been imprisoned there in 1650. Holyoake identified himself with

Fox's fearless exchanges with the local Justice who was, he thought, the first to call Friends 'quakers'. Fox 'never quaked before anyone however savage, nor before any imprisonment however vindictive'.[171]

Trouble always began, Holyoake thought, when beliefs and opinions, like the profits of manufacture, got caught up with structures of patronage and power in such a way that they could no longer be distributed and exchanged freely.[172] When Reason and its Reasoners ruled in unequal forms of association – whether for mutual improvement, fustian manufacturing or social benefit – 'proclamations' and 'demands' could follow. 'The Co-operator makes no proclamations as to his religious opinions and treats any demand of the kind as a social outrage'.[173] 'Interests' could take root all too quickly even within Co-operatives. This is why rules against employees becoming board members existed even among producer or worker co-operatives, including the Hebden Bridge Society. 'Paid servants' could too easily turn into a single, self-interested section ruling a Society.[174] Priesthoods of various kinds had, Holyoake thought, taken power in Christian churches, but not only in them. Robert Owen and Charles Bradlaugh became, in Holyoake's view, too absolutist in their secularism. Anti-Christianity could became as dogmatic as any 'Church Party'. All beliefs needed to be 'rescued from the tyrant and the policeman'.[175] Free association in co-operative forms was well adapted for such work. But while unadulterated truth like unadulterated flour, was a basic human need, it was by no means an automatic product, even in co-operatives. Members needed to guard against impurities, whether from powerful patrons of the movement like the Christian Socialists with their own agendas extrinsic to the movement or from powerful business leaders in the Co-operative Wholesale Society. The art of co-operative association included protecting members against truths which, whether coming from inside themselves or from others set in authority over them, could turn too easily into vested interests. Hence the importance Holyoake attached to this-wordly Societies constructed in such a way that individual beliefs and external commitments could contribute to and not obstruct social rather than exclusively economic growth. At one point Holyoake even bracketed Robert Owen with Thomas Hughes: they both tended to mix 'polemical controversy' with 'social advocacy' in ways he thought co-operators should guard against.[176]

At the same time Holyoake was no relativist. A 'neutral faith' was no less a faith. There was a difference between 'hostile' and 'generous' toleration. Playing fair was good, but generosity would 'take care that the rival is not killed by fair play'.[177] Toleration was a virtue because 'the first duty of man is the maintenance of his own convictions, the next is respect for those of his neighbours'.[178]

> 'There are some good, well meaning, earnest people who are of opinion that giving preference to your own views in which you believe, over those of others in which you do not believe is intolerance. This is not good discernment. Absolute belief in your own view of truth is *Sincerity*. The belief that no one else can possibly be right is *Infallibility* The refusal to others of a chance of proving their own truth is *Intolerance*. Standing up for your own belief in Truth is not Intolerance but *Duty*.' [179]

In his celebration of an idea which, like any religion, was also a way of life supported by deliberately designed forms of association, Holyoake minted new words for his beliefs. 'Secularism' became the best known of these, and in keeping with his interest in principles in general, he explained those pertaining to secularism in forms which would be available to as many people as possible. *The Principles of Secularism Briefly Explained* went through four changing editions between 1859 and 1881.[180] The first edition came out in five, one-penny parts under the titles 'Definition of terms'; 'Secular aphorisms'; 'Definitions of principles'; 'Secular organisation indicated' and 'Characteristics of secular principles'. 'Limitationism' was another term Holyoake used to describe his beliefs, as was 'Netheism'. In 1858 he called himself a 'cosmist'. George Henry Lewes thought that 'suspensive atheist' best described him.[181]

Holyoake insisted that while co-operation was old, Co-operatives were new. To see them as otherwise was to sell out to the political economists who were eager to vaccinate society against a revolutionary form by saying that co-operation with a small 'c' had always been there. 'Industrial co-operation is not a new name for an old thing, but a new thing under an old name'.[182] It was their existence as recent social inventions by working people that made co-operatives world-making, the term Holyoake used in order to contest the familiar put-down of 'utopianism'.

> 'Gibbon Wakefield says: "Co-operation takes place when several persons help each other in the same employment, as when two greyhounds running together kill more hares than four greyhounds running separately". This is the nature of the Co-operation chiefly known to political economists. But industrial co-operation unites not merely to kill the hares but to eat them. The greyhounds of Wakefield run down the hares for their masters – the new co-operative greyhounds run down the hare for themselves'.[183]

[viii] '...the working people want to do the same'.

Holyoake liked to distinguish between liberal practices which he saw as 'stationary' and 'deliberate' liberalism which did not limit democratic invention but pushed on with it, detail by detail. In an address to the Brighton Liberal Working Men's Committee in 1886 he warned against liberalism as self-serving ideology or vested, stationary interest acting as if its freedoms were *already* universal. 'Liberalism is not yet self-regulating and...is dilatory in understanding its own business'.[184] The expense of elections ruled out working-class Liberal Parliamentary candidatures. So Holyoake recommended that all members of every Liberal Association should contribute to a common fund.[185] As already mentioned, Holyoake gave Samuel Smiles his best-selling book title *(Self Help* has been in print ever since 1859 [186]), but for Holyoake it continued to mean self-government and independence for a whole class of people rather than for a few escapees from poverty. Social mobility was not the goal, although he certainly achieved it in his own life. Changing the destination by the very nature of the vehicle was the task.

In Holyoake's time (and ever since), reformers who were disdainful of shop-keeping – including Robert Owen –'tended not to recognise working-class co-operators' dream of running the world'.[187] While 'character' was important in the co-operative store, Holyoake knew that it could not act independently of circumstance. 'Circumstances' were crucial determinants for anyone as influenced by Robert Owen as Holyoake. This was why Holyoake argued that new circumstances were being created within and by co-operative societies, whose members would surround each other with new ways of arranging for the production, distribution and exchange of goodness as well as goods. Victims were to announce themselves as agents, acting together as subjects rather than as objects of anyone else's benevolence. Once a lasting ecology of co-operative associations existed – and Holyoake encouraged members to believe that it did from the late 1860s onwards – it would be more likely that the 'credit note' for co-operative behaviour with which he thought all humans were born would be redeemed, rather than being sold to selfish, competitive predators.[188]

In an equal society it might be understandable to resist the introduction of the Secret Ballot as John Stuart Mill did, on the grounds that individuals should stand up in public for their opinions, helping themselves. But in the prevailing circumstances co-operators saw protection from patronage as essential. Holyoake chided Mill and Herbert Spencer for 'not thinking that self-help has its limits'… 'There is no sense in telling a man whose legs are broken he ought to walk unassisted'.[189] Holyoake worked with Mill and admired him as 'a great teacher of the people', but he was bold enough to confront the competitive individualism which Mill's work could be used to justify.[190] He differed with Mill 'with diffidence' on such matters as the propriety of oath-taking, and on 'the well-known Utilitarian doctrine that the consequences of an act are the justifications of it'. Utilitarianism, he argued, should not be carried into the domain of morals. 'Truth is higher than utility, and goes before it. Truth is a measure of utility, and not utility the measure of truth. Conscience is higher than consequence'.[191]

Too readily tidied up in our own times as a 'Gladstonian Liberal', Holyoake respectfully – face to face as well as in letters – disagreed with the Grand Old Man on fundamental matters of theology as well as on equality of opportunity, each of them showing and winning consideration, as one intellectual to another.[192] For one whose formal education was a world away from that of Gladstone, the equitability and depth of their exchanges is something to admire in both men. Holyoake's *The Origin and Nature of Secularism* (1896) led to an empathetic exchange between them on their feelings and hopes concerning life after death.[193] Holyoake was unafraid of apparent inconsistency, of fellow-travelling with powerful people among the governing classes and thus losing face with friends and allies. This was especially so in the run-up to the Reform Act of 1867 when he acted as a self-appointed diplomat, shuffling between Home Secretary Spencer Walpole and the Reform League in an attempt to avoid violence in Hyde Park.[194]

It was the absence of equality of consideration between whole classes of people which most offended Holyoake. At his most Liberal, some would say starry-eyed in his relationship with Gladstone, he was also most adroitly committed to his class, 'the working people'. After a breakfast meeting in 1876 he wrote to the great man about 'the conditions of association among the people'. These are, after all, 'the same as among gentlemen':

> 'In a club gentlemen have refreshments according to their taste: read what books they please: discuss what topics they choose. The working people want to do the same. Being crowded in their daily lives, they have no sense of distinctness and deference to each other as gentlemen have. To allure them into association and compass its pleasant perpetuity, it is only needed to concede them the liberties of gentlemen…' [195]

Only! But a start had been made in Rochdale, where microscopes and telescopes were added to the Society's Library in 1861 'so that the co-operator can look into things small and great, far and near. The gentlemen of Rochdale had no such institution for their use'.[196] 'A library', after all, 'is the soul of a store, the soul of a town'. Working people were in some respects ahead of 'gentlemen'. At the store (the co-operator) finds a library, as in Rochdale, larger and richer than the town library itself'.[197] Holyoake played with what would happen 'if workmen were gentlemen' in order to make simple points on behalf of his class. He delighted in upstaging gentlemanly double standards, for example concerning debt, and contrasted them with the prudence enshrined in the Rochdale principles.[198] When co-operators won their independence it would be 'an independence not yet possessed by the middle and upper classes – the independence which pays its way'. 'And even if they were no better than their "betters" they would be entitled to their turn in managing their own affairs'. 'Workmen' were in a different position from 'gentlemen' for the simple reason that they were not gentlemen, and gentlemen were dependent upon this uneven distribution of life chances. Holyoake's was a well-directed, morally-charged question: 'why should the rich be accorded the sole right of governing?'[199]

'In this place and elsewhere', Holyoake wrote in his history of the Rochdale Pioneers, 'I prefer to use the phrase *claim* of the workman instead of the term "right". A right of labour, like a right in politics, is what can be got to be ruled or conceded. A claim is what ought morally to be conceded. But the claim holds good, and is to be persisted in. If workmen were gentlemen in means no employer would dare to disallow it.'[200] 'Means' were the issue, in the sense of facilities or instruments as well as money. If 'physical rebellion' by 'the industrial classes' was not recommended by Holyoake, action against 'authority' was, in order to contest the 'intellectual error, social inferiority and insufficiency of means' imposed upon working people.[201] Holyoake did not want to allow a word like 'responsibility' to be alienated: he wanted everyone to be in a position to take it and own it. Refuting Dr Brindley's anti-secularist lectures on 'Human responsibility and retributive justice' in 1879, Holyoake was clear that he (the secularist) 'teaches that society is responsible for its own condition'.[202]

Holyoake took great pride in the potential of the Societies he helped to generate, and hence of their members. Unusually among cultural critics to the present day, he understood social movements as forms of human creativity or 'moral art' as intricate and learned as any other cultural achievement or work of art.[203] 'The art of association has no professors and no literature'.[204] How the *voluntas* or will of the many might be engaged in world-changing ways was a serious question, requiring invention as well as analysis. 'Each creature has two main qualities – susceptibility and resistance. The capacities of receiving noble impressions, and of insensibility to the ignoble ones, are our best endowments'. So, how to proceed? How best to engage with the agency of human beings not judged to be as capable as their masters?

> 'When thought or circumstances create within us impulses of choice or action, we call that will. As we know other persons to be constituted as ourselves, we strive by reason or by surrounding them with suitable material conditions to create the will we wish to prevail'.

Like co-operative societies, secularist associations 'seek to supply the material and social conditions under which, whatever of goodness (relative or absolute) exists in human nature, may manifest itself unchecked.'[205]

Holyoake enjoyed holding a mirror up to parts of social life well known to activists. For example: the atmosphere created by Cassandras in progressive organisations 'who predict to everybody that the thing must fail, until they make it impossible that it can succeed'. He compared a social movement to a river that 'moves through society as the river does through the land...new outlets seem to open of themselves, and in an unexpected hour the accumulated torrent of ideas bursts open a final passage to the great sea of truth.'[206]

{ 2 }

A useable past?

Introduction

This section offers a reappraisal of Holyoake's work, articulated through his preferred social movements. I look at his life and work in the light of three sets of ideas and the possibilities they suggest: for 'ideas are like seeds'.

The first possibility to consider is that the co-operative movement remains central to the making of an unfinished, associational-socialist alternative to the Marxist revolutionary tradition of *circa* 1848 (building on 1789) and into the 20th century: 1917 (Russia), 1948 (China) 1959 (Cuba) and beyond. Holyoake certainly thought that this was so. From 1839 onwards, his arguments with 'communism' and 'socialism', gathering pace after 1848, were not what progressives have often described as 'reactionary'. In 1897, writing for Leeds co-operators, he described his (and their) alternative way forward, as 'not dreamy but definite, not revolutionary but constructive'.[207] The final part of the final edition of *The History of Co-operation* ('Part III, from 1876 to 1904' penned in his late 80s) began with a two-page chapter (XLI) on the 'transformation of social aims'. His self-conscious play with words as vectors of social struggle was more than usually evident late in his life:

> 'All the fervor and earnestness of early Co-operative Societies was not, as the reader has seen, about Co-operation, as it is now known, but about communistic life... In the "Socialist" agitation taken up by the people, the State was left out and the people came in. Their communities were intended to be independent and controlled by the residents for themselves... This scheme of communist life was sometimes spoken of under the name of "Co-operation", as indicating that the exertions of all must be *co-operant* to the common good. The Rochdale Pioneers founded a new form of Co-operation; their inspiration was communistic... Communism suffered incarnation in their hands, and the new birth was the co-operative store – a far lesser creation; still that was much.'[208]

In 1847–8, Marx and Engels ended their *Manifesto of the Communist Party*: 'in place of the old bourgeois society, with its classes and class antagonisms, we shall have an association, in which the free development of each is the condition for the free development of all'. It is as if Holyoake was pointing to the co-operative movement and insisting that we *already do have* an association in which...[209] There might not be a need for people to mortgage or postpone their (own) future, to separate means from ends, to seek to make a 'revolution' in one, bloody, way and then to inaugurate a fresh regime as if it could be unsullied by its origins. In other words to be their own future. Cooperators were trying to be 'present at their own making'.[210]

The second idea is that the co-operative movement as advocated by Holyoake could be central to the emergence of a coherent, self-regulating, autonomous ethical or moral *tradition*. This is more ambitious than it sounds.

Particularly in Britain, traditions – real and imagined – are commonplace. In *Keywords* Raymond Williams suggested that in British culture 'tradition' tends to be imposed from the top rather than built from the bottom.[211] G.K. Chesterton observed that 'tradition means giving votes to the most obscure of all classes, our ancestors. It is the democracy of the dead. Tradition refuses to submit to that arrogant oligarchy who merely happen to be walking around.'[212] Such a notion fits the co-operative movement well, particularly in a time like the present, of privatisations which insult our ancestors by individualizing the social capital they left us. A tradition in an ethical or moral – even a 'religious' – sense, acknowledged and nurtured by those who belong to it and to whom it belongs, could provide a source of resistance and hope – a space to 'occupy' in the verb chosen by a recent social movement – for present-day activists.

Reading Holyoake I have been struck by the bold, philosophical-moral, rather than short-term, business-history view which co-operators took of their movement in his day. The first chapter of Holyoake's *The Co-operative Movement Today* (1891, 1903), was called 'Famous Precursors of Co-operation'. Holyoake reached back to 'the myth world before Homer' and proceeded to identify ten 'distinguished Social Innovators' across the ages, including Plato, Christ, Thomas More, Bacon, Campanella, Harrington, Bellers and Saint-Simon. He observed that 'only three – Christ, Bellers and Baboeuf – were plebians'. And 'in none of (their) schemes of a new order of society was there any, or very little, of the Co-operative principle of self-help, and self-government'. Co-operative principles are, he insisted, something else.

Christ and the Essenes got short shrift: 'it does not appear that Christ foresaw the discovery of Political Economy and the rise of the manufacturing system, since His plan of selling all you have and giving it to the poor would soon bring society to a precarious level, and add the rich to the population of the poor'. The co-operative principle was not like that. 'To put in the minds of men the idea that the end can be reached at the beginning without labour, concert and patience, has proved disastrous, and filled those of a communistic way of thinking with a foolish expectancy which has led to discord and ruin'.[213] From the mid-century on, Holyoake tended to associate 'communism' with revolutions of a 1789 or 1848 kind and 'socialism' with state action.

In their *Foundations: a study in the Ethics and Economics of the Co-operative Movement, prepared at the request of the Co-operative Congress held at Gloucester in April 1879*, Thomas Hughes and E.V. Neale took an equally long-sighted historical view. They reached back through Catholic Christendom and 'the Mediaeval world' to Greek philosophy. They saw Co-operation and the new 'social state' as inheriting the freedom to associate away from 'the State' won by the Catholic Church, and thus able to construct a state of affairs as novel as Christendom had been. If the commissioning of Holyoake's Lectures on Charity, Truth, Knowledge, Science and Progression by the Manchester Unity of Oddfellows was indicative of a generous ambition among their members, so too was the fact that it was Co-operative Congress which formally commissioned a work with the scope of *Foundations* in 1879. In 1915, Congress also agreed that it should be revised and reissued. These were not texts in search of a comfortable niche for the movement, contained safely within established traditions. *Foundations* was divided into three parts. Part 1 was on The Moral Basis of Co-operation, and its Relation to a) Religious Faith b) Other Philanthropic Movements and c) Socialism, Communism and other Politico-Social Movements. Part 2 was on The Economical Basis of Co-operation and its Relation to a) Competition; b) Current Economic Theories; c) The State. Part 3 was on The Practice of Co-operation: a) In

Distribution; b) In Production; c) In Social Life.

The third idea might be understood as proposing a 'net-like construction with which new experiences can be caught again and again'.[214] My suggestion is that it might appeal to young people across a difficult, conflicted, fragmented twenty-first century world, to articulate a 'religion of co-operation'. If so, Holyoake could become one of its prophets, thereby helping to rescue the notion of 'religion' from dominant definitions and providing extra force or binding for the co-operative movement. 'In one form or another', Karen Armstrong writes, 'religion is humanly universal ... it is also essentially multifarious'.[215]

This might seem an odd suggestion to make in 'secular' times, especially as a matter arising from the life of a man who was sent to prison for blasphemy, spent many days debating with priests and ministers and is most often understood as an atheist. 'Religiousness' intrigued Holyoake. 'All pursuit of good objects with pure intent is religiousness in the best sense in which this term appears to be used. The distinctive peculiarity of the Secularist is... a religiousness to which the idea of God is not essential, nor a denial of the idea necessary'.[216] A 'religion of socialism' reinforced working and progressive middle-class activists during the 1880s and 1890s.[217] Could co-operation be as attractive in modern times, when 'competitiveness', 'the economy', 'the market' and 'the Western way of life' have assumed a quasi- religious status, and when there is a widely-acknowledged deficit in 'Western' democracy as a system capable of attracting popular enthusiasm? Precisely because 'the market' has become a fetish – Adam Smith's Hidden Hand as an object of worship – there may be space for alternative things (relations) to venerate. At a time when members of the political class repeatedly refer to 'our country', and when it is no longer clear who the 'us' is, there is an evident need for 'another country' (past and present) which either once upon a time *did*, or in the future *could* belong to all its inhabitants, equitably and co-operatively.[218] There is a widely-acknowledged shortage of units of 'belonging' able to function as 'bridging' as well as 'bonding' social capital, capable of federating differences *between* their adherents as well selecting *among* them for similarities.[219]

> 'rejoice! For a later
> era will differ
> (O difference that kills,
> or intimidates, much
> of all our small shadowy
> life!)' [220]

The trinity of items to which people are encouraged to belong in 'the West' – the individual (and his or her 'identity'), the family and the nation – play no part in the 1995 *Statement of Co-operative Identity* or in the *Rules* and Laws of the Rochdale Pioneers and their successors. In their place, 'members' and 'membership', of Societies are mentioned seventeen times in the 1995 *Statement*. This statement proposes that actual Societies – as opposed to abstractions like 'civil society' – could constitute an entire society or world-wide commonwealth. This would be achieved by means of co-operation among co-operatives, and by spreading education and information about co-operatives as widely as possible – an honourable occupation for social missionaries. A family, yes, but as Robert Owen said, when expounding 'the religion of his system' to the delegates of the Third Co-operative Congress in London in 1832, the co-operative family was a 'great social family which is now rapidly advancing to a state of independent and equalized community'.[221]

Not only the family but also the community, not only the individual but also society... The question is how to inform as well as intone such commonplaces? Could co-operatives now be part of a necessary if not a sufficient answer? Among the advocates of a twenty-first century, world-wide 'solidarity economy' co-operators have begun to raise the stakes:

> 'Gandhi's formulation was that co-operation was an extension of the principle of self rule or swaraj. He rooted the idea of co-operatives in personal and spiritual and not merely collective terms. This has been a theme of many of the major co-operative movements, secular and religious, of the past 150 years. In other words, co-ops are not merely about collective economic power but about the skills and rewards of being social. It is about the power to be human, not just the power to get more.'[222]

In his 1996 *Background Paper* to the 1995 *Statement*, Ian Macpherson developed the idea of co-operatives understood and *organised* on the premise that 'full individual development'...'can take place only in association with others'. If the full development of 'human personality' in every human being is the goal, as Macpherson suggests, this points to fully mutual forms of association whose members believe in the value of 'equality'. Capitalist firms are responsible to and controlled 'primarily in the interests of capital', whereas 'one of the main features distinguishing a co-operative from such firms is that 'their basis is in human personality' and its equitable development for everyone.

Macpherson explored 'solidarity' as the ultimate ethical value in which co-operative members believe, constructing co-operatives whose assets belong to 'the group' as well as to individuals. Co-operatives are 'affirmations of collective strength and mutual responsibility, and even responsibility to employees who are not members and to the wider society'. Solidarity as a value 'ensures that co-operative action is not just a disguised form of limited self-interest. A co-operative is more than an association of members; it is also a collectivity'... 'Solidarity also means that co-operatives stand together and aspire to a united co-operative movement'.[223]

> 'Since its beginnings, the co-operative movement has encouraged people of different political allegiances and ideologies to work together. In that sense it has tried to transcend the traditional ideologies that have created so much tension, unrest and warfare in the late nineteenth and twentieth centuries. Indeed this capacity to bring diverse people together for common goals is one of the great promises the movement offers to the twenty-first century.' [224]

IIA. An associational-socialist alternative to the Marxist revolutionary tradition of c.1848 to c.1959.

[i] A peaceful path?

Holyoake called the period of co-operative history from 1845 until 1876 'the constructive period'.[225] This period was not about withdrawal from the outside world by going into community. As encouraged by Holyoake the movement was engaged in an ambitious struggle, with allies and against opponents, within but also against the either-ors of market and state. If 'utopian' refers, as Engels thought, to attempts to 'rescue society behind its back', this was not the stance of the seven hundred and ninety-four Societies which subscribed to build Holyoake

House. In full public view, in buildings as proud as any town hall, co-operators traded in necessities central to peoples' needs. These included ideas and facts about each other – in a word, mutuality. Because they were oppositional, and on a scale large enough by the late-nineteenth century to be called 'a state within the state'; and because they constituted their own, large-scale market within 'the' market (the Co-operative Wholesale Society was in the top ten enterprises in the world by the end of Holyoake's life[226]) they were, in turn, attacked in the market by private competitors and shaped within the state by public regulators.

Holyoake was convinced that free, equitable, universal (the Owenite word for global) production, distribution and exchange of knowledge and ideas would produce, above all else, peace. This was a fundamental good, an expectation even, as it was for all nineteenth-century believers in universal freedom based on co-operation rather than competition.[227] Holyoake was not against all military campaigns. For example, he supported the struggles of Garibaldi's Redshirts in Italy for freedom from foreign rule. The flag which Garibaldi gave him covered his coffin in 1906.[228] He attributed unpopular wars – in the sense of wars which were not 'peoples' wars' – to standing armies, bloated States and secret decision-making. His faith was that if arrangements for fully mutual, or free (in the more than capitalist sense of that word) communication were put in place among and between peoples, these would amount to peace. Arms had been crucial in feudal times, but in the middle of the nineteenth century, ideas had become the people's war material, and it was their moral duty to fight for progress by means of the methodical instantiation of ideas.[229] In *The Co-operative Movement Today*, 1903 (first published in 1891) he recalled capital's violence during the first phase of the industrial revolution and the first forty years of his own life.

'Over the whole plain of labour and trade you saw society in conflict. No arms were used, and yet men were struck down; no blood was spilt, and yet men died. Neither giant nor feudal lord were any longer there; a new tyrant reigned in their stead, more omnipresent and pitiless than they – whose name was Capital. Like his predecessors he had relenting moods, and posed as a benefactor when

"With one hand he put
A penny in the urn of poverty
And with the other took a shilling out". '

Since then, Labour had made advances, but 'the right of irresponsible aggressivenesss which capital still has, corrupted it like despotism and made it insatiable...This would have been thought to be social war had it not been called "competition".'[230] By contrast, co-operation had 'cardinal principles' and a 'pacific policy' with which to win the struggle in which it was now engaged. It is no surprise to find Holyoake joining the Garden City Association in his nineties, to help create Letchworth as the beginning of Ebenezer Howard's *Tomorrow: a Peaceful Path to Real Reform* (1898).[231] 'Are there, or ever were, any body of working-people so independent as the co-operators, who not only own property but own themselves?'.[232]

'Force is no remedy here; it may break up, but it can never build up society. It can never relax the cold contraction of error, interest and prejudice; while the geniality of reason, of wise, earnest, persistent, and informing argument, expands the iron heart of the world, so that the inspiration of justice and compassion can enter it, and sooner or later, concessions are made which denunciation and menace could never extort.' [233]

In countries like Britain where tyranny had been superseded, 'murder as a means of progress' was unnecessary, 'a worn-out theory'. It was important, however, to point to governmental hypocrisy. 'Agitators' were not the only advocates of the 'doctrine' of assassination.

> 'Governments hold the doctrine and act upon it. They often cause persons to be put to death on principle. They have often held it to be good policy to kill a few popular leaders in order to strike terror into their followers'.

So have people like Governor Eyre, Charles Kingsley and Thomas Carlyle.

But,

> 'if tyrannicide is to be approved as a policy the business of the despot-ender should be an art, and praise should be given under conditions'.[234]

Invited to join the coming-of-age celebrations of the Hebden Bridge Fustian Manufacturers Co-operative Society in September 1891, Holyoake said 'there were two methods to improve the state of things in the country, co-operation or trade unionism. Or they might employ dynamite. He was for the dynamite of argument'.[235]

Intrigued by 'the English political mind',[236] Holyoake described how one of its characteristics was to exaggerate in order to provoke the violence of radical movements, so as to ratify the state's resort to violence. The strategy was to magnify or invent labour's violent intentions, in order to threaten or employ violence on behalf of property and order. If advocates of 'physical force' among, for example, Chartists and Reform

Leaguers in the 1840s and 1860s threatened revolution by means of physical force, government repression could be justified. 'Communism' was a bogey seventy years before 1917. 'Socialists and Nihilists' could also serve as bogeymen, not only in Britain.

> 'A little outrage of speech or act on their part is made to go a long way by classes more dangerous then they, who, unwilling to accord redress, are glad of pretexts of repression. Alarmed power has many friends...Despotic "Order" has its Robespierres as well as Anarchy. A great cry goes up in the Press against assassins, while few cry out against the oppression which creates the assassinations of despair... The armed and conspiring Buonapartes, Bismarcks, and Czars are bloodier far than the impotent and aspiring poor'.[237]

The revolutionary year of 1848 inspired great fear, notably among Christian Socialist friends of co-operation, among whom Thomas Hughes became particularly vocal.[238] In the months preceding the Chartists final great demonstration on Kennington Common on April 10th 1848, 'the conclusion to which the Chartist leaders came was that the Government wanted to create a conflict, shoot down a number of the people, and then proclaim to Europe that they had "saved society" by murder'.[239] Whatever the intricacies surrounding 'the 10th April of Spencer Walpole' twenty years later – and Holyoake's exact role in them, seen as too accommodating by those to his Left [240] – his position became self-consciously non-violent, in a demonstrative, Gandhian sense. He advised Chartists not to strike back when and if they were struck. 'Many of them, I knew, were willing to die for their country, if that would save it. They would serve it much better by dying without resistance than dying with it. If any were killed whilst walking in the procession their comrades should move quietly on. Nothing would tell more strongly on public opinion than such heroic observance of order'... 'Hetherington, one of the bravest in the ranks, told me he would do it'.[241]

Twentieth-century violence, verbal and political, terror for its own sake from Left and Right, was more than a glint in the late nineteenth-century eye. It was present on the Left, most clearly among some anarchists and syndicalists, and in the fulminations against those who were anathematised as 'reformists' by revolutionaries who followed Marx.[242] By the end of his life, signs of violence as romance or cult were apparent to Holyoake. But, while open to classical justifications of tyrannicide, he was clear that co-operators built Societies for bread, knowledge and freedom – where the freedom to do so had been won – in other ways. 'Co-operators help themselves by Commercial and Industrial Associations, neither making war on Capitalists, nor supplicating aid from the State'.[243] Holyoake knew about politicians' threats and 'unprincipled' counter threats made on behalf of 'the working men'. Particularly in England, they would not be popular.

> 'When a politician does not well know what to say against an adversary's measures, he calls them "socialistic"... In former days, when a clerical disputant met with an unmanageable argument, he said it was "atheistic", and then it was taken as answered. In these days the perplexed politician, seeing no answer to a principle pressed upon him, says it is "communistic"...
>
> One thing may be taken as true, that the English, whether poor or rich, are not, as a body, thieves. Now and then you find some in both classes who have a predatory talent, which they do not hide in a napkin. Statesman may sleep in peace. The

working men will never steal knowingly, either by crowbar or ballot-box. Tories and Whigs have robbed them; and I think I have seen the Radical hand with marks about it, as though it had been in the people's pocket – doubtless in some moment of patriotic aberration. Nevertheless, the common sense of common men is against peculation'.[244]

Even within the movement, 'socialist theory' could be used as a punchbag by co-operators who resisted sharing their surplus with producers as well as with consumers:

> 'A favourite argument against the labourer's claim of sharing in the profits of his labour, was that of calling it a "Socialist Theory". Of course it was a "Socialist Theory". All co-operative stores are founded on the same "Socialist Theory" which gives profits to purchasers as well as to capitalists'.[245]

[ii] *Not only the political but also the social.*

There was, Holyoake thought, an important distinction between 'social' and 'political' reform, as regarding their respective routes as well as their results. He shared the suspicion of political reform shown by early co-operators, including the suspicion felt by some of Robert Owen's followers of Owen's search for all-at-once, top-down, total transformations, and the suspicion of 'the Charter and nothing but the Charter' felt by some Chartists.

A reserve of probing, somewhat Socratic scepticism stayed with Holyoake for much of his life. This was characteristic, perhaps, of a dedicated *writer* for whom the word *social* was multivalent. In old age he warned against the idea that even co-operators' 'social remedy would do everything for the people'. Nothing could do everything. As he had done in Chartist times, Holyoake continued to argue that political reform had to be worked for step by step alongside everything else. It was exclusivity, or what he called 'half-mindedness' that was wrong. He could not help admiring Lord Shaftesbury, allowing him a 'moral affinity' with co-operators. But then again, 'he was 'essentially and exclusively a social reformer and took no part in political amelioration'. So he was unable to identify with any popular aspiration 'for such power as should enable (people) to have a political voice in the determination of their own destiny'.[246] For Holyoake, completeness, the whole distance, was all. But so too was every step.

In ways that have 'perplexed and perturbed' tidy taxonomists among his readers, Holyoake picked his co-operative way: neither a Social Democrat, nor a Tory Radical, nor a simple Liberal, nor a Spencerian individualist.[247] While there was 'undoubtedly a deep and honourable sentiment of humanity in the heart both of the Conservative, Socialist and Christian philanthropist' and while Kingsley's fictional 'Churchman's Chartist' and George Eliot's 'Positivist Chartists' were fine figures, 'they were no more like the true Chartist than a hardy mountain plant is like a hothouse tulip.'[248] In *Bygones Worth Remembering* his analysis of what we would call the cultural politics of John Ruskin, J.M. Ludlow and 'the Chartists of fiction' in Kingsley's *Alton Locke* and Eliot's *Felix Holt* anticipated Raymond Williams's work in *Culture and Society 1780–1950* (1958). 'The real Chartists – like the Co-operators – sought self-government for the people by the people', by contrast for instance with 'that nobly organized kind of passive competence which Mr Ruskin meditated for the people'.[249] Holyoake's language in *Bygones* was oddly prophetic of the blood of twentieth-century world war, although he did not anticipate the gold which capitalists would forge from it. To resile from politics was becoming increasingly dangerous. 'I always dissented from this doctrine (of exclusively social reform), and resented it... as the politician will come some day and throw away the savings of a century into a sea of imperial blood'.[250]

From his earliest days in Birmingham when he sought Christian truth by sampling his local churches and chapels, Holyoake believed that Christianity and war were incompatible. At the end of his life he combined rule by the wealthy, declarations of war ('few know wherefore') and private and public debt, in the same paragraph.[251] More often, he argued that it was the lack of open and shared 'intelligence' – a word Holyoake often used to mean education and knowledge – which produced international violence. So he campaigned against government taxes on every form of communication, whether railway travel, newspapers, stamps or advertisements. For 'twenty-four years chairman of the Travelling Tax Abolition Committee' he wrote a *History of the Travelling Tax* for the CWS *Annual* in 1901.[252] 'Clandestine commissions' between business people were intolerable, even more so when they took place between co-operative societies.[253] It was only as regards the Secret Ballot, for which he argued strenuously against all comers including Mill and Bright, that Holyoake defended secrecy. This was to protect working-class people against the coercive power of their patrons and employers. As already mentioned, he found resistance to the Secret Ballot by alleged – and Liberal – democrats offensive. 'It is insanity of individuality which wantonly enters upon unequal conflicts; and open voting is of that nature... It is madness, not manliness, in a man who opposes his single head to twenty swords... Secret suffrage is the needle-gun which places the proletariat and the proprietor upon an equality in the electoral combat... The State ought to keep faith with the elector one minute in every three millions of minutes which elapse on the average between one General Election and another'.²⁵⁴

Peace between peoples or nations was one thing. Peace between social classes meant the avoidance of violent acts. For Holyoake, however, this did not involve the surrender of his own class to their alleged superiors. Peace in his sense involved the mutual transformation of each existing class. Contradictory 'interests' could find forms of association in which to recognise each other *as* contradictory, which they could not do 'under competition'. This is what 'unity' meant. In the co-operative movement it meant the 'unity of industrial interests' within and between Co-operative Societies, a unity which was structurally prevented within the wider, capitalist society. In the secularist movement it meant 'the unity of principle which prevails amid whatever diversity of opinion may subsist in a Secular Society, the bond of union being the common convictions of the duty of advancing the Secular good of this life... To seek human improvement by material methods, irrespective of any other opinions held, and irrespective of any diversity of reasons for holding these'.²⁵⁵ In a characteristic Holyoake maxim, 'the solution of the problem of union can only be effected by narrowing the ground of profession, and widening that of action'.²⁵⁶

Societies were needed which had sufficient autonomy from the dominant society surrounding them to encourage a 'harmonization of interests... by providing a common framework' within which to embody a post-capitalist, co-operative (and 'secular') 'order' among working people.²⁵⁷ Unity depended on a degree of autonomy or 'independence', another co-operative value. Independence meant a state (of affairs) where the religion and politics of working people could not be dictated to them 'by employers, squires and magistrates'. Hence the utility of Co-operative Halls 'where we can hear the thing we will, on any day we will.' Independence had to be made everyday rather than being the product of an all-at-once revolution or *coup*. 'Do not believe that justice always comes uppermost. It never does until it is made to come. The Old Pioneers knew this'.[258] Holyoake showed what he meant by the limitations of dominant meanings of revolution when he suggested that the only such event he had ever been involved in was the removal of Palmerston from power in 1865.[259]

Fully 'social' transformation had to be mutual, ending the very idea of a separate *labouring* class divested of the full humanity (and the profits of capital) which were currently the property of 'gentlemen'. The end in view, an association of all classes and all nations, was not contradicted by the means – associations of all classes and all nations.

Consciousness, or intelligence, was fundamental. At one time Holyoake was prepared to advocate education or 'knowledge' as a qualification for extending the franchise to working people. 'Associative intelligence', like 'associative communication'[260] was a primary product of co-operatives. To use a Marxist distinction, it was basic rather than superstructural – as basic as groceries. In Leeds, 'intelligence was becoming a commodity supplied by the Society.'[261] After all, it was, 'a co-operative investment' as material as any other.[262]

The 'positive moral and social culture' for which Holyoake worked was a way of life with its own loyalties, solidarities, markets within 'the' market and state formations within 'the' state. This new way of life was already replacing the human deformations of the capital-labour relation. Labour had begun to employ capital, paying it no more than a fair wage. 'At first (co-operators) were not willing to pay interest for it (capital). Now they are willing to hire capital to prevent capital hiring them'.[263] It was the combination of immediate economic rewards and epochal change which

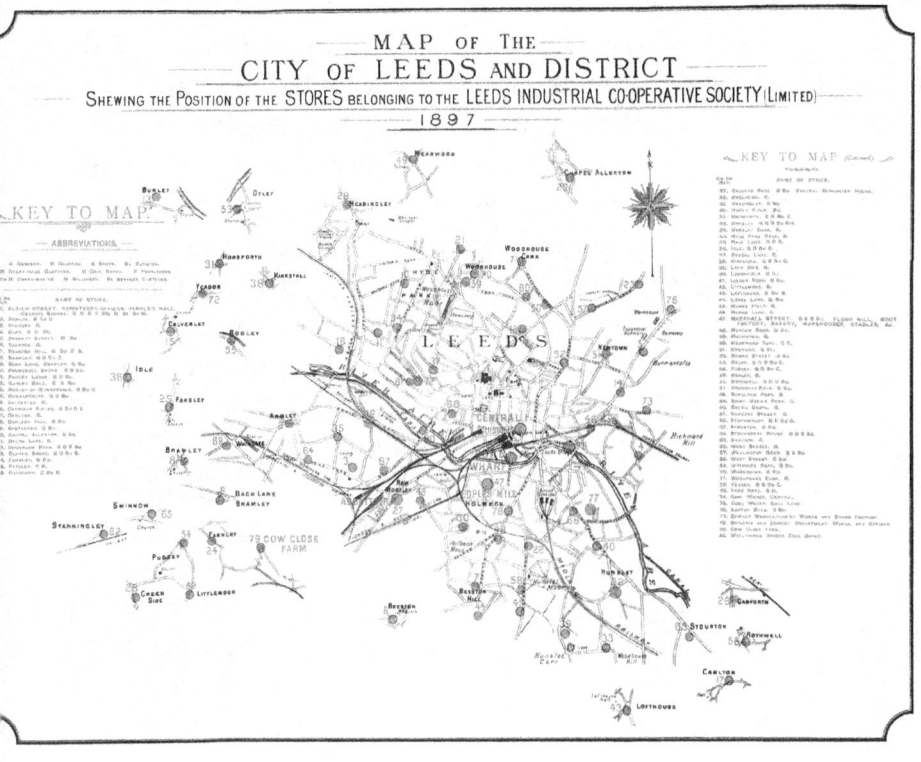

Map of the City of Leeds and District, showing the scatter and density of the Society's presence in 1897

made co-operatives compelling. Leeds Co-operators were told that they had in hand 'a new system of association and business'. The map of the city, folded into their celebratory History showed members how far they had already got. It was dotted with Central and Branch stores.[264] Derby members were invited to understand that the new 'Order of Industry' which was to replace the 'Order of Capital' was to be as different from capitalism as feudalism had been, to encourage the thought that 'co-operation has no reason to fear the competition which it supercedes'.[265] The change might take a long time to complete, as capitalism's 'great arch' had done. But 'without doubt the hire system of labour will be superseded by the self-employer of labour in co-operative workshops, as surely as the feudal and vassal system has been superseded by hired workmen'.[266] But whereas the transition to capitalism had required the 'organisation of arms', the transition to 'Industry' could only endure through 'the organisation of ideas'.[267]

More than a century later, 'socialism' is most frequently seen as a failure, anyway impossible and fortunately dead, surviving only as a label used by regimes in order to conceal nightmares. In the 'free world' the very idea of socialism remains a chimera feared by those in power more than it is longed for by those out of it. Socialism's surviving missionaries represent it either as an inevitability regardless of how they behave; or as a struggle against the USA and 'the West'; or as a struggle in the head as much as on the ground; or as the taking, winning or capturing of power at some date in the future, whether by revolution or election. 'Coming into' power will be followed by the introduction of Policies by Political Parties which may or may not carry the socialist label on their tin.

When *social* change is practised by means of 'way of life' decisions taken by plain people every day, for example in co-operative, fair trade, transition town, and other green organisations, its significance as something more (not less) than 'political' and 'economic' activity goes largely unnoticed. Throughout his life Holyoake celebrated such ordinary-but-extraordinary practices. 'Progress' was a human struggle not a Law; it was being developed by working people as an art. In one of his most memorable sayings he declared that 'in politics nothing approaches; everything has to be fetched.'[268] 'Progression depends upon ourselves'.[269] 'Utopianism is not my idiosyncracy. But I have confidence in endeavour. Continuity of ameliorative effort is the sole enthusiasm that can serve the cause of societarian improvement'.[270] Like most co-operators between the mid-nineteenth and the early twentieth centuries, Holyoake resisted the 'socialist' label, while from time to time referring more favourably, as did William Morris, to 'communism'. This was different from what he thought of as Carl *(sic)* Marx's 'imperialistic communism and state socialism' – a judgement based more on some of Marx's acolytes than on any of his texts.[271] In an essay on 'Co-operation and Socialism' in 1890, Holyoake was careful to differentiate between older, co-operative and newer, 'state-helping' socialisms. He was kinder to Proudhon and Marx than he was to Lassalle and to Frederic Harrison, a Positivist whose case against Co-operation was that it was doing too little and taking too long to do it.

> 'This objection proceeds from theorists who believe they have an infallible, all-sufficient remedy of their own for social evils. Socialistic theorists are mostly social Tories who seek the control of the people... It is a common infatuation of excellent persons who have great schemes of their own, to disparage all others, and get them out of the way, that they alone may run the world. Co-operation is content to make a

plea for itself, doing what it can, and hoping others may be able to do it better'.[272]

This is how Holyoake wanted things remembered in *Sixty Years of an Agitator's Life*:

> 'English Communists' were quite different from the 'newspaper definitions' from which they suffered. 'They had a passion for industry, and sought only an equitable division of profits'.[273]

In the same work he looked back to his employment in 1841 as a socialist lecturer or missionary in Worcester:

> 'Persons favourable to the organisation of the socialist state, who Robert Owen had incited to action, came to be called "Socialists". Mr Cobden spoke at times in the House of Commons in condemnation of them without appearing to be aware that there never were any agitators in England of the kind he had in his mind. Continental Socialists meditated rearranging society by force. There never were in England any philanthropists of the musket and the knife. English socialists expected to improve society by showing the superior reasonableness of the changes they sought. A small branch of these propagandists existed in Worcester'.[274]

Holyoake subscribed to the 'political anti-politics' or 'social radicalism' of what he called 'the enthusiastic period' of co-operative socialism which lasted until the mid- century.[275] He carried its structures of thought and feeling with him for the rest of his life while maintaining an open dialogue, not always consistent on his side, with Liberal and other politicians in the interests of a larger 'outside' for co-operation. He wrote to Gladstone in 1881: 'I maintain always and everywhere that the people should keep the State, not the State the people'.[276] On a more detailed level, he thought dilutions of full co-operation needed to be watched, acceptable though they might be to well-placed friends in London. So too did organised attacks on the movement. Holyoake pointed out the limitations of not-quite- co-operatives to Gladstone. Civil Service Supply Associations (today's social enterprises) were attractive simulacra of the real thing. So Holyoake wanted Gladstone to raise his sights above 'London Co-operation' to 'the higher' or Rochdale forms of co-operative.[277] London's was 'another form of Co-operation (which) has grown up among the middle and upper classes, very useful in its way.'[278] 'Civil Service storemen are mere shopkeepers and are not to be counted.'[279]

To the extent that the higher co-operation threatened competitors, they did not hesitate not only to simulate but also to attack co-operatives through the market and by the use of state power. In 1890, when the Grocers' Association lobbied to get references to the co-operative movement removed from H.O. Arnold Foster's *The Laws of Everyday Life*, written for the use of schools, Holyoake replied with a pamphlet on the *Conspiracy of grocers against public education: the suppressed chapters on Co-operation in 'The Laws of Everyday Life'*.[280] In his eirenic way, he felt that the legitimate interests of small 'private traders' needed to be considered too. Emergent capitalist chains needed to be dealt with as the antagonists of the small grocer as much as they were the enemies of co-operators. He spent some spirit on this matter in his old age.[281] It was as if Holyoake could be considerate, sometimes emollient and 'moderate' – in ways which giants like the CWS could use in their branding materials – precisely *because* he knew how big and full of futurity the Co-operative big tent was. The Burnley

Society were proud of their 'Self Help' shoes; the CWS sold boxes of 'Holyoake' shoes, and used his words on a postcard advertising 'the essence of co-operation'. The promise was 'no disturbance in society... no secret associations' but 'such share of the common competence as labour shall earn or thought can win, and *this it intends to have*' (my italics).

After 1848, how co-operative associationism related to emergent forms of socialism became a *leitmotif* in Holyoake's work.[282] The question became: what were 'the chances of obtaining an English Republic by moral means'?[283] In July 1843 in his journal *The Movement,* Holyoake had attributed to 'socialism' 'the capacity...to build up individual as well as general character, to serve as a complete body of moral, political and social philosophy.'[284] As socialism began to associate itself with what he saw first as 'revolution' and then as a smothering state, he took issue with it more and more, as he tried to kindle first the secularist and then the co-operative movement as the carriers of his 'complete body'. Revolutionary forms inherited from 1789 were not likely, he thought, to produce sustainable social transformation in Labour's interest. 'The French revolutionists of 1793 were insurgents created by oppression, who having no experience of the limitations of freedom contrived to make liberty a greater terror than despotism'.[285] This explains his references to 'mere' socialism as something less not more than co-operation. Whereas 'it is the pure cant of capitalism to persuade men that it is noble to work for nothing'... 'co-operation alone teaches the art of attaining equality without revolution by simply retaining earnings in the workman's own hands'.[286]

> 'Co-operation proceeds by self-help, and socialism by the method of State help. They differ more deeply than that, for

ADVERTISEMENTS.

THE BURNLEY "SELF-HELP"
Cotton Spinning & Manufacturing Society Limited,
HEALEY ROYD MILL, BURNLEY.

MAKERS OF

Oxford Shirtings, Flannelettes, Silesias, Linenettes, Lustres, Dyed Sateens, and Silketeen Linings; also Grey Cloths in Jeans, Twills, and Plains.

ALL COMMUNICATIONS TO OFFICE, MANCHESTER.

National Telephone, 138 Burnley.
National Telephone Co., 3,010 Manchester.

Registered Office:
19, MARSDEN SQUARE, MANCHESTER.

Members should ask at their Stores for the

"SELF-HELP"
═ BRAND ═
Boots and Shoes

All Goods Hand-made.   Satisfaction Guaranteed.

Eccles Industrial Manufacturing Society Limited.
Established 1861.
Works and Offices: SILK STREET, ECCLES, near MANCHESTER.

MANUFACTURERS OF

TOILET, SATIN, ALHAMBRA, HONEYCOMB, TAPESTRY, AND GRECIAN QUILTS.

Quality and Price of Goods will bear a favourable comparison with any other Manufacturers.

The Co-operative Wholesales — Manchester, London, Newcastle, and Glasgow — are appointed our Sole Agents to Societies.

Holyoake shoes (from the National Co-operative Archive)

co-operation seeks to supersede competition and socialism merely seeks to equalize its weapons, so that the war can be carried on with greater advantage...We stand by the side of self-help, and seek to supersede the vicious, warring, self-ish, peace-destroying element of competition, and to introduce the spirit of amity, considering the welfare of others as well as ourselves. Within legitimate limits we shall avail ourselves of the help of Parliament. We claim that the State should be impartial to us, and remove any disability. We mean to make our fortune by our own devices, and if we employ ourselves wisely, we shall be able to do this.'[287]

If revolution was not the same as co-operative radicalism, neither was the vote. 'Suffrage' was not the end of social politics. 'The working class accept the vote', he wrote to *The Times* and other papers in 1871, 'not because it will very early benefit their order, but because it is an indispensable condition to their being able to benefit themselves'.[288] Delegate democracy was practised by co-operators and unnecessarily denigrated by their rulers in government.[289] 'Representative Government confers upon the English citizen *one minute of liberty every seven years* (his italics). It is not much to ask. It is little to be content with. It is a wondrous proof of the people's docility that they yield obedience on such terms'.[290]

[iii] *A state within a state.*

The extraordinary ambition behind the 'associated efforts' of relatively small Co-operative Societies working within the Rochdale tradition gets increasingly hard for modern consumer co-operators to remember, let alone modern liberal radicals. It was a working-class man, Mr H.Whalley, President of a relatively small West Riding Society, the Denholme Industrial Co-operative Society Ltd – hardly a revolutionary cell – who concluded his Holyoake-like, jubilee history of the Society between 1880 and 1930 with these words:

> 'Since our Society was started in 1880 practically all the surplus of £106,609 has been returned to the members... Part of the surplus, however, has been left in the Society as an investment... We also co-operate with other societies in owning and controlling the greatest concern in this country, viz., the Co-operative Wholesale Society, and have as much interest in this institution as any other society of equal size. By this working together, many of the commodities we sell are manufactured expressly for our use and with our capital, so that we both own and control the means of production and distribution, which is of tremendous importance to the workers...(who) by loyally supporting their own shop...can claim all the advantages that associated efforts can give'.[291]

On several occasions Holyoake expressed his pleasure at Lord Rosebery's acknowledgement, speaking from the platform at Co-operative Congress in 1890 in Glasgow as an eminent Liberal statesman, that the co-operative movement amounted to nothing less than a state within the state. 'I have always wished', Rosebery said, 'once at any rate, to be face to face with the citizens of that State within a State, which is called the Co-operative Movement'. Holyoake used this as the epigraph for his book on *The Co-operative Movement Today*.[292] In 1897 he told Leeds co-operators that 'if Lord Rosebery was right in saying this, the Leeds Society may be described as a city within a city, a new city within the old, having its own laws, its own government and revenues which it does not have to earn, and which increase while they sleep – provided they buy at the store'.[293] Holyoake's sense of the presence of the movement in his *History* of the Pioneers is palpable, even provocative. Did it provoke the building of the magnificent Town Hall in Rochdale as a civic response to an independent, would-be hegemonic, working-class social movement?

> 'The Central Store stands at the junction of St Mary's Gate and Toad Lane, presenting a copious frontage to both roads, and raising its head higher than any building in the town. Standing on the site of the old theatre and the Temperance Hall, all know the place, and if they did not they can see it. It has been proposed to erect an observatory upon it, and furnish it with powerful telescopes …
>
> Close to the river, and in a central part of the town, are the Society's manufacturing departments, newly arranged and rebuilt, comprising tobacco manufacturing; bread, biscuit and cake baking; the business of pork butchering, currant cleaning, coffee roasting, coffee and pepper grinding; and in the same yard are the stables and slaughter houses; the whole being so arranged that the produce of each department can be delivered at the shops with the precision of a machine'.[294]

Rosebery's conjunction was *within*: 'within a state'. In keeping with his deliberate rather than stationary liberalism, Holyoake pressed on. At this point his ambition – beyond rather than within – sounds more like that of the man he sometimes railed against, J. T. W. Mitchell of the CWS, than that of men with whom he mostly fellow-travelled like E. V. Neale of the Co-operative Union. Changing the whole system in labour's interest rather than capital's was not generally the tone in which Christian Socialists spoke. Co-operators, wrote

The scale of the presence of the Rochdale Society by 1868

Holyoake, aimed to 'influence the State, cover the State, and eventually change the "system" prevailing in the State.'[295] Holyoake seldom abstracted 'the state' even in theory, wary as he was of plain people abstracting it in practice. State Socialists, he thought, tended to apostatize the state, thereby encouraging 'feudality', or dependency, out of which English working people were growing, helping themselves by means of co-operatives.

'In other countries, despotism, tempered by paternal government, trains the people to look for State redress and State management. Thus the mass of the people... regard the State as the source of evil or good'.[296] Never a systematic thinker himself, Holyoake identified the idea of 'system', like Dickens, as a modern, but also as a somewhat regressive phenomenon: hence the inverted commas. The idea of 'system' was, of course, fully present, not to say overwhelming, in the work of his machine-loving mentor, Robert Owen, with his *New System of Society*. And Holyoake paid tribute to Owenite 'socialist advocates' in a characteristically intricate way:

> 'Whatever faults they else might have, (they) had at least done one service to employers – they had taught workmen to reason upon their condition – they had shown them that commerce was a system, and that masters were slaves of it as well as men...masters could not always do quite as they would any more than their servants'. It followed that 'if the men became masters tomorrow, they would be found doing pretty much as masters do now'.[297]

Owen 'was eager to apply his system to society, which system he believed to be an alembic in which the baser metals of the world might be put and changed to gold'... 'No wonder the principles on which he produced these results took in his mind the shape of a "system."'²⁹⁸ Holyoake enjoyed thinking aloud about whether Co-operation amounted to a system or not. In the local shop, at the level of 'co-operative storekeeping' working against 'competitive shopkeeping'...'each has a different system', the day-to-day components of which Holyoake was unafraid to expound. He thought that Derby co-operators would do well to see themselves as 'outside the competitive system'. 'The Co-operator... is a member of another system.'²⁹⁹ *The Leader*, for which Holyoake wrote under the pseudonym 'Ion' during the early 1850s and of which he was an editor, called itself 'Socialistic' and, making an interesting distinction, favoured the 'doctrine' while not having any 'system' of Socialism. Holyoake's agenda was to give the people, by means of 'equality of intelligence', 'the power to develop a system'.³⁰⁰ He sharpened his wit on Owen's way of applying system to society. It could too easily leave people without their own handle on the future, or as Holyoake put it 'you lost your needle in the wool'. 'It was said of Montaigne that his sentences were vascular and alive, and, if you pricked them, they bled. If you pricked Mr Owen's, when he wrote on his system, you lost your needle in the wool.'³⁰¹

Holyoake's sense of how capitalists had become trapped in their own system was part of his sense of where the writ of moral agency ran and where structure or 'circumstance' set limits to it. He called Chapter 10 of his History of the Pioneers 'The Rochdale System', knowing how incomplete it was. If it was to become complete, members needed to affirm individual and associated agency every day and everywhere, in the workshop as well as in the store. But the whole, or in Owenite language the 'universal', had to exist in part before it could exist as a whole. 'Market-making and workshop-making, producing and consuming, make up the whole of industrial and social life, which can be (and is in many Stores) locally organised'.³⁰² He encouraged the members of the Leeds Industrial Co-operative Society in 1897 to see themselves as part of 'the great working class union' through which they were making and re-making themselves.³⁰³

IIB. Towards an autonomous, ethical or moral 'tradition'?

[i] 'Tradition'.

Traditions in the ordinary sense of the word are easy to grasp, particularly in Britain where so many have been invented.³⁰⁴ Holyoake mostly used the word in this day-to-day sense, while he also nurtured something more ambitious, rooted in his stories – which he told like generative myths – of the Rochdale Pioneers:

> 'In the arid plains of English industry Co-operation broke out like a spring, here and there, at long intervals; only of late years has it furnished a confluence of waters sufficiently to irrigate the parched fields of labour. ... No doubt, if historians had troubled themselves to observe industrial aspects in former centuries, they would have seen Co-operation, in one form or another, creeping up to them for notice. Not getting it, the rise of that form of industry by concert and consent is indicated mainly by tradition and fugitive records'.³⁰⁵

In 1890 Holyoake published a collection of essays most of which had appeared in *Co-operative News*, called *Self-Help a hundred years ago* in which he told of figures like Dr Shute

Barrington (1734-1826), 'the first co-operative bishop', putting them into a family tree or 'consecutive record of hereditary opinion' concerning Self-Help. Holyoake thought it would help members of 'that vast network of Distributive Stores which has now overspread Great Britain, constituting a self-helping movement ... the like of which has arisen in no other nation on earth', were they to acquaint themselves with figures like Bishop Barrington, Count Rumford and Sir Thomas Bernard. 'Forgotten narratives' could 'excite admiration', from times when 'self-respect was hardly born':

> In those days people in low circumstances believed that rich persons were always to exist, and that the poor would never cease in the land. And until co-operation came and proved itself a new force of industry capable of delivering the people from poverty, it did seem that their destiny was precariousness, to be sometime delivered by benevolence'.[306]

The moral philosopher Alasdair MacIntyre offers a considered idea of what constitutes a philosophical, ethical or moral tradition, renders its contents rationally adaptable, and makes it available (or not) for the future.[307] It was his use of 'tradition' which helped me to look again at the scope of the co-operative movement as 'this new order of life'. It was also his sustained preoccupation with 'the political and social structures of the common good', combined with his refusal of instant (and nearly all contemporary) answers which encouraged me to encourage Co-operators to risk more than their (our) *business* or *economic* ambition. 'What are the types of political and social society that can embody those relationships of giving and receiving through which our individual and common goods can be achieved?'

'What kind of society might possess the structures necessary to achieve a common good... If at this point we turn for assistance to recent social and political philosophy, we will be for the most part disappointed, since with rare exception work in that area ignores questions about the common goods of association and relationships that are intermediate between on the one hand the nation-state and on the other the individual and the nuclear family. Yet it is with just this intermediate area that we shall need to be concerned... the sharing of a common good that is constitutive of a type of association that can be realized neither in the forms of the modern state nor in those of the contemporary family'.[308]

What, I kept asking myself – knowing how I would be answered in 2017, even from within – what about the Co-op?

Although he would resist any such label, MacIntyre may be understood as something of a co-operator and mutualist. Co-operators could collect the references to effective forms of mutual activity among plain people which recur in his work, if always (so far) only partially successful. Like Holyoake, MacIntyre is scrupulous when he described how 'plain people' (he prefers 'plain' to 'ordinary', 'most', 'masses' etc.) associate for virtuous purposes. He is also vigilant about false paths frequently taken, and insists on the nature of humans as rationally dependent animals. He is for mutuality and against individualism. While resisting the 'communitarian' label sometimes attached to his work, he defends 'present utopianism' against utopianism 'of the future' in a way which chimes with Holyoake's preference for the phrase 'world-making'. 'Trying to live by Utopian standards is not Utopian, although it does involve a rejection of the economic goals of advanced capitalism.'[309]

So I began to ask: what might the co-operative movement do with – and do *to* – the idea of a tradition in MacIntyre's philosophical, history-of-ethics sense?[310]

'A tradition is constituted by a set of practices and is a mode of understanding their importance and worth; it is the medium by which such practices are shaped and transmitted across generations.'

'Traditions may be primarily religious or moral (for example Catholicism or humanism), economic (for example a particular craft or profession, trade union or manufacturer), aesthetic (for example modes of literature or painting), or geographical (for example crystallising around the history and culture of a particular house, village or region).'[311]

Could the co-operative movement be understood as a tradition in one or more of these settings: most ambitiously as a moral *and* economic tradition in its own right which consciously challenges the social (or anti-social) division of labour between such (traditional) categories? After all, the co-operative movement is, at best, as co-operative and mutual in its manner and procedure and as reasonable as Alasdair MacIntyre suggests that virtuous philosophical traditions – such as his own Aristotelian Thomism – should be.[312] Might it be possible in the future to subscribe, with rationality and commitment equal to that shown by MacIntyre to Catholicism, to an independent, Co-operative tradition to which Holyoake might then be seen as an early witness?

'Long before the French used the phrase "solidarity", the early co-operators understood it. Whether or not they could unite all hearts they believed Co-operation could unite all interests, which was plainly impossible under competition. The Co-operation which they sought was a new force of Industry which should attain competence without mendicancy, and temper inequality by equalizing fortunes. Its main principles are Concord, Economy, Equity and Self-help'[313]

As always, Holyoake's self-consciousness about words helps: he was right to draw attention not only to French uses of 'solidarity' as developed by Emile Durkheim and his radical co-operative disciples during the late-nineteenth and early-twentieth centuries but also to early co-operators' (Saint Simonians as well as Owenites) prior understandings of the idea. 'Organic' as opposed to 'mechanical' solidarity is a defining distinction for modern co-operators to return to.[314]

After setting out 'the values of self-help, self-responsibility, democracy, equality, equity and solidarity' on which 'co-operatives are based', the 1995 International Co-operative Alliance *Statement of Co-operative Identity, Values and Principles* lists 'the ethical values of honesty, openness, social responsibility and caring for others' which 'in the tradition of their founders, co-operative members believe'. What is the weight of that usage of tradition? Could a developed sense of an independent, synoptic co-operative tradition deepen the movement's presence within individuals; in their Societies as lasting collectivities as well as *ad hoc* associations of individuals; and in the wider society they transform by their presence? Can Holyoake's work be read as intimating such a possibility? 'Solidarity' would be fundamental to answering such a question. In his 1996 *Introduction* to the 1995 ICA *Statement of Identity* Ian Macpherson explained how:

'This value has a long and hallowed history within the international (co-operative) movement ... The solidarity value draws attention to the fact that co-operatives are more than just associations of individuals; they are affirmations of collective strength and mutual responsibility... Solidarity is the very cause and consequence of self-help and mutual help, two of the fundamental concepts at the heart of co-operative philosophy. It is this philosophy which distinguishes co-operatives from other forms of economic organisation'.

There is no doubt that during its first industrial revolution phases the co-operative movement grew among 'politically protestant' groups which were familiar with the creativity of nonconformist associational forms rooted in dissenting beliefs, values and principles.[315] In Britain the movement was strongly connected to wider secular and religious stirrings among an insubordinate 'lower' or 'labouring' class. In Holyoake's case, 'the habit I had acquired of frequenting chapels and missionary meetings led me to attend political assemblies'.[316] In MacIntyre's work, a philosophical, ethical or religious tradition is nothing less than a body of enquiry into 'what practical rationality is and what justice is'. This is how Holyoake saw the body of enquiry and organisation he named as 'secularism'. Traditions are bound to 'differ in their catalogs of the virtues'. Holyoake knew this. While he enjoyed making such catalogs, he also had an abiding wish to unite the items in them. *The Reasoner*, published regularly between 1846 and 1861 and intermittently thereafter, was arguably Holyoake's greatest achievement. One way of understanding this journal is as the site of a wordsmith's rather than a whitesmith's foundry. On such sites an amalgam of material energies could be prepared: from Owen's social teaching, to a new movement which Holyoake named as secularism, to his own 'deliberate' liberalism and a new/old co-operative movement. To use one of the images he liked, a river ran through Holyoake's mind, of which his own versions of Owenism, Chartism, Secularism, Liberalism and (strongly during the final forty years of his life) Co-operation were seen as tributaries.[317]

'In each (tradition) intellectual enquiry was or is part of the elaboration of a mode of social and moral life of which the intellectual enquiry itself (is) an integral part, and in each of them the forms of that life (are) embodied with greater or lesser degrees of imperfection in social and political institutions which also draw their life from other sources'.[318]

The notion of 'a mode of social and moral life of which intellectual enquiry is an integral part' recalls the 'complete body', with which Holyoake endowed co-operative socialism in 1843. In the passage already quoted, he described this as 'the capacity to build up individual as well as general character, to serve as a complete body of moral, political and social philosophy'.

MacIntyre understands Buddhism, Liberalism, Marxism, Catholicism, Utilitarianism and other such philosophies and religions, as traditions in this ambitious sense. Could Co-operation join such a list, perhaps encouraged by its recently-added *–ism*: 'co-operativism'. Would this be more likely to open it out, as in 'open co-operativism',[319] or would it turn it in on itself, as traditions tend to do? The question remains open.

At their best, cohesive, ambitious traditions grow and give way to other traditions by asking questions of a real world and its social formations. They dare to oppose and seek to replace each other where necessary. Traditions which do not make sense or hold together philosophically – including those which settle as 'religions' – are, to MacIntyre's mind, ready to fall apart. They should give way to others on a terrain

The Essence Of Co-operation

CO-OPERATION supplements political economy by organising the distribution of wealth. It touches no man's fortune, it seeks no plunder, it causes no disturbance in society, it gives no trouble to statesmen, it enters into no secret associations! It contemplates no violence, it subverts no order, it envies no dignity, it asks no favour, it keeps no terms with the idle, and it will break no faith with the industrious: it means self-help, self-dependence, and such share of the common competence as labour shall earn or thought can win, and this it intends to have.

—*George Jacob Holyoake*.

The CWS uses Holyoake as part of the brand: no threat, but a promise of truth, in the way that he admits that his own Thomist-Aristotelian Catholicism would, if its theology proved not to be philosophically reasonable.[320]

When it is most dynamic, a tradition compares and contrasts the beliefs and practices of other traditions, in the Societies (churches, 'schools' of philosophy, movements and so on) through which they work. Traditions are capable of co-operating even if they do not always do so, by looking outside themselves for answers to questions other than their own – indeed to the questions themselves. A Co-operative tradition, predisposed by its ethic to welcome dialogue and *difference*, could be preeminent in this regard. Richard Sennett's emphasis on *dialogic* communication in his work on 'the rituals, pleasures and politics of co-operation' is a fine recent example of this.[321] The answers given by rival traditions to 'what practical rationality is and what justice is', are seen, at best, as adequate or empty in ways which are open to reasoned analysis and sustained philosophical argument. Rather than zapping each other, rival traditions, at least in MacIntyre's sense of how they should behave, relate to each other co-operatively in a land of reason rather than of unboundaried relativity. Throughout its existence, this is what *The Reasoner* in its different guises tried to do.

[ii] Traditions: some signs and symptoms.

If co-operation in general and co-operatives in particular *were* to see themselves and be seen as constituting a free-standing tradition, which was able to stand alongside and challenge others of an equally ambitious kind, what would be the signs and symptoms, or anticipations, to look for in Holyoake's work and in the wider movement of which he was part?

Language is a good place to start. A self-conscious contest over key words and key concepts, with an emergent set of meanings pressing against a dominant set, is one indicator of a tradition seeking its own space and components in and against other traditions. A second indicator would be *ways of telling*. Fable, anecdote and parable – stories told in such a way as to be memorable and movement-building – are characteristic of the early, 'constructive' period of many 'faith traditions'. Holyoake's writing teems with these. A third indication would be repeated efforts to list or codify values and principles, in the co-operative case culminating over a century later in formulations like the 1995 ICA *Statement*. This is a self-conscious pulling together of different nations' co-operative traditions, making an 'identity' out of British, Danish, French, German, Canadian variations as well as many other traditions across countries in the developing world. A fourth indicator might be the degree and intensity of preoccupation in any emergent 'tradition' with the relation between values and practical, organisational principles. Ethical traditions ('religious' ones even more so) tend to make the relation between the values their adherents believe in and the precise forms in which they associate (for business, mutual improvement, worship, solidarity etc.) axiomatic, even sacred. Their history – especially their schisms and secessions – is, at times, largely *about* such relationships. I will take these four possible signs and symptoms in order.

[iii] Language and contested meanings.

Holyoake delighted in words and phrases, often claiming to have coined new ones. Never mind words like 'netheism', he claimed to be the first to use current phrases like 'purchasing power'.³²² He came back and back to the words 'capital' and 'capitalist', often with a capital letter, explaining how Co-operators use them in senses quite different from those whose interests lie in Competition. He insisted on 'co-operatives' as opposed to the abstract 'co-operation' in the same way that, for Owenite socialists, 'Societies' meant associations with kinetic energy in them. Among co-operators, the words 'share', 'profit', 'dividend' 'member' and 'owner', carry co-operative rather than capitalist meanings. It is interesting that 'the divi' hardly appears in its now-classic 'Co-op' sense in Holyoake's *History* of the Pioneers, even after decades of complaint by Christian Socialists among others that working-class members were only joining Societies because of it. 'Sharing profits on purchase' was a contemporary way of putting it. In a speech in 'the great meeting hall of the Central Stores' at the end of a Conversazione which concluded the 1892 Co-operative Congress in Rochdale, Holyoake remembered how,

> 'It was not dividend which mainly inspired them, for they had never seen it, and they detested the competitive underhandedness by which they saw others acquiring profit…Let us keep to their methods and we shall see the day which they desired to see – when principle shall rule in this movement, when the humiliation of hired labour shall cease, when worker as well as purchaser shall share in the profits created, when the penury of the many shall terminate, and the scandalous fortunes of the few be impossible, under the co-operative law of the common interest, inspired by goodwill and governed by equity'.³²³

Although 'the Co-op' in our time has been in danger of naturalisation as part of English 'heritage', along with old people's 'divi' numbers, the Movement has never entirely allowed itself to fit in comfortably. Its inheritance is to differ over fundamental meanings. Twenty-first century members have retained a sense of this in difficult times. When crisis overtook the Co-operative Group and its Bank during 2013-2014, some members organized to show that if executives and consultants from the financial services industry were to succeed in making the Group fit dominant PLC models, they would remove its reason for being.

Active members know that they cannot let their movement fit neatly into dominant categories of the 'economic', 'business', 'charity', 'the trust model', 'partnerships', 'voluntary organisations', the 'third' or even the 'mutual' *sectors*. They aspire to be more than a 'sector' whether 'public' or 'private': they insist on being both. To have anything that resembled a member-owned, member-controlled co-operative bank admitted within the rules for Clearing House Banks was hard enough in the first place, long before the recent banking crisis.[324] In the face of opposition, no dynamic, ambitious Society which attempts, in Holyoake's phrase, to 'cover the state' can afford to be an island. Members, however awkwardly, have to stake out their own space for meanings as well as for material supplies, and insist on them in a sea of opposed meanings. At each stage of the growth of co-operative societies during Holyoake's time, the next step was contested by law or regulation, whether it was the right of Societies to assign a percentage of their profit (trading surplus) to the education of their members; their claim not to have members' dividends or interest-payments taxed as individual income; their legal entitlement to own land, *as* Societies; their wish to engage in wholesale as well as retail trade; or their ambition to form mutual banks or credit unions. Holyoake in 1892: 'the subjection of the slave was defended by a pretended law of "economic subordination". That was the way the philosophers of slavery put it at last. We have all heard this doctrine of capitalism and cupidity defended in our movement in the name of "economic science"'.[325] As Holyoake saw it, a fundamental 'economic' fact like debt, if incurred on any scale by working-class co-operators or their Societies, entailed an anti-social relationship. It meant that members lost ownership of themselves, let alone of their Co-operatives. 'How can he talk of independence who is the slave of the shoemaker and the tailor? How can he subscribe to a political or social society, who cannot look his grocer in the face?' [326]

If philosophical and ethical questions as large as the nature of principle itself, and then of a *co-operative* principle are in play, contests over meaning will inevitably be hard fought, particularly at times when class, on all sides, dares to speak its name. Holyoake experienced a society at war with itself during the first thirty years of his life and, although in a state of greater equipoise during the 1850s, 60s and 70s, it was still structurally conflicted. In this setting, unity, union, concord, solidarity, fraternity, equitability, mutuality (not a word Holyoake used much) and independence were to be celebrated. But as *future* energy (John Stuart Mill's 'the futurity of the working classes'), rather than as *fact* or achieved destinations. Holyoake 'sought everywhere the principles and feelings that united people rather than the oppositions that divided them'.[327] These were the tools for encouraging working people and their allies to transform society, by using some of its core ideology (including 'unity', 'union' etc.) as catalyst. Hence the question to Gladstone: why shouldn't working people have and hold, here and now, on their own behalf, North as well as South, all the *social* goods which gentlemen assume to be their property, by right? 'Feelings that united people' were not, for Holyoake, a way of making society feel nice about itself, they were the stuff of change, within Co-operative Societies and thence to society.

Chapter XX of Holyoake's *History of Co-operation* is an essay on the 'Nature of Co-operative Principle'. Two quotations will show what he meant by 'English Co-operation' as popular agency rather than reformers' plans. Principles are to be understood as rules of action, the reorganization of society as something to be earned:

> 'A principle is a sign by which a movement is known, is a rule of action, and a pledge of policy to be pursued. To be a man of principle is to be known as a person having definite ideas, who sees his way and has chosen it, while others are confused he is clear. While others go round about he goes straight on... Having no clear discernment of the nature of principle, the unreflecting think one object as good as another, or better, if they see immediate advantage in it.
>
> Co-partnery is not Co-operation. Co-partnery proceeds by hiring money and labour and excluding the labourer from participating in the profit made. English Co-operation never accepted even Louis Blanc's maxim of giving to each according to his wants, and of exacting from each according to his capacity. This points to the reorganization of society. English Co-operation gives nothing to a man because he wants it, but because he earns it.'

Another quotation from the same chapter shows what Holyoake meant by the contest over meanings, between Co-operation in particular and the easier, more fashionable notion of co-operation in general. There was 'confusing chatter in the highest quarters of literature', detrimental to 'industrial Co-operation' as practised 'among those who do the work':

'Co-operation is a very different thing from Co-operation as defined in dictionaries. When several men join in moving a boulder, because one alone could not stir it, it is called Co-operation. In this way a bundle of sticks bound together present a force of resistance which separately none could pretend to, and in this sense sticks are as much co-operators as the men. But industrial Co-operation means not only a union for increasing mechanical force, but for obtaining the profit of the transaction, and having it equitably distributed among those who do the work. It is not knowing the difference which causes such confusing chatter in the highest quarters in literature about "Co-operation being as old as the world" and "which has been practised by every people"'.[328]

Management gurus today, though mainly interested in competitiveness, continue to welcome 'co-operation' alongside comfortable phrases like 'working together' and 'partnership'. The word 'coopetition' has been coined again and again since 1913, notably in a best-seller of 1996 which offered 'a revolution mindset that combines competition and co-operation'.[329] In a text which was widely discussed during 2012, *Together: the Riches, Pleasures and Politics of Co-operation*, Richard Sennett managed to celebrate his subject with scarcely a mention of the actually-existing co-operative movement.

[iv] Ways of telling.

'The real peril of the historian is that he may paralyse his readers by tameness, or kill curiosity by monotony.' [330] The best way to explore Holyoake's ways of telling as tradition-building is to read – to give it its full title once more – *Self-Help By the People: The History of the Rochdale Pioneers 1844-1892* from beginning to end. In its 1907, 'tenth edition revised and enlarged', it feels like a Co-operators' *vade mecum*. It angles for member-readers' attention, more in the manner of an almanac than a history book. The Pioneers produced their own *Almanac* year by year. Chapter III of *Self-Help By the People* is headed: 'The doffers appear at the opening day – moral buying as well as moral selling'; chapter IV 'The Society tried by two well-known difficulties – prejudice and sectarianism' and chapter V, 'Enemies within and enemies without, and how they all were conquered'.

Modern historians have enjoyed correcting the legend of Rochdale, while not always appreciating its power *as* legend. The Pioneers were not the first to base dividends on purchase and Holyoake exaggerated his own role in Rochdale to the extent that people continue to think he was himself a Pioneer... and so on. (He may have lectured there in 1843.[331]) Well before 1908, however, the legend was in full spate: 'the gracefulness of his story led to its reproduction in every European language – creating quite a sensation among the workmen of Lyons – while in England it was a seed from which sprang 250 co-operative societies in two years'.[332] 'Probably no little brochure of the kind has ever done so much effective propaganda.'[333]

In the absence of an anthology, examples from this and his other books may serve to illustrate Holyoake's approach, as a moralist and story-teller. The co-operative movement's life has been constructed by and with stories, including Holyoake's own life – told by Edward Owen Greening as *The Story of the Life of George Jacob Holyoake* 'prepared for the Holyoake Centenary Celebrations at Birmingham on the 14th of April 1917 at the request of the Co-operative Union Ltd'. Among Holyoake's own stories, take, first, his favourite fable concerning 'ridiculous humility', or what his followers could think of as the parable of the fish. Holyoake intended this for

The Doffers appear on the opening day of the Original Toad Lane Store in Rochdale, a drawing from Holyoake's History of Co-operation

times like our own when capital has been 'corrupted... like despotism', is 'insatiable' and 'holds in its hands the food of the people and the means of labour'.

'The pioneers of this movement, seeing that capital governed the world, and workmen had none, bethought themselves how they might acquire it. They saw that capital was an excellent thing. A savage can catch only ten fish a day. The capitalist lends him a net and he catches 200, when the capitalist takes 190 of the fish for the use of the net. That is a good thing for the capitalist. But in due time the capitalist buys the river, when he is able to – and when it suits his purpose he does – exclude the savage from catching fish any more. That is a bad thing for the savage. The policy for the savage to pursue is to get capital and buy his own net, and keep all the fish he catches. This is the theory of Co-operation.

Then the question arose, how were the savages to buy nets who had no money? No avenue seemed open to any human eye whereby capital could come to workmen; no telescope could reveal it on the whole horizon of industry. The Pioneers had no funds, nor had they any credit. Money-lenders never looked in their direction. Nor could they hope for gifts. The philanthropists were scarce in the workmen's quarters. Plainly there was no help save by creating capital; and there was no method of doing this except by collecting a few shillings to buy some provisions wholesale, sell them to each other at shop prices and save the difference. To many this has seemed ridiculous humility, but it was the only form of self-help open to them, and honest self-help is never ridiculous. Thus was discovered the art of creating capital by those who had none.' [334]

Next, the story of why Gruyère cheese 'should be the favourite cheese of co-operators', for 'it is the first cheese made on their system':

> 'Considerant gives an interesting account of the fabrication of Gruyère cheese in the Jura mountains: "The peasants rent a small house, consisting of a workshop and a dairy, with a cellar. In the workshop they place an enormous copper, destined to receive the milk of two hundred cows. A single man suffices to make two or three cheeses of from sixty to eighty pounds weight. These cheeses are placed in a cellar to be salted and cured. Every day the quantity of milk brought to the dairy is noted on two pieces of wood – one for the milker, the other for the manager. It is therefore known exactly how much each family contributes. They can even keep an account of the relative qualities of milk by means of an acrometer. They sell wholesale to the merchants. They deduct rent, fuel, and implements, pay the manager in proportion to the general result, and divide the rest among the families, proportionately to the value of their respective investments." '[335]

Thirdly, the tale of the silk-handkerchief, a story of necessity as the mother of co-operative invention, or how to turn an inequitable market into an opportunity for labour:

> 'Efforts were then being made in London (during the 1820s and 30s *sy*) to establish an agency for the sale of co-operative manufactures. In 1830 the distressed co-operators of Spitalfields and Bethnal Green weavers produced a co-operative silk handkerchief. It was an article that only ladies and gentlemen would buy in sufficient numbers to be of any advantage; but the disastrous proneness of enthusiasm to be

instant in season and out of season, led to there appearing upon it a design representing the inordinate possessions of the upper classes, so that no gentleman could use it without seeing the reproach'.[336]

Next, an allegory of the Tyne Bridge and 'pacific policy': 'so it is with social forces':

'Formerly the religion and politics of the working people were dictated to them by employers, squires and magistrates'. Now, 'in all the far-reaching dominions over which her Majesty, as Queen or Empress reigns, are there, or ever were, any body of working people so independent as the co-operators, who not only own property but own themselves? Nor will they depart from the pacific policy by which it has been won. A few words will illustrate this':

'Most readers know the High-Level Bridge spanning the Tyne, at Newcastle. Between its ponderous parts, as anyone may see, are spaces left for its expansion. Were all the great populations of Newcastle and Gateshead to pull with their fiercest strength, they could not draw these separated parts together. Were all the mechanical force Sir William Armstrong could bring from the Elswick Works applied to the task, it could only break the bridge, it could never close those openings. Yet, when summer comes, the warm, diffusing, zephyr-like breezes – silent, undemonstrative, unseen, unheard – close the apertures by their all-penetrating, all subduing, irresistible warmth. So it is with social influences. Force is no remedy there; it may break up, but it can never build up society. It can never relax the cold contraction of error, interest or prejudice; while the geniality of reason, of wise, earnest and informing argument, expands the iron heart of the world, so that the inspiration of justice and compassion can enter it, and sooner or later, concessions are made which denunciation and menace could never extort'.[337]

Finally, an intricate 'what if' or counter-factual sermon by Holyoake. This is a story of what went wrong in the case of an Owenite project which had had great potential. The story as told by Holyoake is designed not so much to get the facts right, as in a conventional 'History of...', as to suggest how 'the cause' might have benefited and could still benefit, if only co-operators could live up to a self-denying, social or associational ethic. If they could refrain from colluding in dominant ways of writing the history of social 'failures', anti-competitive experiments would, Holyoake suggests, prove to be more sustainable.

'The cause' in this case was the proto-co-operative, Owenite socialist invention of Labour Exchanges in which productive labour-time (registered in Labour Notes) could be exchanged by working people for other necessary goods. The real story, Holyoake thought, was of a defeat inflicted by a greedy rentier, one Mr Bromley, which could have been interpreted – or perhaps even turned out – better. Whether or not Holyoake got the details right is not the point here or elsewhere in these fables.[338] It is the moral of the tale as he draws it which matters.

The story began with 'splendid and capacious premises' in Gray's Inn Rd', owned in the early 1830s by Mr Bromley. These premises stood empty for a while. Mr Bromley encouraged Robert Owen to move in, rent-free to start with and without any schedule of fixtures or definite agreement as to terms and tenure of future tenancy.

'For a year and a half Mr Owen used the place as the grand central institution for promulgating his system'. 'Lectures were delivered there on Sundays and other days. Great festive celebrations were held; and many of the most eminent men of that day and of subsequent years were among the occasional frequenters of the meetings. Trade unionists, social, political, religious and philanthropic reformers of all schools, found welcome and hearing there. No opinion, Tory, Radical or religious, and no want of opinion, was a bar to friendliness and aid, provided the object was one intended to benefit the public'.

However, it was taking the Labour Exchange there that brought the Institution (of which London never had the like before or since) to an end. The Exchange prospered. Mr Bromley spotted an economic opportunity. He was 'satisfied Mr Owen had discovered a mode of making money which was unknown to him'. So he put the rent up, put an exorbitant price on the fittings and demanded a high price for Owen to buy the place. Owen kept him quiet for a while with £700 from his own pocket. The directors of the Exchange refused to take any further lease on the premises at the inflated price being asked. Mr Bromley became impatient for repossession. He sent in a heavy mob. The police were called, some of the rioters, probably on both sides, were taken before the magistrates and 'the same discredit occurred' as though Mr Owen had paid nothing. The directors of the Exchange resolved to move to Blackfriars Rd. But in spite of rumours of closure, business continued to go well in their final days in Grays Inn Rd. This excited Mr Bromley still more to get hold of the business of labour exchange. So he unilaterally announced the closure of the existing Exchange and the opening of the 'National Land and Equitable Labour Exchange Company' on his premises. Holyoake's interpretation ran as follows:

'Here was a well-laid scheme which was really a tribute to the value of exchanges... This practical man, unembarassed by any scruples, thought that if the plan succeeded so well when weighed with Mr Owen's unpopular principles, the world would flock to the same standard when a neutral flag was displayed. He, however, overlooked that outrage, though it sometimes succeeds, is often a dangerous foundation to build upon... Mr Owen's disciples were not all philosophers either. They made their outrage felt and rubbished the new scheme far and wide... They spoke so unpleasantly of the new project and its ingenious projector, that he got few exchanges, and lost his good tenants without getting any other... He found that he had not only alienated those who had made the exchange system popular; he had alarmed the public by the spectacle of violence, police cases and failure. The National Company fell into well earned contempt and distrust, and the Grays Inn Road buildings became an obscure, woebegone, deserted, unprofitable holding.'

'No doubt Labour Exchanges died there'. The moral Holyoake drew is unexpected. Rather than adding to indignation over Mr Bromley, he drew his co-operative readers' attention to themselves, *their* present and future. Above all, Holyoake was interested in 'social devices' and how best their proponents should behave in order to help such devices to work in and against anti-social, competitive conditions. As an organic intellectual, he was interested in the anti-'social' (in his sense of that word) – or in what we would call the ideological – construction of the case against emergent co-operation by its dominant competitors. From the point of view of his *class* project, he was interested in the politics of defeat rather than the inevitabilities of 'failure'.

'Had Mr Owen's friends been self-denying, stilled their hatchet tongues, and have promoted the success of the

Equitable Exchange, the cause might have been saved. They did not comprehend that steam was not a failure, though a thousand experiments broke down before a single steamship sailed or railway car ran; that new medicines as often kill people as cure them before cautious, patient, experimental physicians discover the right way of administering them. Yet no one decries the curative art. But in social devices the first scoundrel or the first fool – the first thief or the first blunderer, who by over-confidence, fraud, or ignorance brings a scheme to immediate grief, sets the world against it for generations, and journalists evermore speak of it as that "abortive failure which was tried long ago and brought ruin and ignominy upon all concerned." '³³⁹

If, as Holyoake advised, power could not be 'taken' all at once, by those who, in his time, were 'out of power', and if the dangers of working people being assimilated to, or captured by, power were as great as their 'taking' it... ways of telling had a special kind of weight. Telling things differently was one, available way of changing things. If small narratives could be told by plain people not in control of The Grand Narrative, they could at least provide one way of building a tradition through which ways of telling could develop into ways of living. Stories from within a growing tradition constitute its progress: they 'make up' a movement, as part of its future conditional tense. As in the parts for different instruments and voices in a musical score, or actors' scripts in a play, they constitute the conditions of its present and future production. They inform what it could and will be like, when and if...

[v] Codification, or cataloguing the virtues.

Traditions, as distinct bodies of enquiry into 'what practical rationality is and what justice is... differ', MacIntyre suggested, 'in their catalogs of the virtues'.[340] As part of establishing their distinct identity as a tradition, among themselves and against rivals, would-be adherents of an emergent tradition tend to meet in successive councils, congresses, conferences, corroborees – seen in retrospect as cumulative – to argue and agree about lists of virtues, values and principles. 'There is an evolution in definitions', Holyoake wrote, 'as in other things, which it is useful to trace. There is need of this, for principles like "Truth can never be confirmed enough/Though doubts did ever sleep".' [341]

The evolutionary process is uneven and intense, the stakes high. After all (Holyoake again): 'a principle is a sign by which a movement is known, is a rule of action, and a pledge of policy to be pursued.[342] The journey from pre-Rochdale 'Articles', 'Laws', 'Regulations' and 'Rules' to the 1995 ICA *Statement* is interesting in this setting, not only for the nature of each step but also because each step was seen at the time, and may be understood now, as part of a series. Each statement of Principles was seen as contributing to an operational ethic and an identifiable spirit – the co-operative ethic and the spirit of associationism? – better adapted for challenging the ethic and spirit of capitalism in its beliefs and ways of organising.[343]

Looking back to co-operation before Rochdale in the 1908 edition of Part 2 of his *History of Co-operation* Holyoake quoted 'One of the People' who, writing in the *Co-operative Miscellany* of 1830, had asked 'What is Co-operation?' 'Certainly many did make the inquiry', he wrote. The answer that 'One of the People' gave in 1830 was, in Holyoake's opinion, 'rather a travelling definition, it moves about a good deal and has no fixed destination':

> 'Co-operation in its fullest sense is the opposite of Competition; instead of competing and striving with each other to procure the necessaries of life, we make common cause, we unite with each other, to procure the same benefits'

This was all very well but 'it does not disclose how the "common cause" is made'. Fortunately, 'this writer gives an explanation of the method of procedure – namely, that a co-operative society devotes the profits of the distributive stores to productive industry and the self-employment of the members of the societies'. And, in spite of the fact that the self-employment of members was 'the greater and more important part of the plan' and had been 'but scantily realised' during the seventy years since 1830, 'the educated co-operator has always borne it in mind, and it remains as a tradition of Co-operation that production and self-employment go together.'[344]

During the years immediately before Holyoake's conversion to and employment within the Owenite movement, the first series of Co-operative Congresses was held, between 1829 and 1832.[345] At the third of these, held in London over seven days in April 1832 and the last to be held before modern Congresses began in 1869, Robert Owen was in full, prophetic mode.

'With permission of the Congress', he 'read a portion of the creed and duties of the religion of his system; to which he expected not one in that Congress could object'. Seven 'Articles' followed, with Owen pausing between Articles 2 and 3 as if to reassure his audience – the italics are in the printed *Proceeding*[346] – that this was his *'individual opinion'*. He went on to read four clauses, taken from his 'universal code of laws, on the Liberty of Man'. The clauses concerned the equal right of everyone 'to express their opinion respecting a First Cause; and to worship it under any form or in any manner agreeable to their consciences, not interfering with equal rights of others'.

Owen had been under attack at the time, not only from outside the movement, but also from within. Statements like 'the time had arrived when they should bow to no other authority but that of truth', sounded pontifical. And delegates like Mr Thompson would have preferred Owen's notion of Power with a capital 'P' to be expressed as the power of Labour rather than the power of a leader – a change of thinking and language which was adopted by Holyoake during the decades which followed. The first of Owen's Articles read:

> 'That all facts yet known to man indicate, that there is an external or internal cause of all existences by the fact of their existence; that this All-pervading cause of motion and change in the universe, is the Power which the nations of the world have called God, Jehovah, Lord, &c. &c; but that the facts are yet unknown to man, which define what that power is.'

Owen reassured delegates that 'to him it would make no difference whether his friends were Jews, Mahometans, Infidels, Hindoos or belonging to any other sect. He was the last man who would attempt to fetter any man's opinion; for he thought every man ought to be allowed to think for himself, especially upon matters of such weighty importance'. 'Many gentlemen', he went on to admit, 'had entertained an erroneous idea relative to his system, namely, that no person could be admitted into a co-operative community without subscribing to all his principles'.

Congress clearly wanted to insist on the openness of 'the Co-operator' to 'the whole human race', 'whatever views a

Radical Reformer might entertain'. Mr Thompson was moved to say that 'it was not necessary to adopt all of Mr Owen's tenets, in order to co-operate with him'. Another delegate (Mr Wigg) dared to ask whether he (Owen) had 'recanted some of his opinions'. Owen hurried to deny this, and to forestall any misunderstanding he proposed a resolution which was later printed on the front page of the Congress Proceedings:

> 'Whereas the Co-operative World contains persons of all religious sects and of all political parties, it is unanimously resolved that Co-operators, *as such* are not identified with any religious, irreligious, or political tenets whatever; neither those of Mr Owen, nor of any other individual'.

This resolution was carried *nem con*. More than that, it was 'voted to be the standing motto upon such publications as the Congress might issue'. This was an important moment in the codification of co-operative principles and an expression of Co-operators' continuing commitment to 'political and religious neutrality'. In the words of the 1995 *Statement,* the commitment is to the virtue of co-operatives being 'open' as well as 'voluntary'. Learning from Holyoake, this can be seen as a belief in itself, a positive form of neutrality rather than an abstention from faith, and as a way of organizing around such a belief. As noticed already, Holyoake would later develop this as 'a new theory of toleration' which he called 'generous' toleration '.[347]

In a pattern which was to be repeated over the next two centuries, the 1832 Congress set down a numbered list of *'Regulations* for Co-operative Societies'. Immediately after the passing of the 'standing motto' resolution, the Rev. Mr Dunn 'brought up the report of the committee appointed to draw up the rules and regulations for co-operative societies'.

Seven 'fundamental rules and regulations' were presented to Congress as 'recommendations ... to all present and future co-operative societies'. In stronger tones, they were proposed as 'the only constitutional basis upon which their societies can be permanently and successfully established'. Many of the words and phrases used would strike a chord in Co-operative Societies committed to the Seven Principles in the 1995 *Statement*.[348]

The 1995 *Statement* was the first time that 'Values' were codified as such, although they too were implicit in earlier 'Rules'. The first expression of what became 'the Rochdale Principles' is now normally credited either to the Society's *Almanac for 1860* or to an earlier one in which 'the objects of this Society' were clearly stated. These began with 'the social and intellectual advancement of its members'. On the front page of the 1860 *Almanac*, this was followed, characteristically, by the statement that the Society 'provides its members with Groceries, Butchers Meat, Drapery Goods, Clothing, Shoes, Clogs &c'. A notice in the *Almanac* then explained how the Society's capital is raised, how surpluses are distributed and other matters of practical principle. A statement down the left-hand side of the same page, characteristically again, added belief in a 'common bond': 'The present co-operative movement does not intend to meddle with the various religious or political differences which now exist in society, but by a common bond, namely that of self interest, to join together the means, the energies, and the talents of all for the common benefit of each'.

Following consultation with other Societies, the Rochdale Society published Model Rules in 1863, based on their own 1860 *Rules of Conduct*. These became widely known through Holyoake's 'Rules and Aims of the Society' in his history of the Pioneers.[349] As Ian Macpherson explained in his 1996

Background Paper, these Principles were 'derived from the values that have infused the movement from its beginnings' and were 'based on the traditions of a variety of 19th century pioneers'.[350] 'Fashioned as much by generations of experience as by philosophical thought', they constituted 'the essential qualities that make co-operators effective, co-operatives distinct and the co-operative movement viable'.[351]

The most striking feature of the life of the Movement and Holyoake's way of chronicling it, is precisely this mixture of philosophical thought and practical details about how best to conduct the business of a Co-operative Society. A good example is Holyoake's description of the Rules and Aims of the Rochdale Society during the 1850s. He goes through that which was subtracted from profits before they were divided among members; the procedures regarding withdrawal of funds by members in distress; struggles with the local Commissioners of Taxation; and the financial accounts of the Educational Fund. Along with these items he describes how 'in 1855 a co-operative conference was held in Rochdale'. A local Committee was appointed to carry out certain agreed resolutions. Abraham Greenwood, President and James Smithies, Secretary 'published a declaration of the principles on which the proceedings of the said Committee would be regulated'.

> 'We shall quote them to the credit of co-operation. They were these:-
> I. That human Society is a body consisting of many members, the real interests of which are identical.
> II. That true workmen should be fellow-workers.
> III. That a principle of justice, not of selfishness, must govern our exchanges.[352]

From his own account, Holyoake was in Rochdale at times during the late 1830s or early 1840s, but he increasingly took issue with the Society after 1844 – as he did later on with the CWS – for staying with the division of profits on purchase to the exclusion of any bonus to labour. There was a Corn Mill and a Co-operative Society before the Pioneers got together, and a Manufacturing Society in the town had also operated in ways he approved of until, as he saw it, departures from principle were allowed to happen. The Rochdale leadership, particularly the Society's President, Abraham Howard (not himself a Pioneer) took issue with Holyoake in 1861 and (in Holyoake's opinion) continued to pay too little attention to him and his views when Congress met in Rochdale in 1892. To say the least, relationships were uneasy.

In 1861 Holyoake wanted to correlate the religious affiliations of members of the Rochdale Society with their positions on 'industrial partnerships' or the 'bonus to labour' controversy. Known sometimes as 'the Labour Question', this had been a live issue in Rochdale before the Society became a global emblem of consumer co-operation. In September 1861, the Society's Secretary, William Cooper, supplied Holyoake with data for an article in *The Counsellor*, a journal with which Holyoake worked: his research was designed 'so that when you knew the religious composition of a Society you might know what the prospects of the recognition of labour in manufacturing might be'.[353] When this early essay in the sociology of religion came out 'it caused quite an upset'. Cooper was given a month's notice which was later rescinded. President Howard issued an official statement which was neatly copied into the Society's Minute Book. Holyoake published this in *The Counsellor*, combined with a stern letter from Howard. In a note, he assured readers that the letter 'concluded with some sentiments I very cordially agreed with and had never transgressed against'. In the *History of the Rochdale Pioneers* he suggested that *The Counsellor* was 'a quiet quarto journal, in which secular, co-operative, political, and religious writers endeavoured to give guidance to working men on public affairs, without dictation, assumption, arbitrary authority, or invective. Those who gave advice or suggestions in it were understood to examine both sides of the question on which they presumed to offer an opinion'. 'There was not a word of criticism or inculcation of any sectarian principle in anything I published. All I sought was an estimate of the tendencies of sects in regard to industrial partnerships, just as the chemist would estimate the specific gravity of the different liquids with the view to determine their value in different experiments'.

This defence allowed Holyoake to express views on *difference* and positive neutrality which were parallel to those which had taken root in the 1830s and were strongly held in Rochdale in the 1860s. The strength of their expression by Howard and by Rochdale members at a monthly and then at a quarterly meeting in a special resolution, can only have pleased Holyoake. His views on individual ('sectarian') religious or political opinion and on the dangers of allowing either to be vested as an interest within co-operative societies had clearly been assimilated. The special resolution was contained in Howard's letter to *The Counsellor:*

> 'That our president be instructed to entirely repudiate a statement said to be furnished by our financial clerk, Mr Wm. Cooper, and which appeared in a publication denominated the Counsellor, for September 1861, such statement being considered detrimental to the interests of this Society; also that the people of this country in forming new co-operative societies, be recommended to seek their members from all

classes and conditions of men.' I beg to inform your readers that the principles of the Rochdale Co-operators are—1st, not to inquire into the political or religious opinions of those who apply for membership into ours or any of the various co-operative societies in our town; 2nd, that the consideration of the various political and religious differences of the members who compose our societies should prevent us from allowing into our councils or practices anything which might be construed into an advantage to any single one of each sect or opinion. The result of these principles has been that in the discussion and determination of all the great questions which have divided us, there might be seen ranged on both sides men of various creeds and opinions. That our policy has been such I need only quote from an article which appeared in the Equitable Pioneers' Society's Almanac, for 1860, where the writer is, for the time being, the mouthpiece of the Society. He says—'The present co-operative movement does not intend to meddle with the various religious or political differences which now exist in society, but by a common bond, namely, that of self-interest, to join together the means, the energies, and talents of all for the common benefit of each.' The co-operator does not seek to inforce or carry out any particular doctrines of any particular individual.' We think that all such statements and recommendations [Mr Cooper made none] in your article of September can only be followed by mischievous effects, and ought not to have been made by those professing themselves the dearest friends of our hitherto successful principles. I recommend, in the name of the Pioneers and Co-operators of Rochdale, all new societies never to inquire what politics or what religion the persons applying for membership are, but take all those who are willing to subscribe to the rules.—I am, dear sir, on behalf of the Society, yours most respectfully, ABRAHAM HOWARD, President." [354]

Holyoake continued to try to communicate, abbreviate and codify *co-operative* principle as a subset of 'principle' in general. In *The Co-operative Movement Today* (1890 and 1903) he listed no less than fourteen principles on which the Rochdale tradition was based.[355] 'The traditions of Co-operation were in the minds of these Pioneer weavers'. In the same book he reduced the Movement's 'main principles' to four: Concord, Economy, Equity and Self Help, and then to two, Economy and Equity.[356] This was a movement 'whose inspiration is fraternity, whose method is economy, whose principle is equity'. For Derby members the two 'principles' become Participation and Education.[357] Holyoake celebrated the Leeds Society for codifying their practice in 1847. He called a chapter of his history of this Society 'the Wonderful Rules'.[358] By the time the final edition of the *History of Co-operation* came out, Holyoake noted that 'Rules' etc. were 'now generally known as the principles of co-operation'.[359] This must have been due in no small part to his own mind- set and persistence.

As already noted, Holyoake's wish to codify went back to his youth. When he was a young man in Birmingham, and before he encountered Owenite socialism, Holyoake searched among the plentiful raw materials for an ethic of association in Protestant Britain – the churches and chapels within travelling distance of his home. He was looking for values and principles which worked for and against working people's self-belief and self-organisation, in this world rather than the next. The small-master culture in which Holyoake was brought up was full of available forms of proto-democracy, different from the forms of social capital which flourish in Catholic cultures and which encourage different kinds of co-operative. In 1838 he and three fellow students at the Mechanics Institute 'all lived together in an associated house in Sun Street West in Birmingham'. Goss saw this later as a small Owenite community.[360]

Having sampled the life of as many churches and chapels in Birmingham as he could, he ended this stage of his journey with a synthesis of his own, mostly secular, values and principles. In search of a satisfactory set of beliefs, he drew up ten 'articles which he considered all that was necessary to believe in, to obtain salvation.' He then prepared another series of 'articles of faith' which he thought were essential for all those who professed Christianity to absorb and practise. They were all principles of action as much as statements of belief. Number seven was unambiguous: 'the inconsistency of war with the principles of Christianity'. Number two anticipated his life's work. It was about *agency*, but also about *everyone*. 'Every individual is capable equally of doing that which is good as that which is evil'.[361]

Holyoake's habit of returning to underlying principles grew stronger as a result of his mathematical studies at the Mechanics' Institute. Frederick Hollis, a Sheffield Owenite, thought that this characteristic made him a suitable person for appointment as a Social Missionary in the city. 'Don't say you can't', he encouraged Holyoake in 1840. 'I know you can. You know what you would have to teach and expound, and you are aware that your previous studies have so habituated you to return to *first principles*, and that is all you have to do in "Social Lecturing"'.[362] Later in life, the six Objects of his publishing venture based at 147 Fleet St from 1853 to 1861 were equally suggestive of a self-consciously codified ethic. For example, number six committed him and his brother to 'maintaining an organ which should be open to all writers, without regard to coincidence of opinion, provided there was general relevance and freedom from odious personalities'.[363] For the world outside Co-operation, Holyoake's *The Principles of Secularism Briefly Explained* was probably his most important individual writing, as distinct from his editorial work. 'Believing in the possibility of a neutral faith, Mr Holyoake here endeavours to define and consolidate his position.'[364] A secularist should 'neither ignore nor deny the future and the spiritual'. These are, however, 'independent questions': the secularist 'concerns himself with present time and material existence'. In 1881 Holyoake published a *Code of the tenets or governing principles of the Society of Secularists set forth in ten articles*. This dealt 'with the Being of God, self-dependence, knowledge, morality, religion, training of children, responsibility, good and evil, and secular sufficiency'. No wonder G.W. Foote, who later became President of the National Secular Society, found Holyoake's secularism in the 1870s 'too catholic'. 'Instead of narrowing the basis of secularism to a mere intellectual attitude towards the doctrine of Deity (he) widens it so far as to include everything and anything'.[365] Opening the Secular Hall in Leicester in March 1882, Holyoake called his speech 'Secularism – a religion which gives heaven no trouble'.[366]

[vi] *Principles of organisation – as the contested embodiment of values and beliefs.*

The art of association is a 'moral art': 'philosophy' rather than 'vanity or caprice' 'originates the principle on which we associate'. Such phrases recur throughout Holyoake's work.

Deeply-felt contests about the relationship between the values adherents believe in and how they think they should morally (and/or must rationally) organise to embody those values are another sign of an autonomous tradition in the making. Alongside values and principles, there is pressure to meet immediate needs in society as it is, whether personal or associational. That there will be contradictions and disagreements is to be expected. If a tradition is taking root, however, there will be a shared sense of a singular whole. Disagreements will be about how best to embody a common set of purposes. To the extent that an inheritance is alive as more than habit, these differences <u>matter</u> to would-be adherents or members. Debating points are made from all sides, but they are experienced as more than that: in Holyoake's words, as 'philosophy' rather than as 'vanity or caprice'.

Traditions in the sense I am exploring here either wilt or gain energy from struggles among their adherents about perceived departures from the truths they attempt to hold in common. Throughout Holyoake's lifetime, co-operators would disagree with each other, sometimes passionately, particularly over rewards to producers at the workplace and purchasers at the store. But disagreements were 'held' as well as 'divided': held within shared *co-operative* notions of virtue, as opposed to competitive, individualist, capitalist or other-wordly notions. And they were held within developing codes of values and principles open to differences about ways of organizing, behaving in and 'owning' co-operatives. At their height during Holyoake's lifetime however, differences were sometimes also expressed as denunciations and even as anathemas against views which in religious terms would be called heresies. Denunciations led to calls for the expulsion of heretics, but for the sake of the survival of an *idea* of the whole. In the eyes of those who worked with an idea of completeness – a new Order of Life, a 'social society' – heresies arose, to be seen by holders of the whole truth as lopsided or partial truths. In his most prophetic mode, Holyoake was fierce about these.

In his time the burning issue was how the values of co-operation related to whether Societies were organised in one way rather than another: for example as predominantly consumer rather than producer, or 'bonus to labour' cooperatives. This is 'an important part of the history of British co-operation, probably the single most important issue that was confronted' during the second half of the nineteenth century.'[367] It survived as a sub-current through the following century and still flows in more subdued ways today. Participants clearly felt that they were contributing to a whole new society, possibly first named as the 'co-operative commonwealth' in 1866.[368] Both sides were capable of going out of their way to include, and sometimes to exclude their opponents, in order to construct (or *make* as in Holyoake's 'the many make the few') Societies with the potential to replace society as it currently existed. And both sides were capable of anathematising the other as obstinate individuals – sometimes as an obstinate *class* of people who self-interestedly adhered to part of the truth rather than to its whole.

There were empirical questions at stake, even when they were expressed in highly charged, ideological ways. There still are such questions – matters of detail about how best to achieve complete co-operation as an immanent 'order' consisting of 'universal' membership of Holyoake's social society. Should it be product by product, trade by trade, site by site, location by location, factory by factory, shop by shop, or Society by Society? Should individual members benefit as workers making a specific product, in a specific trade and in the most suitable location? If so, who should be counted among producers? After all, as Isaac Earnshaw, a Leeds Co-operator, dared to suggest in 1890: 'all this noise was made on behalf of a mere fraction of those engaged in the movement. If labour is entitled to participate as such, he did not see the difference between the man who made the goods, the man who packed and unpacked them, and the man who handed them over the counter'.[369] And, as Beatrice Webb wondered when she argued against producer co-operation, was it to be mines for the mineworkers, sewage for the sewage workers, local government for the local government workers and so on? What was equitable, or efficient, about that?

The questions became sharper and bigger during the second half of the nineteenth century as the movement grew in size. Was it more equitable from a gendered and household point of view, as well as more likely to replace the competitive system economically, if members were to associate around distribution and use rather than around production? Could consumer Societies legitimately employ labour to make everything they needed ('the CWS for Everything') without simply reproducing the capitalist wage relationship? Advocates of the CWS route to the commonwealth argued that it was open to workers in CWS works (and in workshops directly owned by consumer Societies like Rochdale's), to be members of those (mainly retail) Societies which would, in the end, exchange among themselves everything they needed and nothing which members had not made, in works which their Societies owned either in primary or secondary ways. Taking the CWS and Rochdale 'consumer' route, labour would be rewarded. But the reward or 'bonus' or dividend to labour would be distributed at the point of use rather than at the point of production, through the store or shop rather than through the workshop. A whole *system*, a complete *community*, an entire *society* would result from a singular, giant (Co-operative Wholesale) Society, consisting of all the Societies in (corporate rather than individual) membership of it. J.T.W. Mitchell wanted to 'prevent the accumulation of wealth in any particular channel'. 'What we wanted to accomplish by co-operation was absolute equality in the distribution of wealth, though that hardly seemed possible'. Sharing a platform with Tom Mann in Bristol in 1893, Mitchell explained that by means of the CWS and its member Societies, 'we want to put the profits of trade into the pockets of the people, not a section of them':

> 'Until the people get hold of trade profits they will never be able to undertake the productive business of the world. Mr Carnegie of America said that a thousand pounds in the hands of one person would do more good to the community than a thousand persons owning a pound apiece. That was absolutely untrue. It would be better still if the £700,000,000 of the British Debt were owned by the 40,000,000 of British people, than to belong to a small section of the community. Co-operators want to use the best means to get the entire wealth of this country, land and everything else, into the possession of the entire body politic'.[370]

When Thomas Hughes went for the CWS in his inaugural address to the Co-operative Congress of 1887, Mitchell was stung into a hugely ambitious defence of the Society which he Chaired. He wanted the Wholesale to start works in every town where they would pay. He wanted them to make everything their members wore. 'He advised co-operators never to be satisfied until they got control of the entire banking, shipping and every other interest in the country'

> To whom does profit and the increment of value belong? We hold that, as it was created by the industrious classes, it belonged to them. Profit was made by the consumption of the people, and the consumers ought to have the profit. *But what was the difference between the people and the industrious classes?* (my italics) [371]

Tom Mann was one of the Commissioners appointed to the Royal Commission on Labour in 1893-4, and Mitchell was called to give evidence. 'May I put it this way', Mann asked Mitchell: 'that your distributive co-operation is merely preliminary to productive co-operation?' Mitchell: 'that is so'. Mann: 'then productive co-operation is exactly what you are driving at?' Mitchell: 'exactly'.[372]

Key questions which were raised by co-operators can be itemised, even though, as Mitchell well knew, the answers were not so easy. Why should some abilities and skills and some locations and products receive rewards ('rents', of ability, climate, geology etc.) greater than others, within a common, co-operative movement, rather than all members benefitting equitably according to their needs, inputs and loyalties? Within what precise arrangements of production and distribution could 'self- employment' take on a collective, co-operative meaning, as opposed to an individualist competitive one, with Labour employing Capital across the piece as well as in small units of production? [373] How can autonomy and efficiency best be reconciled, along with individual and collective freedom, while Societies continue to have to work against capitalist competition, capitalist 'rationality'? How can the 'iron' laws of organisation, and no less rigid 'laws' of economics be bent to breaking point, every day by living members of co-operatives and mutuals, as opposed to the 'revolutionary' promise of their rupture all at once, one day in the future, by their childrens' children? How can 'complex co-operation' best develop within large-scale, capitalist industry, bringing forward the social inventions necessary to prevent selfish, sectional interests vesting themselves in Co-operative Societies as much as elsewhere? How is it best to prevent established memberships pressing for unrealistic dividends and therefore prices, at the cost of a wider, less prosperous membership? How can successful producer co-operatives avoid becoming 'Working-Class

Limiteds'?[374] Equally, how can successful consumer co-operatives avoid becoming commercial-populist 'Friends of the People' stores, like Lewis's in Manchester, acting *for* customers rather than belonging *to* members? [375] How can *size* be dealt with co-operatively, steering between the weaknesses (and strengths) of 'small is beautiful' and the strengths (and weaknesses) which result from 'the bigger the better'?

Answers to such questions, right and wrong, inform the history of co-operatives. If there is to be another way of doing things (making relations) in the long term, it is worth listening to the principled and practical ways in which complex questions were debated among co-operators in Holyoake's lifetime. The discussion was more considered than producers' *versus* consumers' co-operation. In the Scottish Wholesale Society, 'bonus to labour' was paid from November 1870 onwards. In April 1884 a special meeting was held 'to revise the rules on this head'. In his *Co-operative Production* (a neglected 839-page book published by Oxford at the Clarendon Press in 1894) Benjamin Jones, a London-based CWS co-operator and employee, set out the 'contradictory opinions' expressed in a 'long and interesting discussion' in 1884. *Co-operative News* covered the event in full. The issue was how to determine and distribute 'profit' in a complex Society which produced goods as well as distributing them.[376] In the context of Holyoake's thinking, it is the fact that there was such a detailed discussion which is the point, together with its communication to the wider movement in as live a way as possible, and its resolution by means of votes at members' meetings.

One answer to the growth of vested interests among co-operative activists has been to prefer delegate democracy to representative democracy.[377] And one answer to the problem of size has been to prefer horizontal federation within and between co-operatives to vertical integration of the kind which capitalist companies went for during the late-nineteenth century and towards which the CWS increasingly tended.[378] 'Federation Street' forms part of the co-operative complex in Manchester. It is a stone's throw from Holyoake House. At its productive height, early in the twentieth century, should the giant CWS have federated its productive works more deliberately, in ways J. T. W. Mitchell resisted? This was suggested by the advocates of producer co-operation. It would have allowed individual workers in profitable works such as the Crumpsall Biscuit works in Manchester to share its profits directly. Proposals were put to the Society by J. C. Gray along these lines in papers he prepared in 1886.[379] But CWS leaders like Mitchell feared that this would weaken the CWS's growing capacity to challenge capitalist ways of doing business on (to us) an unimaginably large scale? Perhaps the Co-operative Group should have done the same with the consumer Societies it rescued one by one a century later, thus allowing its Regions more autonomy and their members more direct control, along the lines of the relative autonomy achieved by its North-Eastern Region between 1968 and 1996.[380]

These were the real issues which were contested in Holyoake's time and, at best, worked through in detail on the ground: in Hebden Bridge, Leeds, Derby… and a thousand other Societies. They were also argued out ideologically, although probably more often at Co-operative Congress than at local Society level. By 'ideologically' I mean that they were constructed on both sides as heady 'positions', even as entire, self-righteous moralities, rather than as contradictions to be worked through practically in order to further the co-operative ethic and the spirit of associationism.[381] *'Isms'* and *'Ists'* were bandied about in a setting which was at the same time critical of such abstractions. On the one hand CWS loyalists and consumer co-operators were constructed by their opponents as 'materialists' or, more politely, as 'federalists'. On the other hand, 'bonus to labour', Labour Association, producer Co-operators were constructed as 'idealists' or 'individualists'.[382] From each side a whole truth, intensely believed-in and too important to be diluted, was felt to be threatened by a lop-sided truth. Class and power were also in play, sometimes concealed by ideology and sometimes coming through in spite of it. 'I was reared in the workshop', as Holyoake liked to point out, 'Neale, Ripon and Hughes weren't'.[383] The North versus London and the South, workers versus professionals and titled folk, 'our rulers' versus 'the people': these tensions bubbled away, never far below the surface.

For the passion' on these matters, writes Bibby, 'we can look to Holyoake'.[384] Speaking to a Hebden Bridge audience at an event in October 1887 to name the Fustian Society's new engine he said:

> 'Labour is taken without security, is given no interest, has neither first or second award of profit, and can be cast off as a week's notice... Capital has no care nor toil to perform. It lives in opulence or saunters into sunny climes. All the while labour is chained to the workshop. From morning to night it toils out its dreary or cheerless years. All the strength and light of its life, which it will never see more in this world is unrequited. All that capital does for labour is to feed it, so that it can work, and only as long as it can work, and then leaves it to die. All the profit which labour has created by its ceaseless and cheerless industry is swept away by capital, even to the last penny, and paid over the counter to its banker. Is this fair play to labour? Is this equity to industry? Yet there are some who tell us that this should be the co-operative policy in our workshop. '[385]

As already emphasized, Holyoake felt strongly about rewarding producers as well as purchasers. He was fully capable of prophetic denunciation of 'half-minded' proponents of the purchaser (not yet known only as the 'consumer') side. Yet he also retained an inclusive commitment to a movement made in common, in the end made with everybody – with 'humanity' itself.

His voice is still the most articulate surviving expression of the ways in which unity within a single field of force was sought and sometimes assumed, despite defeats. Edward Owen Greening's judgement about Holyoake's careful – not always consistent – alignments during the long battle between 'the idealists and the practical parties' is probably right. 'In these discussions Mr Holyoake adopted a characteristic attitude: he took the side of the "bottom dog"'.[386] Holyoake's understanding of 'unity' and 'union' as distinct from homogeneity has already been highlighted. Single-issue agitations, whether for the repeal of the Corn Laws, for an Independent Labour Party or Votes for Women were predicated on 'pressing a single political purpose to the extent of over-riding other just reforms'. Joseph McCabe, his first biographer, argued that evaluating such agitations was a matter of 'political morality' to Holyoake. This insight helps our understanding of his whole project.[387] Against the divisions of labour and the 'structural differentiations' of the first industrial revolution in Britain, Holyoake continued to witness to the evident possibility of an inclusive social movement on behalf of labour, and then of All Classes and All Nations. He saw secularism, 'deliberate liberalism', campaigns for free trade in ideas *and* co-operatives as evidence of a self-helping sociality in practice. He felt he was working towards the same end among Secularists as among Co-operators, recalling both movements to their 'original broad base' against leaders whose interests lay in narrowing them down.[388] 'It is the mark of the quack mind to pretend that one thing will do everything'. And he observed that 'It was common to find reformers each convinced of the excellence and perfection of his own plan, and each having great distrust of the plans of others. This is not the way of the co-operator. He knows that society has been and is being improved by a million agencies and by the genius of a million minds'.[389]

Holyoake felt that only the Co-operative Movement as a diverse whole could act as the productive end of the associational project. McCabe, a 'Free Thinker' and Spiritualist rather than a Co-operator, thought that an 'age of specialism' had set in by the 1880s. Sadly, 'it was useless now to hold these things together'; by 'these things' he meant all the movements which interested Holyoake. Writing in 1908, McCabe reached for what would later become common uses of the term 'cultural' (e.g. politics, industries, traditions, even 'materialism') to describe Holyoake's integrative project. 'The real reform open to him' after the 1880s, 'was to initiate a cultural movement that should make theological criticism a part of its positive educational work'.

> 'The time had come for his ideal to break up into its constituent aims. Co-operation was now embodied in a powerful specific movement: education had passed into the hands of national administrators: political work of any shade had vast organisations to promote it. It was useless now to attempt to hold these things together'.[390]

Yet interestingly, from the 1880s onwards, it was within the co-operative movement that Holyoake chose to renew his work for the cause which in 1875 he had called, 'that new power of industry which will grow mightier year by year'.[391] There was never any doubt that his commitment was to Labour in general, and to labourers in the workplace in particular. He urged that they should receive more than their wages: the wage was a subordinate relationship to capital as well as an insufficient reward for labour. 'Wages are but a trade charge, merely the rent of the human machine, and are not more than keeps it in efficiency, and not often that'.[392] 'Industrial Co-operation – voluntary concert, with equitable participation and control among all concerned in any enterprise – is a definition that would now be accepted by political economists and journalists.' [393]

In his dispute with Abraham Howard during *The Counsellor* episode in 1861, Holyoake said 'there was not a word of criticism or inculcation of any sectarian principle in anything I published'. There may not have been, in that instance. But 'sectarian' energy, differentiating believers from other believers with whom they are *au fond* in agreement, is part of the alchemy of any ambitious tradition struggling to establish itself in the interests of world-making. This is well illustrated by Holyoake's views of the Rochdale Pioneers, both for and against, and as a tradition-maker more than a local historian.

He devoted pages of his history of the Pioneers to denouncing the defeat of profit-sharing in Rochdale. The pilgrims had not always made progress. Well before the end of Holyoake's life they strayed, permanently as it seemed, from the original path of complete 'voluntary concert.' Chapter XVIII was called 'Halting on the Way'. He pointed out that: 'A co-operative society is one which shares its profits equitably with all engaged in creating them, in labour and trade'. The Rochdale Society never did, and yet – this is the point – Holyoake built them up in the eyes of the world. A Co-operative Manufacturing Society in Rochdale had conspicuously failed the test, and a Flour Mill had also gone wrong. 'Co-operation means more and higher' than 'persons who, being directors or shareholders in a co-operative company, and knowing it to be so and joining it as co-operators, turn the principle and betray it or destroy it'. Co-operation 'means the recognition of the workmen, not indirectly – not in some infinitesimal, impalpable, hypothetical, and abstract way – but directly, plainly, personally, absolutely, permanently, as owner of an equitable share of the profits of labour'.[394]

Not only but also: quoting Tennyson's *In Memoriam* on the final page of his history of the Pioneers ('Our little systems have their day;/They have their day, and cease to be'), Holyoake continued to mix denunciation with celebration of Rochdale in the name of 'the co-operative law of the common interest'... 'Let us keep to their methods'.

> 'The Rochdale system of co-operation was the littlest, the obscurest, the most unfriended, the most disregarded, most contemned, the least hopeful, the least likely to succeed of any system ever devised by man. Yet it has not 'ceased to be'. On the contrary, it continues to grow, and it is even now the most prosperous system yet devised for the amelioration of the workers of England.'

> 'Let us keep to their methods and we shall see the day which they desired to see when principle shall rule in this movement, when the humiliation of hired labour shall cease, when worker as well as purchaser shall share in the profits created, when the penury of the many shall terminate, and the scandalous fortunes of the few be impossible, under the co-operative law of the common interest, inspired by goodwill and governed by equity.' [395]

This was intended not only as a singular truth, but also as a reconciliation which was, after all, part of the singularity of that particular truth, namely: that it was *co-operative* rather than competitive. Holyoake's energies flowed this way and that. No wonder he owned up, as we have seen, to a 'wilfulness of opinion' which he knew would disturb his readers.[396] Sectarian energy came out again strongly from the mid-1890s onwards, during the early meetings of the International Co-operative Alliance, and well into Holyoake's old age. The Alliance began as a grouping of producer, bonus-to-labour, co-partnership Co-operators wanting to promote their cause. Holyoake worked with them in his most denunciatory vein. When it looked to be moving away from his imperatives he referred to the ICA as the International Commercial Alliance.[397] At one point he argued in favour of precluding corporate membership of the Alliance altogether (notably that of the Co-operative Wholesale Society, but the Pioneers would have been excluded too), in favour of individual members only. Holyoake thought that corporates might 'transform the co-operative movement into a commercial movement. He did not want to see it narrowed down to Balloon Street '.[398] In the end the Alliance chose not to have any individual membership.

When the Labour Association to promote co-partnership between Labour and Capital was founded, Holyoake used a characteristically joined-up metaphor when he spoke at the Association's annual meeting for 1894-5:

> 'Co-operation may be likened to a train, which when it started from Rochdale had two classes of carriages – one carrying Stores, the other carrying Workshops. When the train arrived at Manchester the Workshop carriages were uncoupled and left behind... We have sent down the line the strong new engine of the Labour Association bearing the wholesome name of Co-partnership, and attached the abandoned carriages to it.'[399]

At an early Co-operative Congress, in 1873, the Christian Socialist J.M. Ludlow had proposed the exclusion of all but 'bonus to labour' Societies from Congress. Passionate though he was on this matter, Holyoake argued for a more balanced, 'concert' approach.

> 'As co-operation is the concert of capitalist, producer and consumer, all three had a claim to the division of profits, and after paying capital for its use and providing for the education of the worker... the surplus should be divided between the producer and the customer.'[400]

At Hebden Bridge in 1887, Holyoake argued that just as sharing profits with customers had achieved success for distributive co-ops, the same principle was succeeding with workers in producer co-ops. 'The great leaders of the Wholesale Board had by the efficiency and force of that organisation helped to make co-operation what it is'. So 'it only remained for them' to share the capital which 'they had helped to create' with their workers.[401] The adverb was typical of Holyoake: 'only'. This was the same appeal to people's reason, freedom and better nature which he had made in the letter to Gladstone already quoted: 'it is only needed to concede them (the workers) the liberties of gentlemen'.

Holyoake and Mitchell clashed at Co-operative Congress in 1890. And Holyoake railed against the CWS in *Co-operative News* throughout the early 1890s. After twenty-five years of service, he resigned his seat on the Central Board of the Co-operative Union because of the growth of CWS influence within the Union. He argued that the Sectional Boards of the Union were acting as if they represented the CWS and not the Union. Loyalty to Congress decisions was at stake. The first Congress of 1869 had advised the formation of partnerships of industry and participation in profits. 'We teach the stores to be loyal to the Wholesale, but the Wholesale is not loyal to the Congress. The CWS had refused 'during sixteen years to carry out co-operative principles in our workshops'.[402] Appropriately, it was the Co-operative *Union*, led by producer advocates like J. C. Gray of Hebden Bridge who worked hardest on behalf of a common movement at this time.

The Huddersfield Co-operative Congress of 1895 was planned as an occasion for conciliation. Two of the leading protagonists had died, Neale in 1892 and Mitchell in 1895. A committee was set up to bring things together. Holyoake shared the wish for Congress to move on. Cajoled by Gray, he argued at Congress for conciliation between the two sides of the movement. He 'would not go back upon the past but look forward to the future of this mighty movement.' [403]

Holyoake could be critical of what he called 'co-partnery' co-operation when it went so far as to gloss over the prevailing antagonism (what social scientists now know as 'structural violence') between labour and capital. While a keen supporter of the Labour Association, he would probably have expressed unease at some point during its subsequent evolution into twentieth-century 'industrial participation' designed to increase productivity by means of 'workplace engagement'. This was not his idea of the destination of the co-operative movement fought for by the Pioneers: 'they have "taken their own affairs into their own hands", and what is more to the purpose, they have kept them in their own hands'.[404] Holyoake was not afraid of saying that 'at best unmitigated competition was war, and though war had its bards and its heroic memories, there was murder in its march... Humanity was imposture if progress could not be accomplished by nobler means'... 'Co-partnership Co-operation... is the Peace of Industry'. But if a truce was to be found in 'the never-ceasing conflict between Labour and Capital' it would have to be a lasting one, a new Order of Industry rather than the old one patched up. There was a delicate line to be drawn every day in the lives of associations by and for labour, between tactical acceptance and strategic rejection of 'Competition' – in other words between an ethic of temporary accommodation with antagonists who we see today and a permanently supine stance towards Capital's twists and turns. This is a necessary contradiction to negotiate in the development of the co-operative ethic and the spirit of associationism rather than a weakness in any single individual's stance. Holyoake admired and anticipated 'concord' while drawing attention to its absence. In his Inaugural Address delivered at the nineteenth annual Co-operative Congress in 1887 he argued that 'the co-operator is not against capital. Capital is exactly like fire – an excellent servant when it warms the inmates but a bad one when it burns down the house'. This was not the same register that Thomas Hughes slipped into, for example after the 'Black Monday' socialist demonstration in Trafalgar Square in 1886. In March that year he told a Hebden Bridge audience that 'a great deal of cant was talked by these Socialists about capital and labour. The foundation of such talk as went on in Trafalgar Square was the notion that there was an antagonism between capital and labour.'[405]

Holyoake ended his history of the Pioneers by quoting the speech he made on the last night of the Rochdale Congress of 1892, during a 'Conversazione' in the great meeting hall of the Central Stores in Rochdale:

> 'every man who has a larger income than he could obtain by his own labour, must derive it from the underpaid labour of others... Co-operation is intended – and if it be not a fraudulent thing it is pledged to put the fruits of labour into

the hands of the workers. It is intended to do what Mazzini told the Italian workmen co-operation could do – 'Unite Capital and Labour in the same hands'... The remedy is the association of labour and the division of the fruits of labour between the producers in proportion to the amount and value of the work done by each'.

I will leave Holyoake's question where he left it, first for his audience in 1892 and then for the readers of his Pioneers' History: 'what hinders this division being general now?'[406]

IIC. A religion of co-operation?

[i] 'Religion'.

'Secularism, a religion which gives heaven no trouble' is the arresting phrase, already quoted, used by Holyoake at the opening of the Secular Hall in Leicester 1882. The idea of a 'religion of co-operation' – 'this new order of life, it is appearing' – gradually emerged as an unexpected by-product of my renewed interest in Holyoake following the UN Year of Co-operatives in 2012.

Provoked by his use of 'religion', as his Leicester audience in 1882 may also have been, it seemed worthwhile to try to 'mainstream co-operation' in ways other than as a more (or less) successful business form, co-existing with others. Learning from Holyoake that *difference* or positive neutrality lies at the heart of co-operative belief and practice, 'religion' in the sense used by Thomas Hughes and Edward Vansittart Neale in their *Foundations* (1879 and 1915) became of great interest.[407]

Holyoake was an advocate of *unity* and *union* based on common interest, in Societies, secularist as well as co-operative out of which the dynamism and adhesiveness of a this-worldly faith could develop, but which were also open to diverse – eccentric in its proper sense – beliefs and activities among their members: 'open and voluntary', as the 1995 *Statement of Co-operative Identity* phrases it. The aim of any adequate association, whether secularist, co-operative or even organisations such as the Athenaeums which sprang up in many Victorian towns, was 'to supply the material and social conditions under which, whatever of goodness (relative or absolute) exists in human nature, may manifest itself unchecked'. Holyoake saw Athenaeums as 'a type of a Secular Society'.[408]

I first studied Co-operative Societies in the English town of Reading at the end of the nineteenth and the beginning of the twentieth centuries. I wanted to understand churches and chapels in the context of voluntary, commercial and local-state organisations whether 'for' or 'of' working-class people. So the Reading Co-operative Society became important in my *Religion and Voluntary Organisations in Crisis* (1971). I later included co-operatives in a study of 'the religion of socialism' in Britain during the 1880s and 1890s.[409] Surprising people attached surprising hopes to the co-operative movement during those years. Tom Mann – a revolutionary socialist in what became the very different, Communist Party tradition – was excitedly evangelical about Co-operation during the 1890s. Percy Redfern, who later became a dedicated CWS official and its first historian, described his own spiritual outlook during the same years in a fine autobiography: *Journey Towards Understanding* (1946). Working with a group of Tolstoyans in Croydon was part of Redfern's journey towards the CWS.[410] For all his Liberalism and critique of emergent forms of Social Democracy, Holyoake was also argumentatively engaged with William Morris's (and Karl Marx's) socialism during the same years; with Robert Blatchford's *Clarion* newspaper, the I.L.P's journal *Labour Leader* and with other signs of the excitement of the 1880s and 1890s.

When I re-read Holyoake, his continuing concern with religion came out as clearly as his critical preoccupation first with 'social' and later with socialist ideas. 'In my youth I had borne the burden of theological hopes and fears until my mind ached, and if I could lead others into a simpler, surer and brighter way, I was wishful to do so'. This is what impelled Holyoake to set down his *Principles of Secularism* in 1859.[411] The idea of the secular *versus* the religious soon became as simplistic to me as it was to him. Moving beyond that antinomy is also now more fashionable than it has been for many years among writers on religion, and to a lesser but growing extent among writers on radical politics.[412]

The category 'religion' is under review more generally now, in ways which could disclose unfamiliar possibilities. If 'it' – religion – is regarded as being always x y or z, or if it always does x y or z, or if it is no more than an error out of which humans grow, then further consideration of it is a waste of spirit. In other words, if 'essentialist', 'functionalist' or 'rationalist' takes on religion are the only plausible ones, there is no reason to think further on these matters. A piece like Holyoake's *The uselessness of prayer* could provide a suitable terminus.[413]

The essentialist puts religion in a neat definitional box. The box generally contains God (One or many); set forms of worship and church (without 'churches' or something like them, no 'religion'); the supernatural; and self-defined or received 'religious' beliefs accompanied by anathemas against 'unbelief' by Christians and others. Religion essentially is…. A single definition follows.[414]

The functionalist puts religion in a social or psychological box. This box contains how 'it' (religion) makes and maintains a social order, prevents or generates change, resolves cognitive and social dissonance, comforts and integrates believers regardless of reason. 'Religion essentially does...'. A single function follows.[415]

The militant rationalist puts religion in the past. As a chapter in the human story, religion is seen as 'early', not to say primitive. As a mistake in the human exercise book, as it were, 'religion' has been corrected by 'science'. Where religion lingers it is, in genetic terms, recessive. By now in reason's journey towards total understanding, it should be over and done with. Less dogmatic versions of secular rationality distinguish between *a* religion and 'religion' in general, and/ or between organized, deist 'religions' which are past their sell-by date, and individual spirituality which is still acceptable or even quite *à la mode*.

A particular view of modernity and 'progress' goes with secular rationalisms. Advocates of this view sometimes put on religion's clothes. This was notably the case in Holyoake's time among Utilitarians (including some Owenites); among Positivists (including some people very interested in Owen); and then, towards the end of the nineteenth century, among neo-Hegelian Idealists. Rational Religions, Religions of Happiness, Temples of Reason and the religions and churches of Progress and Humanity were familiar to Holyoake as his fellow travellers or mentors, as of course were Christian and other types of Sacred Socialist.[416] Holyoake took pleasure observing these beliefs and practices. He liked recounting their stories. He was sometimes sympathetic, never arrogant and always entertaining to read on such subjects.

In the twenty-first century religion has refused to go away. For good as well as obvious ill, it is present in strength, for example among 'extremist' youth, millenarians and 'endists' of many kinds, including fundamentalists, pentecostalists and followers of flourishing, world-wide absolutist faiths, whether scripture-based or church-based.[417] In Gregor McLennan's view we are riding a 'post secular wave'.[418] Would-be revolutionary religious movements, often anti-Western and not only Muslim, are now read by sober commentators as modern and understandable rather than as 'medieval', and merely disagreeable.[419] Sociologists of religion, with Max Weber as one of their founding fathers, continue to offer intricate taxonomies of 'religious rejections of the world and their directions.'[420] This-worldly cults, sects, churches and denominations are classified and studied in action. They are then contrasted with other-worldly examples of these different types of organisation. These are then further differentiated as socially 'active' or socially 'passive', with no doubt among unbelievers as well as believers about their individual power and social potential.

Inclusive, multi-dimensional, substantive descriptions and analyses of religion are now in full play: religion as what Peter Berger calls 'social reality', rather than as regressive delusion.[421] Durkheim's work remains influential in this setting.

> 'In answer to the question: What is the (elusive) object of this more or less universal activity, Religion? Durkeim said: There is a real object, and the object is Society. "Religion is a system of ideas with which individuals represent to themselves the society of which they are members, and the obscure but intimate relations which they have with it". "Religion is... the system of symbols by means of which Society becomes conscious of itself; it is the way of thinking characteristic of collective existence."'[422]

The question about contemporary societies and individuals has become 'what form does their religion take?' rather than 'do they have any?' And the answers need not focus on formal churches or denominations. Contemporary concern is as much with less formal cults and sects; with basic human needs and practices, individual as well as collective; and with differing versions of the 'common sense' which holds dynamic social movements and societies together, for better as well as for worse.

For fifty years now, 'secularisation' has been a contested concept among students of society rather than an assumed process.[423] 'Do you believe in...?' was the question which assaulted Holyoake, in court rooms and elsewhere. But even committed 'religious' writers now want to prise religions, including Christianity, free from the baggage which attaches to yes or no answers to simplistic questions about 'belief'.[424]

[ii] *Co-operation, religion and Holyoake.*

In December 1878, as already observed, at a time of dynamic growth in the co-operative movement, the Southern Section of the Central Co-operative Union resolved that a 'manual' on *Foundations: A Study in the Ethics and Economics of the Co-operative Movement* would be commissioned by the Union. The Southern Section was the area of the Union most directly linked into Christian Socialism. An outline by Thomas Hughes and Edward Vansittart Neale was approved in February 1879, referred to the United Board and thence to the Co-operative Congress of 1879. In the first edition of the resulting book, which stayed in print and was revised in 1915, Hughes and Neale observed that:

'Co-operation, as it is presented in these pages, is an attempt made by men profoundly convinced of the eternal reality of moral truth, to embody the high ideal of duty in institutions applying to the daily events of our ordinary lives' ...

'Our Societies have come to acknowledge that the mere fact of membership in a retail store involves more than paying ready money, attending once a quarter, and drawing dividends. As the years pass they find themselves constantly brought into new and more intimate relations with their fellow-members, in their own association and in the Union. In the primary sense of the word, *id quod religat,* 'that which binds together', they have already found that co-operation has been a religion to them...'[425]

At Hebden Bridge in 1898 one of the aristocratic patrons of the movement, Earl Grey, said that 'Co-operative production furnished each man with an ideal which became to him a religion.'[426]

Such sentiments came *to* the co-operative movement from above rather than from below: they referred to 'them' not 'us', to 'him' rather than 'me'. But Holyoake, in spite of his rather different relationship with Labour, also seldom passed 'the religious question' by on the other side of the road. This is another good reason for re-reading him today. He behaved to patrons as if on level terms, and bridled at the tone of voice of the movement's aristocratic friends, and of the entrist motives he detected among Christian Socialist co-operators. Holyoake thought there were better reasons for eliminating poverty than progressive Anglicans' concern to end working-class alienation from the established church. His sense of putting Capital in its necessary but subordinate place was strong: people were manifestly and already able to help each other to arrange their own means of production and reproduction, whether of knowledge, belief, governance, candles or treacle. So Holyoake acted as if the meanings currently enclosed by 'religion' and the churches were worth rescuing from their other-worldly devotees. Religious meanings needed to be disentangled from existing arrangements of power, and from the ecclesiastical, tithe-collecting landlords he had felt angry about since his childhood years.[427] For Holyoake religion was, in MacIntyre's sense, 'an essentially contested concept', intimately linked to unequal relations of wealth and power perhaps more than it is for us now. It was, in Raymond Williams's sense, a 'keyword'. Keywords were, for Williams, words which carry significant social (or anti-social) meanings. But they were also words 'the problems of whose meanings seem inextricably bound up with the problems they are being used to discuss'.[428]

As became clear during *The Counsellor* episode in 1861, Holyoake was an instinctive sociologist or taxonomist of religion in Max Weber's sense. He was interested not only in what kinds of behaviour were supported by what kinds of organisation – a question which defines and divides many religious traditions – but also in the 'theodicy' question. That is to say he was interested in what people thought about, and how they organised in the face of, the unequal distribution of life-chances. This is one way of describing Holyoake's lifelong project. Weber considered it to be the dynamic behind the evolution of most religions.[429]

Holyoake delighted in amusing tales about phenomena which were eventually to feed into Weberian and post-Weberian classifications of 'religious rejections of the world and their directions': this-worldly and other-worldly, active and passive, exclusive and inclusive forms for the organisation of belief and social activity. His descriptions of the Ham

Common Concordium and of the life of Peter Baume have already been quoted. Sociological work on types of religious organisation was integral to Weber's historical work on the breakthrough of capitalist 'rationality' to which *The Protestant Ethic and the Spirit of Capitalism* was only a preface.

Holyoake first used the term 'secularism' during the early 1850s. He began to organise under its banner in 1852. In an 'Introductory Sketch' to Holyoake's life published soon after his death, his bibliographer Goss described Holyoake's idea of secularism as:

> 'the study of promoting human welfare by material means. Secularism relates to the present existence of man, having for its object the development of the physical, intellectual and moral nature of man to the highest point as the immediate duty of society inculcating the practical sufficiency of natural morality apart from Atheism, Theism or Christianity'.

Only the best for everyone – to be achieved here and now, by themselves and for themselves – was good enough. Secularism was 'a system of secular principles apart from atheism and theism, maintaining that wherever a moral end was sought, there was a secular *as well as a religious* (my italics) part to it'.[430] Holyoake confessed to having a religious as well as a secular mind; it was just that he wanted a division of theoretical and practical labour between them. He devoted a chapter of *Sixty Years of an Agitators's Life* to the 'Origin of Secularism 1850–1890'.[431] This included a re-appropriation of 'religion' on behalf of 'the common sense and best sense of all sorts and conditions of men'. Holyoake wanted to prise it away from astrologers, priests and other professionals, preferring to rely on experience rather than expertise, just as Quakers and other Protestant churches did. In his view, deeply-held beliefs at work within associational forms that were deliberately designed to put them into practice – which is one way of describing what religions consist of – were worth struggling for. Holyoake fought to fashion them at every stage of his life. It comes as no surprise that the eminent Rochdale Quaker, Liberal Parliamentarian and industrialist, John Bright, whom Holyoake was unafraid to disagree with as well as to praise, called him 'a very good Christian, and (he) does not know it'.[432] Nor is it surprising that the Methodist Radical leader Hugh Price Hughes acknowledged in the *New Review* that 'Mr Holyoake taught us many years ago those truth of Secularism which are happily no longer neglected by Christian teachers'. Holyoake was clearly pleased to quote his comment in *Sixty Years*.[433]

Holyoake worked alongside Mazzini but also challenged him on matters of theology. He never trusted 'providence', for example, any more than he trusted those provisions – candles and treacle – which were supplied to co-operators from sources outside their own movement. Unlike Mazzini, he did not believe in a supply-line from God to 'the People', through which He distributed his chosen future for humanity: in Holyoake's version of the religion of humanity people were their own agents, not God's or History's.[434]

> 'Providence procrastinates. No peril stirs it, no prayer quickens its action... Men perish as they supplicate. In danger the people must trust in themselves'.

> '...what were called spiritual means could not be depended on; the preacher who put his trust in aid from above still found it necessary to take up a collection' [435]

Doing good 'by *material* means (Holyoake's emphasis) is the simple test'.[436] This world (now) was not to be separated from the next world (then): the material world includes the spiritual. Everyone's creed was to be their own. Education would help this to become possible. Hence the need for Co-operative Societies to set aside part of their dividend for educational purposes. Fully individual creeds could only be articulated within a dedicated social movement of which they were one product.

> 'The *moral* (my emphasis) test of the Scriptures was sufficient, and the only one that had popular education in it, and needed neither ridicule, nor scorn, nor bitterness to enforce it, since it had the commanding advantages of appealing to the common sense and best sense of...men of Christian or of Pagan persuasion...'[437]

Being able to be 'different from other people' in associations which worked against the interference of un-elected Authority was essential. 'Those who believe because others believe the same are without claim to authority.'[438] If there was to be a religion of co-operation, free communication between people with diverse stories and beliefs would be its defining precondition: hence Holyoake's campaigns against stamp duties on newspapers, for workmen's fares on railway transport and for inclusive school text books. Free communication would also be a continuing product of co-operatives. Hence his commitment to the reading rooms, libraries, meeting rooms and halls integral to the local branches of co-operative societies as well as to their central premises. *Meetings* were among the things (relations) which co-operatives made. All members of co-operative societies as accessible, knowable communities should be in the best possible position to help each other to produce, distribute and exchange this, among other human necessities. This is what Richard Sennett meant by 'dialogic' communication in *Together: the Rituals, Pleasures and Politics of Co-operation* (2012). Co-operative communication could be fully mutual, neither top down nor bottom up, in economic, material matters (demand and supply) as much as in matters of political (and spiritual) governance. Holyoake would surely have welcomed the United Diversity Co-operative in twenty-first century London (uniteddiversity.coop) as well as the Jainist-Hindu concept Aneskantavada which states that no single perspective on an issue contains the whole truth. Ideally this should result in a tolerant approach to the doctrines of other faiths. In his 1996 *Background Paper* to the 1995 *Statement of Co-operative Identity*, Ian Macpherson observed how, 'Co-operatives around the world ... have developed within a rich array of belief systems, including all the world's great religions and ideologies.' To quote him again,

> 'Since its beginnings the co-operative movement has encouraged people of different political allegiances and ideologies to work together. In that sense it has tried to transcend the traditional ideologies that have created so much tension, unrest and warfare in the late nineteenth and twentieth centuries. Indeed this capacity to bring diverse people together for common goals is one of the great promises the movement offers to the twenty-first century'.[439]

Holyoake was critical of 'modes of accounting for scriptural doctrine' such as the 'Higher Criticism' disputes between Christians and anti-Christians concerning the interpretation of ancient texts. Whose knowledge? And for whom? were the questions. Higher Criticism 'cannot be made intelligible and convincing except to students of very considerable research... (They) could never command the popular mind nor enable a working man to dare the understanding of others in argument... If I find maxims obviously useful and true, judged by human experience, I adopt them, whether given by inspiration or not. If precepts did not answer to this test, they were not acceptable, though all the apostles in history had signed them'.[440]

In order to communicate as widely as possible, Holyoake chose *Chambers Encyclopedia* to publish an essay on Secularism. As ever unafraid of eminent authorities, he asked Professor F. W. Newman (1805–1897) to look at this work. The Professor, the Cardinal's brother, went through many *Phases of Faith* (the title of his autobiography) on a journey from Calvinism to Theism. He 'regarded all who believed that duty to man is prior in time and importance to duty to God as Secularists'. Holyoake wondered about that, 'in this sense he (Newman) might be so classed himself, though he maintains Theism with a noble earnestness... That the secular form of opinion implies Atheism is an error into which many fall. Secularism, like mathematics, is independent of theistical or other doctrine'. Holyoake's lack of deference was evident again: he told Newman (who was an eminent mathematician among many other things) that 'Euclid did not ignore the gods of his day; he did not recognise them in geometry. They were not included in it.' He followed this by teasing Bradlaugh, his co-worker in the secularist cause: 'At one time the only two men of note in England who maintained that the Secular was Atheistic, were Dr Magee, the late Archbishop of York, and Mr Bradlaugh'.[441] Holyoake's secularism was nothing less than 'a new theory of secular life'. He regretted that some Secularist Societies, 'simply anti-theological, have taken the secular name, which leads many unobservant persons to consider the term Secularism as synonymous with atheism and general church-fighting.'[442]

Holyoake's lectures to the Worcester Socialists in their Hall of Science in 1840 were thought by Goss to be 'imbued with a highly moral, and truly religious tone of sentiment, which it was his most ardent desire and endeavor to inculcate among his audience'.[443] In the following year, he was invited by the Manchester Congress of the Universal Community Society of Rational Religionists to accept a station at Sheffield. It was in that 'diocese', as it was known, that he served as a 'social missionary'.[444] Looking back on this work later in life Holyoake observed that 'reason in piety was not then understood – faith being regarded as above logic'. This was no longer completely so. In *Sixty Years of An Agitator's Life* he welcomed the fact that some Christian and some Socialist attitudes had changed. Partly because of the secularist movement a new conversation about religion had started. Like Quakers, Holyoake wanted to make the secular sacred as well as the sacred secular.[445] When Bishop Colenso was attacked for examining the Pentateuch in secular historical as opposed to sacred theological terms, Holyoake refrained from attacking religion as such.[446] In fact he welcomed its diffusion, 'if only it be prized from what he considered to be corruption'.[447]

Holyoake's work escapes easy categories, in theology as in political economy, in 'opinion' as well as in association. His was a careful rather than troubled journey between a number of related positions. These included a variant of Unitarianism as a youth and young man; 'reason' as 'oracle' in his twenties (he edited *The Oracle of Reason* for a short time in 1841); detachment from any God-idea following the death of his daughter, Madeline, in October 1842; Owenism, but without the cult of Owen, from the mid-1830s onwards; an ambitious, inclusive secularism from the early 1850s; and the positive neutrality of the co-operative movement at its multi-faith best from the 1860s onwards. Holyoake challenged Bradlaugh's dogmatic atheism in public debate, supported Charles Watts and the British Secular *Union* in 1877 and at the age of 82 became the first President of the Rationalist Press *Association* (my italics). Like Mary Darwin, Eleanor Holyoake retained her Christian faith throughout her husband's journey.

In 1852 the Bishop of Oxford opposed the legalization of the Manchester Unity of Oddfellows on the grounds that if they had approved Lectures written for their members by Holyoake, they must be an atheistic organisation. Holyoake later pointed out that the bishop had not actually read the Lectures. When he did so, he had to admit 'that they were not irreligious – neither were they religious.' The Grand Master of the Order's response was to challenge his Lordship's use of the category 'religious'.[448] Holyoake's view was that 'Oddfellowship, like religion, can only sustain and commend itself by association with morality'.[449] He celebrated the Grand Master's response to the Bishop:

> 'How could the Lectures be "religious" in your Lordship's sense without leading to dissent and theological controversy in all our lodges – which would be an evil and inconsistent with that concord and brotherhood our Order is designed to promote'.[450]

For Holyoake, 'unity' remained a core co-operative value. It was 'secular grounds of tolerance and unity (which) might render co-operative efforts possible.' A specific kind of unity in political as well as in religious organisations was essential if large-scale working-class associations were to be produced and distributed. This was unity of the kind represented by a hand-shake (a common symbol in Friendly Societies) between odd fellows. Branch autonomy, or local government within and permitting 'national' self-government was as important among Friendly Society members as it was among

Congregationalist, Baptist, Primitive Methodist and other associational – properly democratic – heirs to the seventeenth-century revolution in Britain. Perhaps more on its Left wing than its Right, the labour movement in Britain has always subscribed to this difficult ideal. It was nervousness about the achievement of 'unity' in Federations (for example between Districts of miners' trades unions, and between them and other associations of working people including co-operatives) as well as in Unities and Orders of Friendly Societies independent of the state, which lay behind the 'fear of the Ballot' even among Liberal philosophers much admired by Holyoake. The fear was about class and power, and the potential differences between 'the governing mind' and 'the co-operative mind'.[451] Supposing people 'out of power' acted together, with their own Society votes as well as with Parliamentary 'suffrage' when the latter was eventually 'granted' to them? One for all and all for one – associated self-help, achieved by and leading to self-government expressed in dynamic, complex co-operatives – what might happen then?

Such fear was 'as old as England. It is the fear lest another should take his own way, and not take yours. It is in religion as well as in politics, and not easily eradicated'.[452] As Goss pointed out, 'the terrors of the law had been used against Holyoake by professing Christians.' So it was his own experience which told him that 'Christianity can never be wisely investigated while it retains its present principles, for power not reason it is grand evidence'.[453] Holyoake's insubordinate reasoning was perhaps harder to refute and more likely to generate anxiety, because it was so reasonably expressed, in publications like *The Reasoner*.

As already argued, for Holyoake political and religious 'neutrality' was a commitment rather than an abstention, reaching back to the 'enthusiastic period' of co-operative history. Co-operators would delay things if they made 'a profession of theological or political opinion a co-operative object...(and) if every member had to be converted to a given opinion before admission'. 'Opinion' was not what unity meant from a co-operative point of view. Co-operative neutrality was to 'avoid the sleepless resentments of wounded conscience and political conflict perilous to that unity which is the abiding strength of co-operation'.[454] Resentment dissipated personal and associational energy. When Holyoake reached the year 1850 in his 'Historical Chronicle Year By Year' of the Leeds Industrial Co-operative Society, he noted that this was the year that 'contentiousness, common in the commencement of co-operation... asserted itself in Leeds'. So much so that 'a wandering speaker in the town thought Leeds social reformers excelled in the capacity of disagreeing with themselves'. Holyoake's response – as late as 1897 – harked back to Owenite Rational Religion. Leeds members were criticizing each other, he thought, not for their mutual improvement, but to cause each other 'confusion'. This was no part of the associational ethic or the spirit of co-operation. It did not belong to 'the new world spirit':

> 'more or less, this is done everywhere among those under the influence of what we used to call "the old world spirit" which regarded everybody as personally responsible for his peculiarities which he was supposed to have willfully chosen and willfully retained.' [455]

This was the old world spirit which the Reverend Mr Marriott had confronted with such confidence and to 'great cheering', at the debate on 'Political and Religious Opinions at the 1832 Co-operative Congress. This was indeed 'a subject of very great importance':

'whatever views a Radical Reformer might entertain relative to the benefitting of society, it was morally impossible he could ameliorate the condition of mankind so far as the Co-operator, who acted on a system that embraced the whole human race; a system that acknowledged all men to be the creatures of circumstances, and forgave the failings of every one, from the king to the poorest peasant (great cheering)'.[456]

To embrace the whole human race was no mean ambition. Universality was not to be achieved by providence, whether in the shape of Progress, History or God. Social determination (from...) did not eliminate social responsibility (for...), articulated through individual members associated in Societies like the Leeds Industrial Co-operative Society:

'It was one of the main objects of early co-operative lectures to found a new art of association, and those who founded co-operation under Robert Owen had enduring enthusiasm which no difficulty dismayed – no disaster chilled.'[457]

'The unity which is at once strength and peace' could only be realised if 'free thought' was actually – materially – free. That is, if everyone was travelling on 'the same path', side by side not 'high and low'. This is a big ask, much bigger than modern defenders of 'the right to free expression of opinion' dare to understand. In his celebration of the Derby Society, Holyoake praised the editor of the *Derby Monthy Co-operative Record* for his outspoken defence of the most diverse contributions. Co-operative Societies produced free thought among other goods:

'Ideas of piety and politics of the most divergent kind were to be found in co-operative ranks. Official recognition was given to none. Only the principles of co-operation were official ...

Personal beliefs of other kinds had equal respect under the golden equality of toleration which ensures the unity which is at once strength and peace.'

The editor then used four lines of verse to condense what he meant by 'difference' – outside 'the co-operative world':

Man, some unwrought difference sees,
And speaks of high and low
And worships those, and tramples these
While the same path they go' [458]

There is a memorable expression of Holyoake's feelings 'on Theism and Futurity' in his *Sixty Years of an Agitator's Life* [459]. He remembered being regularly challenged during his days lecturing in Sheffield 'by people who thought that they and they alone were in possession of the truth': 'the class of people (who) 'fancy themselves ...all-knowing'. Remembering how he was 'attacked without reason, led him to 'enter the great debatable ground of the existence of Deity and future state' (sic), as follows:

'The universe never impressed me with so much awe and wonder as when I found I could not account for it...I admit ignorance is a privation. But to submit not to know, where knowledge is withheld, seems but one of the sacrifices that reverence for truth imposes on us.'

The future after death is unknown and – a characteristic emphasis – equally so, by everybody:

'All the while the white mystery is still unpenetrated in this life, and we must die to find it out. But a future being undiscovered is no proof that there is no future... all stand before the portals of the untrodden world in equal unknowingness of what lies beyond... In this world which is under our feet we may be equal in friendliness, duty and justice. The reverence of that which is right is no mean form of worship... As we read in the family motto of the Maharajahs of Benares, "There is no Religion higher than Truth", and the only truth which can be trusted is that which can be tested here. The believer said to the prophet:" I will set my camel free and trust him to Allah" Mahomet answered: 'Tie thy camel first and then commit him to God'.[460]

On the face of it, it seems surprising that Holyoake sometimes met blasts of intense fear, capable of turning to violence. He was a down to earth advocate after all: 'tie thy camel first'; 'equally unknowing' and 'reverent-for truth'.

But in his lifetime secularist and co-operative movements were operating within a powerful field of force. At one pole of this field was a specific kind of order, at the other pole the possibility of another Order (of mundane life) altogether. What would happen to social order if it was exposed as less than fully social, or even actively anti-social, by forces ('moral forces' to boot) attracted towards the second pole? And what would happen if those forces, anti-'religious' or irreligious as they often were, were to acquire some of the strengths of a religion? [461]

The aggression, not to say panic, which popular 'unbelief', 'infidelism' and 'blasphemy' excited in Victorian Britain has been well documented by historians.[462] From the French Revolution onwards the fear was like that inspired by 'extremist' threats to 'civilization' at any period of history. As Robespierre put it, 'it is not enough to have overturned the throne; our concern is to erect upon its remains holy Equality and the sacred Rights of man'.[463] Led by Robespierre – until his execution in 1794 – the Jacobins sought to establish a Cult of the Supreme Being to replace Christianity, referring to their messengers as apostles going forth to establish a new religion. In 1793 a Goddess of Reason was enthroned on the high altar at Notre Dame Cathedral: revolutionary leaders used terms like 'credo', 'sacrament' and 'sermon' in their speeches. 'No sooner had the revolutionaries rid themselves of one religion than they invented another'.[464] The French Revolution was, it goes without saying, the primary political event in *The Age of Revolution 1789 to 1848*, matched as it was by the English industrial revolution. The memory of it was all the more threatening to the extent that it had not been against 'religion' *tout court* but for the category 'religion' itself. If the time had come to earth religion in a – perhaps even in the – actually-existing social movement of the here and now… who knew the extent to which the world might be turned upside down? A radical social movement with the capacity religions have shown to spread widely, quickly and deeply might be threatening indeed. Order! Order!

Holyoake was not ignorant of the revolutionary terror with which Robespierre's name still remains so closely associated. 'The inquisitor, the tyrant, the conqueror, the Thug, may be honest… Marat made honesty infamous. Robespierre was honest, who made honesty terrible, whose speeches read like murder, whose sentences drip with blood'.[465] It was the fear of a reprisal of revolutionary violence to property as well as to people across Europe in 1848 which lay behind the Christian Socialist movement's attachment to small-scale co-operative workshops FOR the people during the years 1848 to 1854. In the same way that there was a struggle over 'religion' as a category there was also a struggle over 'co-operation'. It might… what might it achieve? Efforts to educate and contain 'the people' or the 'labouring classes', as opposed to liberating labour *as* a class capable of constructing a whole new Order, ran through the history of co-operation in general and Co-operatives in particular for the remainder of the nineteenth century.[466] This is the tightrope the co-operative movement trod for the next fifty years, and is still treading, if in a more residual way: the line between fitting into and transforming society. It will be apparent by now how Holyoake walked the same tightrope, of tactical acceptance combined with strategic rejection of Competition. When he fell off the tightrope – as people in movements, however 'social' do – it was as often on the new Order side of the line as it was on the old.

Nowhere in Europe from the mid-nineteenth century onwards was the co-operative movement, even its dominant consumer-led form, so integrally connected to a wider working-class, labour or 'social' movement as it was in Britain.[467] This was bound to seem like a threat as well as an opportunity to the powers that be. Could such a movement be safely contained, either by its private competitors or by its public regulators? Twenty-first century co-operators could still be encouraged by a history of their movement which sees it from the point of view of its market competitors and its state regulators, rather through their own downturned and sometimes depressive eyes. Like individuals, social movements with radical potential are subject to mood swings, on a day- to- day basis tending to underestimate as well as, on occasion, wildly overestimating their presence in the world.

Something more subversive than Holyoake's equitable reasoning certainly seemed to spell trouble, for example in a courtroom clash in 1852, a decade after the Cheltenham case cited at the beginning of this book. The clash was between Holyoake and an indignant presiding officer, Commissioner

Phillips of the Bankruptcy Court. Once again, the issue was whether Holyoake 'believed in a God'. Holyoake wished to stand surety for a bankrupt tailor, and wanted to affirm rather than take the Oath – a right which he was to help to establish in law in 1869. Because that right was not available in 1852 he was moved to declare 'that while the oath was legally binding on his conscience, it was not a profession of his faith, and he prays leave to make (that) declaration now'.

'Commissioner Phillips asked Holyoake what he meant. Did he mean that by it not being a profession of his faith, that it was not on the faith of a Christian? Mr Holyoake answered "Yes!". Mr Phillips asked: "What do you call yourself?" to which the answer, "A secularist," was promptly given. Commissioner Phillips then asked what he meant by secularist. Mr Holyoake: "One who gives precedence to the duties of this life over considerations which pertain to another world." Commissioner Phillips: "Do you believe in a God?". Mr Holyoake: 'I am not prepared to say." Commissioner Phillips: "Not prepared to say whether you believe in a God! You put yourself forward in a court of justice, and bring scandal upon it, by saying that that you are not prepared to say whether you believe in the Deity! Go and attend to your 'secular' business!" Mr Holyoake who had some days previously made an affidavit of bail, stood down and made his way out of court, and the insolvent went back to prison'.[468]

Looking back, Holyoake reflected that, had he been 'capable of speaking in strident and imperious tones', he would have met with more aggression and 'mischief ', particularly in his days as a Social Missionary. He set out to diffuse aggression in volatile situations, for example in an episode in Whitehaven in the early 1850s.

There had been religious riots in that town, not for the first time, following an assault on a Unitarian street-lecturer while he spoke on the subject of 'Progression'. A local magistrate had acquitted the assailant. For whatever reason, the topic, the preacher and/or his denomination had been a provocation. Ever since 1842, when the Bishop of Exeter had forced the resignation of William Pare, the Owenite Registrar of Birmingham 'the clergy', Holyoake wrote,' had been an intimidating force in every town, and many alarmed and prudent persons had denied their opinions or explained them away in self-protection'.

In 1851 Holyoake offered to speak in Whitehaven. 'Open, even ostentatious, defiance had merit', Holyoake reflected later, 'and some justification from the point of view of self-respect.' Nevertheless, in his own telling of the story, Holyoake went out of his way to be peaceable, both in the content and delivery of his two lectures in the town. 'I went to reason with them'. The atmosphere was tense. An assault on the lecturer was expected. The unpredictable affiliations of local Irish people and of coal miners added to the mix. Placards put up by socialists stirred things up: 'The Devil and Socialism were in the town'. There were rumours of impending 'blood and slaughter' in the theatre where Holyoake was to speak, and threats to pull the whole building down. He insisted on chairing his own lectures so that no local committee line-up occupying the stage of the hall could incite a response in kind. Holyoake joked that if he was alone on stage a target of one would be harder to hit. 'I preferred to conduct the meeting without assistance... I had long seen that there could never be a quarrel unless there were two parties to it ... and *I* was not going to be one '.

Holyoake's lecture title, no easier to turn into a headline than 'Progression', carefully elaborated his fundamental commitment: 'The Moral Innocency of Speculative Opinion, even the most extreme, when conscientiously entertained, setting forth how far a man might dissent from the Religious Opinions of his Neighbours, and yet hope to live in Truth and die in Peace'. Holyoake thought that his audience was 'astonished at not being outraged', and violence was avoided. 'They saw that a speaker might promote conviction without putting the "Devil" on his placard'.

'My argument was one they could not fight, and did not answer'. He stuck to his subject, in spite of 'the trick... of asking me whether "I believed the Bible to be the revealed will of God" and "Whether I believed in the Resurrection of our Lord Jesus Christ". He had learned from Cheltenham nine years before not to offer any provocation.[469]

Sixteen years later, in 1867, Holyoake found himself 'among the fishermen of Cromer'. As he told the story, he was the guest of a local Quaker. On the Sunday he went to church. It was his custom to look for 'the most distinguished preacher' in any town he visited. This was in keeping with his wish not to exclude Ministers of religion from Co-operative Congresses but rather to have sermons from every denomination.[470]

In Cromer he was greatly impressed by an unnamed Dean whose views chimed with his own:

> 'He said that there was a class of persons of high character, of perfect intellectual probity, who had that living morality which bound society together. Yet they professed not the Christian name. Nevertheless, it must be observed that, while morality bound man to the world, it was spiritual life which bound man to God'

The following day Holyoake was invited 'by many inhabitants of the town, led by local fishermen, to lecture on the "Orators of the English Parliament". Placards were put up announcing the lecture, including outside the Bible Society's Depot. The lecture was to take place in the fishermen's room. During the afternoon the atmosphere changed, 'muffled whisperings were heard behind every counter. The vicar had been in the town'. Seeing the placards, especially the one on the Bible Society's door, the vicar had organised their removal. He evidently 'admitted my subject was not in itself objectionable, but then I might say something else in speaking of it'. Holyoake sent word to the fishermen that if they wanted to withdraw the invitation, he would understand. He knew they might suffer financially from the Vicar's disapproval during lean seasons. The fisherman sent word that they would welcome him in their room. It was to be lit with their best candles.

When evening came, Holyoake walked to the room with his host, 'whose Quaker blood was a little stirred'. It was packed. They were greeted by 'an immense shout of welcome'. The lecture concerned the difference between oratory and public speaking. Holyoake was always interested in communication as art form. 'The exact communication of thought is the real difficulty of all rhetoric. It is the highest effort of art to enable another to see truth as we see it, to conceive a principle as we conceive it... The wonder is not that men misunderstand each other; it is rather marvellous that there are not more mistakes'.[471] In Cromer Holyoake 'pointed out the gradations of that art by which men climb on phrases to power'. It went down well. 'Signs of discernment arose sufficient to satisfy any speaker.'

> 'We said not a word about the vicar. I made no illusion to him, direct or indirect... He was, perhaps, a little apt to forget that the people of Cromer were citizens as well as Christians, and had a right to know what affected them as Englishmen (and) that 'they needed to understand the secular merits of those great men who influence their destinies'.[472]

[iii] Final questions.

'The battles for opinion... have some popular interest when they take a fighting form'.[473] Holyoake determined to act reasonably within a field of force for which he could not be held responsible, in the interest of distinctive, co-operative and secular, values and principles. He continued to insist on this world rather than another; on now rather than then; here rather than hereafter; on the agency of the many rather than the paramountcy of the few, however wise they might be; and on a present social movement rather than a mortgaged future. For most of the time he was unwilling to be drawn to one magnetic pole, in permanent opposition to the other. Perhaps the well-mannered awkwardness of his stance – his 'reverent unknowing' as well as his 'deliberate liberalism' – was a source not only of his sustained energy but also of the amused disdain with which Holyoake was met during his lifetime and by some interpreters ever since.

The change to a whole new order of society anticipated by Holyoake – 'this new Order of life, it is appearing' (1900) – was to be carried by thousands of co-operative societies by means of moral rather than physical force. If it is ever to happen in our time or at any future time, it may require a movement with strong internal as well as external adhesive to bind it together. In the final pages of his *The Protestant Ethic and the Spirit of Capitalism* Max Weber famously wondered whether escape from the iron cage of bureaucratic rationality would ever be possible without an 'ethic' comparable to that which had enabled its construction within incipient capitalisms. R. H. Tawney was also given to wonder whether the conviction which Protestants held, that a new order was divinely ordained by a power greater than their own was one ingredient in 'the rise of capitalism'. Would it be possible, he wondered, for socialists to engineer the rise of their new order without an extrinsic conviction with a force comparable to that of Protestant religion?[474] While writing this book I was asked why I risk practical commitment to co-operatives by putting the Co-operative Movement and its 1995 *Statement of Co-operative Identity, Values and Principles* anywhere near the category 'religion? Surely mainstreaming co-operative and mutual enterprises as economically rational in today's competitive world is hard enough without entering any Other world?[475]

Could moral idealism be unearthed once more, as one of the buried assets of the Co-operative Movement? Could modern advocates of co-operative and mutual enterprises invite loyalty not only to economic rationality but also to a co-operative ethic – even a *spirit*uality[476] – looking for the grace of gods rather different from today's trinity: the individual, the family, and the nation? A more theoretical question: could Weber's taxonomy of 'religious rejections of the world and their directions' be a way of understanding and developing the theory and the practice of co-operatives and mutuals as active rather than passive associations of values and principles, a this-worldly rather than other- worldly faith and practice? What could reinforce them as modern, revolutionary, associational forms capable, in E.P. Thompson's words, of mobilizing a whole class of people (Holyoake's 'Labour') to be 'present at their own making'? In the much-quoted *Preface* to *The Making of the English Working Class*, in which he famously identified 'the enormous condescension of posterity', Thompson also insisted that the working class did not 'rise like the sun at an appointed time'. Working- class people, rather, were present at their own making. But to go back to where I began, Holyoake's *History of Co-operation* (1908): 'Co-operators will never remain leal and true to their Society unless a foundation which never gives way is laid in their understanding'.

More than a century after Holyoake's death, it might be best to admit that we don't know. I know that 'the only way forward is a peaceful transition like Holyoake worked so hard for'.[477] I know that I have watched many co-operators during the last fifty years living out their attachment to their Societies and their Movement *as if* to a religion, with a dynamic faith – often against the odds and after many defeats – as freely chosen, as open and voluntary and as binding as any other religious faith. Encouraged by Holyoake's work, at a time in world history when 'religions' are powerfully present within a morbid social ecology, could there be some future in asking what kind of a benign, this-worldly 'religion' or 'mode of existence' (Latour's phrase, better perhaps than 'mode of production') co-operatives and mutuals could constitute in the future? Of what body or commonwealth could they – might they *already* – constitute the cells?

If my dream of Holyoake's work-in-progress entering the mainstream, carrying a title like *The Co-operative Ethic and the Spirit of Associationism* were to come true, 'The Association of All Classes of All Nations' would be at the centre of an early chapter. This was the Owenite Society which Holyoake joined in 1838. In 2017, can such an Association be so easily condescended to? Was it, or rather, is it – in our extraordinarily disjointed times – really so quaint? At the very least perhaps, a seed, ready to be sown for another season?

Select bibliography and information for further work

The National Co-operative Archive has its own Holyoake Collection. This is managed by the Co-operative College in Holyoake House and held in trust for posterity (with the Pioneers Museum in Rochdale) by the Co-operative Heritage Trust. The archive contains many of Holyoake's publications and some of his papers and correspondence, for example that with Robert Owen and E.O. Greening. The Collection includes some 3,500 letters, catalogued chronologically, with a name index. An alphabetical list of items in the collection is available from Gillian Lonergan at the College. The Bishopsgate Institute in London also has some Holyoake correspondence, for example with Charles Bradlaugh, Hypatia Bradlaugh and George Howell, together with Holyoake's diaries and other papers. The British Library has Holyoake's letters to W. E. Gladstone (Add. MSS 44303-44786) and correspondence with and relating to Harriet Martineau (Add.MSS 42726). There are some letters and papers in the Perkins Library at Duke University.

Where there is more than one edition of a work, as there often is with Holyoake, I have used the most accessible or the latest edition for page references in the footnotes. Holyoake was an inveterate reviser but not a meticulous editor of his own work. The following is a selective list of my own sources to guide future students.

R. Beevers, *The Garden City Utopia: a critical biography of Ebenezer Howard* (London: Macmillan, 1988).

A.E. Bestor, 'The origins of the socialist vocabulary', *Journal of the History of Ideas*, Vol.IX, 3 (1948) pp.259–302.

A.E. Bestor, *Backwoods Utopias, the sectarian and Owenite phases of communitarian socialism in America 1663– 1829* (Philadelphia: University of Pennsylvania Press, 1950).

Andrew Bibby, *All Our Own Work: The co-operative pioneers of Hebden Bridge and their mill* (*London*: Merlin Press, 2015). (Bibby, 2015).

Johnston Birchall, *People-Centred Businesses: Co-operatives, Mutuals and the Idea of Membership* (Basingstoke and New York: Palgrave Macmillan, 2011).

Paul Blackledge and Kelvin Knight, *Virtue and Politics: Alasdair MacIntyre's Revolutionary Aristotelianism* (Notre Dame Indiana: University of Notre Dame Press, 2011).

Barbara J. Blaszak, *George Jacob Holyoake (1817–1906) and the Development of the British Co-operative Movement* (Dyfed, Wales: Edwin Mellen Press, 1988). This book was based on a PhD thesis, 'George Jacob Holyoake: An Attitudinal Study' (State University of New York at Buffalo, 1978).

S.A Book, *Co-operative Values in a Changing World: a report to the*

ICA Congress in Tokyo 1992 (Geneva: ICA, 1992).

Susan Budd, 'The loss of faith in England, 1850–1950', in *Past and Present* no 36 (April 1967) pp.106–25.

Adam Brandenburger and Barry Nalebuff, *Coopetition: A Revolution Mindset That Combines Competition and Cooperation* (New York: Currency/ Doubleday, 1996).

W.Henry Brown, *George Jacob Holyoake* (Manchester: Co-operative Printing Society, 1906), Pioneer Biographies of Social Reformers no 1, and (the same 16-page length) W.H.Brown, *Holyoake the Co-operator* (Manchester, Co-operative Printing Society, n.d.).

Gregory Claeys, *Citizens and States: politics and anti-politics in early British socialism* (Cambridge: Cambridge University Press, 1989)

Stefan Collini, 'The Idea of Character in Victorian Political Thought', *Transactions of the Royal Historical Society*, 5th series: 35 (1985), pp.29–50.

P.Conaty and D. Bollier, *Toward an Open Co-operativism: a New Social Economy based on Open Platforms, Co-operative models and the Commons.*(A Report on a Commons Strategy Group Workshop. Berlin, Germany Aug.27–28 2014), and in January 2015 a Report for Co-opsUK available at commonstransition.org.

Co-operatives UK, *The UK Co-operative Economy 2014, Untold Resilience* (*Manchester*, Co-operatives UK, June 2014).

J.Emmanuel and I.Macpherson, *Co-operatives and the Pursuit of Peace* (University of Victoria: New Rochdale Press BCICS, 2007).

David Erdal, *Beyond the Corporation: Humanity Working* (London: Bodley Head 2011).

W. Hamish Fraser, *Alexander Campbell and the Search for Socialism* (Manchester: Holyoake Books, 1996).

C.W.F.Goss, *A Descriptive Bibliography of the Writings of George Jacob Holyoake. With a Brief Sketch of His Life* (London: Crowther & Goodman, 1908). (Goss, *Brief Life* and *Bibliography*).

Venu Madhav Govindu, Deepak Malghan, 'Building a Creative Freedom: J.C.Kumarappa and his Economic Philosophy', in the *Economic and Political Weekly* (Kumarappa, 2005).

James Gregory, 'The most singular and eccentric little sect of this generation': the White Quakers of Ireland, *c*. 1840–1854', in Joan Allen and Richard C. Allen, *Faith of Our Fathers: Popular Culture and Belief in Post-Reformation England, Ireland and Wales*, (Newcastle on Tyne: Cambridge Scholars Publishing 2009), pp.118–136. James Gregory's article was based on an earlier study in *Quaker Studies*, 'Some account of the Progress of the Truth as it is in Jesus': The White Quakers of Ireland', in *Quaker Studies*, 9,1 (2004), pp.68–94.

Edward Owen Greening, *The Story of the Life of George Jacob Holyoake* (Manchester: Co-operative Union Ltd, 1917).

L.E Grugel, *George Jacob Holyoake: a study in the evolution of a Victorian radical* (Philadelphia: Porcupine Press,1976). This book was based on a 1976 University of Chicago PhD thesis.

Peter Gurney, 'George Jacob Holyoake: Socialism, Association and Co-operation in Nineteenth-Century England' in Stephen Yeo ed., *New Views of Co-operation*, (London: Routledge, 1988), pp.52-72.

Peter Gurney, ' "A Higher State of Civilisation and Happiness", Internationalism in the British Co-operative Movement c.1889-1917', in Frits Van Holthoon and Marcel van der Linden eds. *Internationalism in the European Labour Movement 1830-1940* (Leiden: E.J. Brill, 1988), pp.543-564.

Peter Gurney, 'The Middle Class Embrace: language, representation and the contest over Co-operative forms in Britain 1860-1914, in *Victorian Studies* 37/2 (1994), pp.253-286.

Peter Gurney, *Co-operative Culture and the politics of consumption in England 1870-1930* (Manchester: Manchester University Press, 1996)

Peter Gurney, 'Le debat sur la Co-operation dans l'Angleterre Victorienne et Edwardienne' in *Histoire, Economie et Societe* Economie, 16/2 (1997), pp.12-23.

Peter Gurney, '"Labour's Great Arch" Co-operation and cultural revolution in Britain, 1795-1926', in Ellen Furlough and Carl Strickwerda eds., *Consumers against capitalism. Consumer Co-operation in Europe, North America and Japan 1840-1990* (Maryland: Rowman and Littlefield, 1999).

F.Hall and W.P.Watkins, *Co-operation: a Survey of the History, Principles and Organisation of the Co-operative Movement in Great*

Britain and Ireland (Manchester: Co-operative Union, 1934).

J.F.C Harrison, *Quest for the New Moral World: Robert Owen and the Owenites in Britain and America* (New York: Charles Scribner's Sons, 1969).

Royden Harrison, *Before the Socialists: Studies in Labour and Politics 1861 – 1881* (London: Routledge and Kegan Paul, 1965).

G.J.Holyoake, *The trial of George Jacob Holyoake, on an indictment for blasphemy, before Mr Justice Erskine and a common jury, at Gloucester, August the 15th, 1842, from notes specially taken by Mr Hunt* (London: The Anti-Persecution Union, 1842). (Holyoake, 1842 trial)

G.J.Holyoake, *The lectures used by the Manchester Unity of the Independent Order of Odd Fellows, sanctioned and approved by the Bristol A.M.C., June, 1846* (London: John G.Hornblower,1846). (Holyoake, 1846 *Lectures*)

G.J Holyoake, *The Organisation of Freethinkers* (London: J. Watson, 1852).

G.J. Holyoake, *Organisation: not of arms –but ideas* (London: J. Watson, 1853).

G.J.Holyoake, *The principles of secularism briefly explained* (London: Holyoake and co, 1859) Subsequent editions followed in 1860, 1870, 1871 (revised) and 1881 (revised) (Holyoake, 1859 *Secularism, Principles).*

G.J. Holyoake, *The Trial of Theism* (London: Holyoake and Co, 1858), also published in a Trubner edition in 1877. *The Trial…*

was originally published fortnightly, in 22 penny parts of 8 pages each. It examines at least ten schools of theistical thought with which Holyoke had been brought into controversy and 'may be considered a history of a fifteen years' discussion and propagandism, giving in a revised form, the chief articles on theological subjects which he had written during this period'. See Goss, *Bibliography* p.23.

G.J.Holyoake, *Code of the tenets or governing principles of the Society of Secularists set forth in ten articles* (London: Society of Secularists, 1881).

G.J.Holyoake, *Hostile and generous toleration (a new theory of toleration)*, (London: E.W Allen, 1886).

G.J.Holyoake, *Deliberate liberalism: four instances of it* (London: John Heywood, 1886).

G.J.Holyoake, *Self-Help a hundred years ago* (London: Swan Sonnenschein, 1890). 1st edition, 1888. (Holyoake, *Self Help a hundred years ago*).

G.J.Holyoake, 'State Socialism', in *The Nineteenth Century: a monthly review*, June 1879, pp.1114–1120. (Holyoake 'State Socialism' 1879).

G.J.Holyoake, 'Co-operation and Socialism', in James Samuelson ed. *Subjects of the Day*, no. 2, August 1890, pp.89–104. (The whole of this issue of *Subjects...* was on 'Socialism, Labour and Capital'. (Holyoake, 'Co-operation and Socialism', 1890).

G.J. Holyoake, *The origin and nature of secularism; showing that where freethought commonly ends, secularism begins*, (London:

Watts & Co, 1896). (Holyoake, *Secularism, Origin and Nature*).

G.J.Holyoake, *The Jubilee History of the Leeds Industrial Co-operative Society from 1847 to 1897 traced year by year*, (Leeds: Central Co-operative Offices, 1897) (Holyoake, *Leeds* 1897.)

G.J.Holyoake, *Against clandestine commissions, mainly in the interests of co-operative societies* (London: Gay and Bird, 1899). There were two editions of this in the same year.

G.J.Holyoake, and Amos Scotton *The Jubilee History of the Derby Co-operative Provident Society Limited 1850–1900*, (Manchester: Co-operative Printing Society, 1900). (Holyoake, *Derby* 1900).

G.J.Holyoake, *The Co-operative Movement Today*, (London: Methuen, 1903) The first edition was in 1891. (Holyoake, *Co-operative Movement Today*).

G.J. Holyoake, *Anti-Boycott Papers* (Manchester: Co-operative Union, 1903).

G.J Holyoake, *Bygones worth remembering* (London: T. Fisher Unwin, 1905). Two volumes. (Holyoake, *Bygones*).

G.J.Holyoake, *Sixty Years of an Agitator's Life* (London: T. Fisher Unwin, 1906) 1st edition, 1892. Holyoake began writing this book in 1881. Divided into two, differently-paginated parts, bound within the same volume. (Holyoake, *Sixty Years*).

G.J.Holyoake, *Self-Help By The People: The History of the Rochdale Pioneers 1844–1892* (London and New York: Swan Sonnenschein, 1907). The 1907 edition is the 3rd reprint of the 10th edition of Parts 1 and 2. The first edition of Part 1 was in

1858. (Holyoake, *Rochdale Pioneers*).

G.J Holyoake, *The History of Co-operation, revised and completed* (London: T. Fisher Unwin, 1908). Holyoake began this work in 1873; the first edition of vol.1 was in 1875 and of vol.2 in 1879. In the 1908 edition, the volumes (now Parts) are bound together but the pagination is separate. (Holyoake, *History of Co-operation*).

G.J. Holyoake, *The Organisation of Freethinkers* (London: J. Watson, 1852).

The following Holyoake publications have been digitized on a website assembled by Gerald Massey: http://geraldmassey.org.uk/holyoake/index.htm:
Sixty Years of an Agitator's Life
Bygones Worth Remembering
Among the Americans
The Rochdale Pioneers
The Jubilee History of the Leeds Industrial Co-operative Society
The Jubilee History of the Derby Co-operative Society
The History of Co-operation
Public Speaking and Debate.

Thomas Hughes and Edward Vansittart Neale, *Foundations: a study in the Ethics and Economics of the Co-operative Movement, prepared at the request of the Co-operative Congress held at Gloucester in April 1879, revised in 1915 by A. Stoddart, A. and W.Clayton* (Manchester: The Co-operative Union, 1915). 1st edition 1879. (Hughes and Neale, *Foundations*).

International Co-operative Alliance, '*Co-operative facts and figures*' http:ica.coop/en/whats-co-op/co-operative-facts-figures.

Kelvin Knight, *The MacIntyre Reader* (Cambridge: Polity Press, 1998).

J.E.M.Latham, *Search for a New Eden, James Pierrepont Greaves (1777–1842): The Sacred Socialist and His Followers* (London: Associated University Presses, 1999).

Michael Lewis and Pat Connaty, *The Resilience Imperative: co-operative transitions to a steady-state economy* (Gabriola Island, BC: New Society Publishers, 2102).

The London Co-operative Society, *Articles of Agreement for the formation of a community on principles of mutual co-operation within fifty miles of London, drawn up and recommended by the London Co-operative Society* (London: 1825 LCS Articles 1825).

Alasdair MacIntyre, *After Virtue: a study in moral theory* (London: Duckworth, 1981) 3rd edition 2007.

Alasdair MacIntyre, *Dependent Rational Animals: Why Human Beings Need the Virtues,* first published 1999 (London: Duckworth, 2009), especially Chapter 11, 'The political and social structures of the common good', pp.129–146. (MacIntyre, *Dependent* 2009).

Alasdair MacIntyre, *God, Philosophy, Universities: a Selective history of the Catholic Philosophical Tradition* (London: Continuum, 2009).

Ian Macpherson 'Co-operative Principles for the 21st Century: Introduction' (made available by the ICA, 11 Sept. 1995) and 'Background Paper to the Statement on the Co-operative Identity' (made available by the ICA, 8 Jan. 1996) http://

www.uwcc.wise.edu/icic/issues/prin/21-cent/intro.html, (Macpherson, *Introduction*, 1995) (Macpherson, *Background*, 1996).

Joseph McCabe, *Life and Letters of George Jacob Holyoake*. Two volumes. (London: Rationalist Press Association and Watts and Co., 1908) (McCabe, *Life and Letters*).

John Stuart Mill, Chapter on Socialism, in J.M.Robson et al eds., *The Collected Works of John Stuart Mill* (London &Toronto: University of Toronto Press, Routledge and Kegan Paul, 1963–1991).

John Stuart Mill, *Principles of Political Economy* (most available, 7th edition 1973 from Augustus M. Kelley reprints, Clifton, New Jersey).

F. Molina, and J.K. Walton, 'An alternative co-operative tradition: the Basque co-operatives of Mondragon', in A. Webster, A. Brown, D.Stewart, J.Walton and L. Shaw, *The hidden alternative: Co-operative values, past, present and future* (Manchester: Manchester University Press, 2011), pp.226–251.

A.S. Mulhall and A. Swift, *Liberals and Communitarians* (Oxford: Blackwell, 1992).

R. Murray, *Co-operation in the Age of Google: a report for Co-operatives UK* (2010). (The original, 150-page draft of this Report contains material not included in its ultimate publication).

Robin Murray, 'A different way of doing things', in *Red Pepper* May 2012.

Denis G. Paz, ed. *Nineteenth-Century English Religious Traditions, Retrospect and Prospect* (Greenwood Press, Westport, Connecticut, 1995).

Gordon Pearson, *The Road to Co-operation: escaping the bottom line* (Gower Publishing, Farnham Surrey and Ashgate Publishing: Burlington USA, 2012).

John Restakis, *Humanizing the Economy: Co-operatives in the Age of Capital* (Gabriola Island BC: New Society Publishers, 2010).

Edward Royle, 'George Jacob Holyoake and the Secularist Movement in Britain 1841-1861' (PhD thesis, Cambridge University, 1968).

Edward Royle, *Radical Politics 1790-1900: Religion and Unbelief* (London: Longman, 1971). [Royle, 1971]

Edward Royle *Victorian Infidels: the origins of the British secularist movement 1791-1866* (Manchester: Manchester University Press, 1974).

Edward Royle, *The Infidel Tradition from Paine to Bradlaugh* (London: Macmillan, 1976).

Edward Royle, *Radicals, Secularists and Republicans: popular freethought in Britain 1866-1915* (Manchester: Manchester University Press, 1980).

R.Sennett, *Together: the rituals, pleasures and politics of co-operation* (London: Allen Lane, 2012).

Synergia: the Synergia Steering Group e mail exchanges from

2013 to 2016, of which I was a consumer rather than an active producer were invaluable. Synergia is a network which seeks to answer two questions: what is the new Co-operative Political Economy and how does it work? And, what is the best way to harness the power of digital technology as a tool for linking global knowledge to local action? Driven by Pat Conaty, a Fellow of the New Economics Foundation and an Associate Researcher for Co-operatives UK, Synergia is supported in the UK by Co-operatives UK, The Plunkett Foundation, Schumacher College, and the P2P Foundation; and in Canada by Athabasca University and its Research Fund; by the BC-Alberta Social Economy Research Alliance (BALTA); and the Canadian Co-operative Association (ACCA).

E.P.Thompson ed. *Out of Apathy* (London:New Left Books, Stevens and son, 1959).

E.P.Thompson, *William Morris: Romantic to Revolutionary*, (London: Merlin Press 2nd edition, 1977), 'Postscript 1976', pp.763-816.

W.P. Watkins, *Co-operative Principles Today and Tomorrow* (Manchester: Holyoake Books, 1986).

A. Webster, A. Brown, D. Stewart, J.K. Walton and L. Shaw eds. *The hidden alternative, Co-operative values, past, present and future* (Manchester: Manchester University Press, 2011).

Raymond Williams, *Culture and Society* (London: Chatto & Windus, 1958).

Raymond Williams, *Culture* (London: Fontana, 1981).

Stephen Yeo, 'Towards Co-operative Politics: using early to

generate late socialism', in *Journal of Co-operative Studies*, 42.3 (2009), pp.22-35.

Stephen Yeo, 'Co-operation, Mutuality, and the Democratic Deficit or Re-membering Democracy' and 'Theorizing Co-operative Studies: obstacles and opportunities for twenty-first century Co-operative and Mutual Enterprises', in Ian Macpherson and Erin Mclaughlin eds. *Integrating Diversities within a Complex Heritage: essays in the field of Co-operative Studies* (British Columbia Institute for Co-operative Studies, University of Victoria, Canada, New Rochdale Press: 2008), pp.223-276 and 345-389.

Endnotes

1. Edward Owen Greening, *The Story of the Life of George Jacob Holyoake* (Manchester, Co-operative Union Ltd, 1917), p.9. This book was 'prepared for the Holyoake Centenary Celebrations at Birmingham, on the 14th April 1917, at the request of the Co-operative Union'. In subsequent Notes I will refer to it as Greening, *Holyoake* 1917.
2. Greening, *Holyoake* 1917, p.9.
3. C.W.F.Goss, *A Descriptive Bibliography of the Writings of George Jacob Holyoake. With a Brief Sketch of His Life* (London: Crowther & Goodman, 1908), p.xiii. To compile his invaluable bibliography and 'Introductory Sketch', Goss reviewed 'over 400 books, pamphlets and magazine articles'. (The Introductory Sketch is paginated separately from the Bibliography. I will refer to them in subsequent Notes as Goss, *Brief Life* and Goss, *Bibliography*).
4. W.H.Brown, *George Jacob Holyoake* (London and Leicester: C.W.Daniel and Leicester Co-operative Printing Society, n.d. but 1906), p.13.
5. 'Death of Mr G.J.Holyoake. A Peaceful End to a Strenuous Career. Chartist, Journalist and Social Reformer', *Co-operative News*, 27 Jan.1906.
6. G.J. Holyoake and Amos Scotton, *The Jubilee History of the Derby Co-operative Provident Society Limited 1850–1900* (Manchester: Co-operative Printing Society,1900), p.18. In subsequent Notes I will refer to this as Holyoake, *Derby* 1900. The 'new Order of Labour' quote is taken from a last 'Preface, 1906' to the 'revised and completed' edition of *The History of Co-operation* (London: T. Fisher Unwin, 1908), p.xi. In subsequent Notes I will refer to *The History...* as Holyoake, *History of Co-operation*.
7. I take 'resources for a journey of hope' from Raymond Williams, *Towards 2000* (London, Chatto & Windus, 1983) and from R. Gable ed. *Raymond Williams: Resources of Hope: Culture, Democracy, Socialism* (London: Verso, 1989). In the CWS magazine, *The Wheatsheaf*, vol.II, no.1, (May 1898), p.162 a co-operator insisted that 'Co-operation is not an –ism'. 'Among all the contending –isms clamouring for support, the ordinary working man may well be perplexed, wondering which of them is the most likely to fulfill the promises of its advocates, and in many cases be may refuse to discuss or adopt any of the systems offered him'.
8. A phrase used by Holyoake at Co-operative Congress in Halifax in 1874, in a contribution concerning co-operative education, quoted in

Co-operative News, April 25th 1874, p.230.

9. For more on 'outside' natures, see G.J. Holyoake, *The Jubilee History of the Leeds Industrial Co-operative Society from 1847 to 1897 traced year by year* (Leeds: Central Co-operative Offices, 1897), p.60. In subsequent Notes I will refer to this as Holyoake, *Leeds* 1897.

10. For 'open co-operativism', and a 'solidarity economy, see Pat Conaty and David Bollier, *Toward an Open Co-operativism: a New Social Economy based on Open Platforms, Co-operative models and the Commons*, initially a Report on a Commons Strategy Group Workshop. Berlin, Germany Aug.27–28 2014, subsequently a paper for Co-opsUK available from Co-opsUK and at commonstransition.org. See also: Michael Lewis and Pat Connaty, *The Resilience Imperative: co-operative transitions to a steady-state economy* (Gabriola Island BC: New Society Publishers, 2102); John Restakis, *Humanizing the Economy: Co-operatives in the Age of Capital* (Gabriola Island BC: New Society Publishers, 2010); Robin Murray, *Co-operation in the Age of Google*, a report for Co-ops UK. The original draft of this fundamentally important work began, 'after many years of beating against the wind, there is a gathering sense within the co-operative movement that – ideologically, politically and commercially – the wind has turned, that there are opportunities for the movement to regain the momentum it had during its first flowering in the second half of the nineteenth century, and its rise to retailing leadership in the first half of the twentieth.'

11. Capitalists pulling the roof of the world down on everyone's heads rather than relinquishing their own power is a phrase from an 1886 lecture by William Morris used in my 'News from Nowhere - An Appreciation', in *News from Nowhere* no. 2 (Brighton: News from Nowhere, n.d. [1971]) pp.6-11.

12. I have taken this quote from John Restakis from an e mail string on behalf of *Synergia* dated April 15th 2014.

13. G.J.Holyoake, *Sixty Years of an Agitator's Life* (London: T Fisher Unwin, 1906), p.xi. In subsequent Notes I will refer to this work as Holyoake, *Sixty Years*. For more on 'outside' natures, see Holyoake,*Leeds* 1897, p.60.

14. Giovanni Belardelli, *Mazzini* (Bologna: Societa editrice il Mulino, 2010) pp.101–2. Ivano Barberini, President of the ICA until his death in 2009, established the Fondazione Ivano Barberini, based in Bologna, for the study and spread of the history and culture of Co-operation. A leaflet explaining its scope and aims in 2012 was called 'La memoria del futuro'. In an early poem called 'To Him I Sing', Walt Whitman

included a line which read, 'I raise the present on the past'.
15. The reference to this reading aloud in 1875 is in G.J.Holyoake, *Bygones Worth Remembering* (London: T. Fisher Unwin, 1905) I, p.66. In subsequent Notes I will refer to this work as Holyoake, *Bygones*.
16. Goss, *Brief Life* p.lxv.
17. Holyoake, *Leeds*, 1897, p.104.
18. Holyoake, *Sixty years*, II, p.767.
19. G.J.Holyoake, *The Co-operative Movement Today* (London: Methuen, 1903), p. 145. The first edition of this work was in 1891. In subsequent Notes I will refer to it as Holyoake, *Co-operative Movement Today* 1903.
20. Holyoake, *Leeds*, 1897, p.217.
21. Among many examples, all worth anthologizing, see Holyoake, *Sixty Years*, I, pp.58–9, reflecting on how 'what you most desire, and have long looked for, you never see' in a beautifully imaginative, poetic way; and Holyoake, *Sixty Years* I, vividly characterising his audiences, the 'various classes of hearers' he encountered as a young Lecturer in Sheffield.
22. *Co-operative News*, vol.XXXVII 1906, p.120. I owe this reference to Andrew Bibby.
23. For associationism as practical critique of two, very different socialisms see Stephen Yeo, 'Notes on Three Socialisms, Collectivism, Statism and Associationism, mainly in late-nineteenth and early-twentieth century Britain', in Carl Levy ed., *Socialism and the Intelligentsia 1880–1914* (London: Routledge 1987), pp.219–270; and 'Three Socialisms: statism, collectivism, associationism, in W. Outhwaite and M. Mulkay, eds. *Social Criticism and Social Theory* (Oxford: Blackwell, 1987), pp.83–113.
24. T.W.Mercer, *The Co-operative Movement in Politics*, a pamphlet in the National Co-operative Archive (Manchester: Co-operative Union, 1921).
25. Holyoake, *The Trial of Theism* (Holyoake and Co, Bookseller and publisher 147 Fleet St, 1858), p.176
26. Holyoake, *Co-operative Movement Today* 1903, p.190. The whole of chapter xxiv, pp.179–192 is helpful here.
27. Holyoake, *Secular Responsibility* (London: Trubner, 60 Paternoster Row 1873), p.6.
28. Holyoake, *History of Co-operation*, pp.402–3.
29. G.J.Holyoake, *Self-Help By The People: The History of the Rochdale Pioneers 1844-1892* (London and New York: Swan Sonnenschein, 1907), p.183. In

subsequent Notes I will refer to this as Holyoake, *Rochdale Pioneers* 10th edition, 1907. E. V. Neale was at least as eager in his use of 'association' as Holyoake: 'The associated homes which we imagine around the associated working places produced by our associated system of purchases, may, and we believe would, gradually evolve a tone of moral feeling far higher than is now the custom', in 'Why should the rich interest themselves in Co-operation and how can they promote it' (Manchester, 1877), p.12 ; and 'Association and Education, what they may do for the people: An Address delivered at the 3rd anniversary of the Beccles Co-operative Society, on September 27th 1882' in *Pamphlets on Co-operation 1873–1885* in the Goldsmith's Library of Economic Literature (formerly H.S. Foxwell's book collection), Senate House, University of London.

30. Joseph McCabe, *Life and Letters of George Jacob Holyoake* (London: Rationalist Press Association and Watts and Co., 1908), vol.2 p.23. In subsequent Notes I will refer to this as McCabe, *Life and Letters*.

31. G.J.Holyoake, 'Co-operation and Socialism' in James Samuelson ed. *Subjects of the Day* no.2 Aug 1890, pp.89–104. In subsequent Notes I will refer to this as Holyoake, 'Co-operation and Socialism' 1890.

32. Holyoake, *Sixty Years*, I, p.137.

33. Holyoake, *History of Co-operation*, p.156.

34. Holyoake, *Sixty Years*, II, p.166.

35. The bulk of Holyoake materials are divided between the National Co-operative Archive in Holyoake House, Manchester, cared for by the Co-operative Hertitage Trust and the Co-operative College, and the Bishopsgate Institute in London. The archivists in both places are exceptionally knowledgable and helpful. L. Grugel. *George Jacob Holyoake: A Study in the Evolution of A Victorian Radical* (Philadelphia: Porcupine Press, 1975) provides a starting point, although it does not replace nineteenth and early twentieth-century work. Peter Gurney's work (see this Bibliography, above) is invaluable, as in 'George Jacob Holyoake: Socialism, Association and Co-operation in Nineteenth-Century England', in Stephen Yeo ed. *New Views of Co-operation* (London: Routledge, 1988), pp.52–73; and, particularly 'Labor's Great Arch: Co-operation and Cultural Revolution in Britain, 1795–1926', in Ellen Furlough and Carl Strikwerda, *Consumers against Capitalism: Consumer Co-operation in Europe, North America, and Japan, 1840–1990* (London: Rowman and Littlefield, 1999), pp.135–173.

36. The essay started life as a talk to a 'Mainstreaming Co-operation'

conference in Manchester in 2102, for which see Stephen Yeo, 'G.J.Holyoake (1817-1906): A Resource for a Journey of Hope?', in A Webster, L.Shaw, R.Vorberg-Rugh, *Mainstreaming Co-operation: an alternative for the twenty-first century* (Manchester: Manchester University Press, 2016), pp.46-68.

37. 'Readable but unreliable' is a phrase used by Edward Royle in his *DNB* entry on Holyoake. For the 'respectability' thematic see, among many other places, L.W Grugel, *George Jacob Holyoake: A Study in the Evolution of a Victorian Radical* (Philadelphia: Porcupine Press, 1976).

38. A task complicated by the fact that he used many pseudonyms, including 'Disque', 'Ion', 'Landor Praed', 'A London Zulu', 'One who has seen them before', 'Quasimodo', 'A Student in Co-operation' and 'A Voice from the Crowd', see Goss, *Brief Life*, p.lxxxii. And his editorial interventions were not confined to signed pieces. For a list of his contributions to newspapers, including the pseudonyms used see Goss, *Bibliography*, pp.73-76.

39. Holyoake, *The Common People: a discourse delivered at the Church of Progress, St Georges Hall, Langham Place* (London: Trubner & Co., 1870). In the National Co-operative Archive.

40. Goss, *Brief Life*, pp.lxxviii.

41. Chris Wrigley, 'The commemorative urge: the co-operative movement's collective memory', in L.Black and Nicole Robertson, *Consumerism and the Co-operative movement in modern British history: Taking stock* (Manchester: Manchester University Press, 2009), pp.157-174.

42. See Walter Benjamin, 'The Storyteller: Reflections on the Works of Nikolai Leskov', an essay first published in 1936, now in the many editions of his *Illuminations* and other volumes of collected essays. For Benjamin's own short fictions see Sam Dolbear and others, eds., *The Storyteller, Walter Benjamin, Tales out of Loneliness* (London: Verso, 2016). For creativity and the 'ordinary' see Raymond Williams, 'Culture is Ordinary', first published in Norman Mackenzie ed. *Convictions* (London: MacGibbon and Kee, 1958) and 'The Creative Mind', in Raymond Williams, *The Long Revolution* (London: Chatto & Windus, 1961), pp.3-41.

43. For this argument, see Stephen Yeo, 'Socialism, the State and some oppositional Englishness', in R.Colls and P.Dodd, eds., *Englishness, Politics and Culture 1880-1920* (London: Croom Helm, 1986), pp.308-369.

44. J. Baernreither, *English Associations of Working Men* (London: Swan

Sonnenschein, 1889). This was an English edition revised and enlarged by the author from a German edition published in Tubingen in 1886. The project was conceived on a visit to England in 1883. J.M Ludlow, an early Christian Socialist supporter of small-scale co-operative workshops and the first Chief Registrar of Friendly Societies prefaced the English edition: 'I know of no book, in our own or any other language, which takes so large and clear a view of the great associative movement of the English nineteenth century working class in all its forms as this of Dr Baernreither's. Baernreither saw England as 'the theatre of a gigantic development of associated life, which gives to her labour, her education, her social intercourse, nay to the entire development of her culture, a pronounced direction, a decisive stamp... The free union of individuals for the attainment of a common object is the great psychological fact in the life of this people, its great characteristic feature'.

45. Holyoake, *Sixty Years*, p.10.
46. Chapters ii, iii, iv, v and vi of Holyoake, *Sixty Years* are vivid sources for 'Artisan life sixty years ago' – the title of chapter vi.
47. The title of the French Labour History journal. Holyoake's enterprises included two trips to North America, in 1879 and 1882, to collect material for a settlers' guide book.
48. These details are in Holyoake, *Log Book No 1* (November 27, 1836) and *Letterbook* (September 14 1839) in the Bishopsgate Institute, and in Lee E. Grugel, *George Jacob Holyoake, A Study in the Evolution of a Victorian Radical* (Philadelphia: Porcupine Press, 1976) pp.4, 9.
49. All these works are in the Holyoake Collection in the National Co-operative Archive, in Holyoake House in Manchester.
50. The words are those of Edward Royle's *DNB* Entry for Holyoake.
51. 'Holyoake Testimonial Fund', a manuscript subscription list from 1853, is in the Holyoake Collection in the National Co-operative Archive, as is a printed balance sheet from (the same?) Testimonial Fund in 1877.
52. Maximilien was run over by a taxicab in Bloomsbury in 1857. See McCabe, *Life and Letters*, I, pp.199–200, 210.
53. McCabe, *Life and Letters*, I, p.126.
54. These articles are in the NCA.
55. Holyoake, *History of Co-operation*, p.299
56. W.Henry Brown, *George Jacob Holyoake* (London and Leicester, n.d., but 1906), p.15.

57. Holyoake, *History of Co-operation*, p.90.
58. This and the previous quotation are from Holyoake, *History of Co-operation*, pp.609–10.
59. G.J.Holyoake, *Deliberate Liberalism: four instances of it* (London: John Heywood, 1886). Peter Gurney drew my attention to this many years ago.
60. John Osborne dramatized the case in a TV play in 1960 called *A subject of scandal and concern* in which Richard Burton played Holyoake. For the case, see G.J.Holyoake, *The trial of George Jacob Holyoake, on an indictment of blasphemy, before Mr Justice Erskine and a common jury, at Gloucester, August the 15th 1842*, from notes specially taken by Mr Hunt. (London: The Anti-Persecution Union, 1842).
61. While there are signs in Holyoake's late work of the influence of late-nineteenth century 'social liberalism' such as that of L.T.Hobhouse, C.F.G.Masterman and J.A.Hobson, it is tantalizing that he died in 1906, at the very time when 'New Liberalism', was finding its way into practical Politics. As a friendly society member, what would he have made of the clash between the friendly society movement and the industrial insurance industry over the shape of the 1911 National Insurance Act? For this struggle, see Stephen Yeo, 'Working – class association, private capital, welfare and the state', in M.Rustin and N.Parry, eds. *Social Work and the State* (London: Arnold, 1979), pp.48–71.
62. Holyoake, *Rochdale Pioneers*, p.180.
63. For which see G.J.Holyoake, *Working Class Representation: its conditions and consequences: an address* (London: Book Store, 1868).
64. For the waywardness of Holyoake's Parliamentary candidatures, steering between the independence of Labour, 'Lib-Lab' ism, radical and more orthodox Liberalism, see McCabe, *Life and Letters*, 1 pp.40-3. McCabe, like other contemporaries found him irritatingly hard to place, whether on matters of Labour Representation, atheism/agnosticism, or even on how hard to be on CWS thinking as represented by working-class figures such as J.T.W.Mitchell or his fellow socialist missionary John Watts.
65. *Jubilee History of the Denholme Industrial Co-operative Society Ltd, 1880–1930* (Manchester: CWS Printing Works Longsight, 1930), p.10.
66. Holyoake, *Rochdale Pioneers*, Preface to the 1893 edition, pp.x-xi.
67. A legend grew up that 'the gracefulness of his story led to its reproduction in every European language – creating quite a sensation among the workmen of Lyons – while in England it was a seed from which sprang

250 co-operative societies in two years', Goss, *Brief Life*, p.xlviii. It was William Cooper, the Secretary of the Pioneers, who wrote to the *Daily News* in December 1863 stating that 'of 332 Co-operative Societies then on the Registrar's Returns, 251 had been established since 1857, when " Self Help" was published, and, he adds " I have heard several persons ascribe the origins of their now prosperous Society to reading the History". It is typical that Holyoake cultivated the legend; see Holyoake, *Rochdale Pioneers*, Preface to the 1893 edition, p.xi.

68. J.B Smethurst, *A Bibliography of Co-operative Societies' Histories* (Manchester: Co-operative Union Ltd., 1974), available from the National Co-operative Archive.

69. Holyoake, *The History of Co-operation in Halifax: and some other institutions around it* (London: London Book Store, 1867) is a 57pp. item in the National Co-operative Archive.

70. Holyoake, Derby 1900 p.183.

71. Without which E.P.Thompson and John Saville's journal *The New Reasoner*, which ran from 1957 to 1959 following their departure from the British Communist Party, and which led into the *New Left Review*, would surely not have been named as such.

72. McCabe, *Life and Letters*, vol.2, p.327.

73. For Mayhew as journalist-plus, see E.P.Thompson and Eileen Yeo eds., *The Unknown Mayhew: Selections from the Morning Chronicle* (London: Merlin Press, 1971).

74. J.A.Hobson's address is in *South Place Magazine* no.6, March 1906, pp.81–88.

75. This was in a speech in 1864 honouring the burial of Alderman Livesey of Rochdale, a friend of the Pioneers. The speech was reported in the *Rochdale Observer* and reproduced in Holyoake, *Rochdale Pioneers*, p.174.

76. G.J.Holyoake, *A Logic of Facts, or plain hints on reasoning* (London: Watson, 3, Queen's Head Passage, 1848), p.iv. For Holyoake's eloquent sense of class and 'law', 'the London workman' and 'the rich' at the time of the 1889 Dock Strike, see Holyoake 'Co-operation and Socialism', 1890, p.102.

77. Holyoake, History *of Co-operation*, p.217.

78. G.J. Holyoake, *Mathematics No Mystery: or the beauties and uses of Euclid* (London: J. Watson 1847)

79. G.J.Holyoake, *Rudiments of Public Speaking and Debate, or Hints on the Application of Logic* (London: Watson, 3 Queen's Head Passage, 1849).

80. Holyoake *Self-Help a Hundred Years Ago* (London: Swan Sonnenschein, 1890), pp.21-2. 1st edition 1888. In subsequent Notes I will refer to this as Holyoake, *Self-Help a hundred years ago*.
81. Holyoake, *History of Co-operation*, p.292.
82. Holyoake, *History of Co-operation*, pp.591-2, 607-8; see also Holyoake, *Co-operative Movement Today*, p.181.
83. McCabe, *Life and Letters*, vol.1, p.vii.
84. *The Secular Web: a drop of reason in a pool of confusion* http://infidels.org/library/historical/robert_ingersoll/tribute.holyoake, pp.1-7; the words quoted are dated Aug 8th 1888.
85. Holyoake, *The Principles of Secularism Illustrated* (London: Austen & and Co., Johnson Court Fleet St), p.16. In subsequent Notes I will refer to this work as Holyoake, 1859 *Secularism, Principles*.
86. 'the principles of association' 'teach that repulsiveness is a misfortune, and (they) substitute compassion for dislike, patience for anger, goodwill for animosity, confidence for distrust, investigation for suspicion, and generous interest in the welfare of others for indifference to their fate'. Hence the need for 'education to achieve co-operation' in Holyoake, 'Co-operation and Socialism' 1890, p.92.
87. Holyoake, *Bygones* vol.1 pp.152-3.
88. It is interesting that it was A.E.Bestor the educationalist, and in his pioneering book specifically on Owenite and other 'communities', *Backwoods Utopias, the Sectarian and Owenite Phases of Communitarian Socialism in America, 1663-1829* (Philadelphia: University of Pennsylvania Press, 1950) who developed the idea of 'communitarian' socialism as 'a method for the social regeneration of mankind', as distinct from the 'from above' uses of 'communitarian-ism' which became dominant towards the end of the twentieth century. Alasdair MacIntyre has recently challenged such uses too, resisting the idea that his work is 'communitarian' in the modern sense. 'The communitarian mistake (is) to attempt to infuse the politics of the state with the values and modes of participation in local community', MacIntyre, *Dependent* 2009, p.142. Michel Bauwens is also doing much to rescue 'communitarian' economics and philosophy, as is Elinor Ostrom, the poet John Burnside, and Maurice Glasman (in his *Unnecessary Suffering*, London: Verso Books, 1996), all of them reclaiming 'community' for *association* away from professional and managerial *policy*. See also Rory Ridley-Duff 'Communitarian Perspectives on Social Enterprise', in *Corporate Governance* vol.15, no.2 March 2007; and Eileen and Stephen

Yeo, 'On the Uses of "Community", from Owenism to the present', in Stephen Yeo ed., *New Views of Co-operation* (London: Routledge, 1988), pp.229-258.

89. The phrases in this paragraph all come from Holyoake, *History of Cho-operation*, chapter XL pp.607-610.
90. Holyoake, *Co-operative Movement Today*, p.2.
91. Holyoake, *Sixty Years*, II, p.166.
92. Holyoake, *Rochdale Pioneers*, p.46; see also Holyoake, *Self-Help A Hundred Years Ago*, p.202.
93. Holyoake, *Co-operative Movement Today*, p.6.
94. See Goss, *Brief Life*, p.lxxii. *Self-Help a Hundred Years Ago* went through three editions rather quickly, in 1881, 1891 nd 1906.
95. A.E. Bestor, 'The Evolution of the Socialist Vocabulary', in *Journal of the History of Ideas*, Vol.IX, no. 3 (1948), pp.259-302; Raymond Williams, *Keywords: A vocabulary of culture and society* (1976; London: Flamingo edition 1983), entries on 'socialist', 'society' 'sociology' etc.; F.A Hayek, 'The Weasel Word "Social"', in *The Salisbury Review*, Autumn 1983, pp.4-5. In 'Some Elementary Forms of Durkheim', in *Past and Present*, no.95, 1982, pp.3-18 John Bossy uses Williams' *Keywords* entry on 'Society' to trace the parallel history of 'religion': 'but in the long run "religion' has managed to retain at least some of its historic content, "society' has suffered an almost total evacuation'. Bossy's quotations are taken from Durkheim's *Elementary Forms of the Religious Life* (1912), translated by J. W. Swain (London: G. Allen and Unwin, 1915), 2nd edition with Introduction by R. Nisbet (London: Allen and Unwin, 1976).
96. Ian Macpherson' Background Paper to the Statement on the Co-operative Identity' (made available by the ICA, 8 Jan. 1996) p.5 of 16, available at http://www.uwcc.wise.edu/icic/issues/prin/21-cent/intro.html. In subsequent Notes I will refer to this work as Macpherson, *Background*, 1996.
97. Holyoake, *Self-Help a Hundred Years Ago* 1890, pp.200-01.
98. Holyoake, *Co-operative Movement Today*, 1903, p.86.
99. Preliminary thoughts on this are in Stephen Yeo, 'Theorizing Co-operative Studies: Obstacles and Opportunities for twenty-first century Co-operative and Mutual Enterprises', in Ian Macpherson and Erin Mclaughlin-Jenkins, *Integrating Diversities within a Complex Heritage: essays in the field of Co-operative Studies* (Victoria, British Columbia: New Rochdale Press, 2008), pp.345-390; and 'The identity of co-operative

BIBLIOGRAPHY, NOTES & REFERENCES

and mutual enterprises and the political sociology of Emile Durkheim: an introduction', in Lawrence Black and Nicole Robertson, *Consumerism and the Co-operative movement in modern British history* (Manchester: Manchester University Press, 2009), pp.69–85.
100. Holyoake, *Derby* 1900, p.136.
101. Stefan Collini, 'The Idea of 'Character' in Victorian Political Thought', in *Transactions of the Royal Historical Society*, Vol.35 (1985), pp.29–50.
102. For the violence of the 'never –ceasing conflict between Labour and Capital' and how 'there was murder in the march' of unmitigated competition see Holyoake, *History of Co-operation*, 1879 'Preface' to vol.2, p.xviii. For the 'war of Industry against Capital' which will not cease until Co-operative Industry is established, see Holyoake, *Co-operative Movement Today*, 1903, chap. II, pp.6–15.
103. Cited in Stephen Yeo, *Religion and Voluntary Organisations in Crisis* (London, Croom Helm, 1976) p.285.
104. Hughes and Neale, *Foundations* (1879), 1915 edition, p.100.
105. G.J.Holyoake, *Employee interest in Co-operation* (1884), as summarized in Goss, *Bibliography*, p.44.
106. Holyoake, *Rochdale Pioneers*, 10th edition, 1907, p.1.
107. G.J.Holyoake, *The lectures used by the Manchester Unity of the Independent Order of Odd Fellows, sanctioned and approved by the Bristol A.M.C., June, 1846* (London: John G.Hornblower,1846). In subsequent Notes I will refer to these Lectures as Holyoake, *1846 Lectures*.
108. *Co-operative News*, 27 Jan 1906; McCabe, *Life and Letters*, vol.1, p.109.
109. Holyoake, *1846 Lectures*, 'Purple Lecture', pp.9–11. The italics are Holyoake's.
110. Holyoake, *1846 Lectures*. Reading these Lectures I wished I had a deeply philosophical historian at my elbow. Like Alasdair MacIntyre, Holyoake seemed to be working with an idea of what humans and their nature are like when they are most fulfilled, most in line with their 'nature' and purpose. In Holyoake, *History of Co-operation*, p.217 this Aristotelian phrase appears, 'every creature must be allowed to articulate after its kind, and would do better if it only knew how'. This reads differently from Owen's 'doctrine of circumstances', or notion of human nature as a blank slate upon which human's circumstances can be written, and re-written with immediate effect.
111. Holyoake, *Sixty Years*, I, pp.206–11; Goss, *Bibliography*, p.6.
112. Andrew Bibby, *All Our Own Work: the Co-operative pioneers of Hebden*

Bridge and their mill (London: Merlin Press, 2015), p.11.
113. Greening, *Holyoake* 1917, p.22.
114. *Congress Report* (1905) (Manchester: the Co-operative Union Ltd., Long Millgate, 1905), pp.45–50.
115. Marcel Mauss, *The Gift: forms and function of exchange in archaic societies* (London: Cohen and West, 1966), originally published in French in 1925 in *L'Annee Sociologique*. The first English translation was in 1954. See also my 'The identity of co-operative and mutual enterprises and the political sociology of Emile Durkeim: an introduction', in L.Black and N.Robertson eds. *Consumerism and the Co-operative movement in modern British history: Taking stock* (Manchester: Manchester University Press, 2009), pp.86–106. Charles Gide is an under-explored link between Durkheimians and the British Co-operative Movement; see, for example, his *Consumers' Co-operative Societies* (Manchester: Co-operative Union Ltd., 1921).
116. *Co-operative Congress Report* 1905, p.47, held in Paisley. Mauss was also keen to warn his audience, without naming them, about the Webbs' approach to Co-operation: for example in Sydney and Beatrice Webb's best work *Industrial Democracy* (1897). It was as if Mauss was answering the Webbs in his speech at the Paisley Congress, warning workers (Labour) about accepting divisions of labour (structural differentiations) between associations of working people which might reinforce capitalist divisions between people : 'there were in France 200 distributive societies, the members of which thought that politics, socialism, trade-unionism, and co-operation could not be divided, because the working man was a trade-unionist, a member of a friendly society, a citizen, and a co-operators in one and the same moment, and could not be divided against himself'.
117. *Co-operative News*, Dec 17th 1904, pp.1532–3
118. The Address is in the 1906 *Co-operative Congress Report*, pp.36ff.
119. Holyoake, *Rochdale Pioneers*, 'Preface' to 1893 edition, p.vii.
120. Holyoake, *History of Co-operation*, p.403.
121. Holyoake, *Co-operative Movement Today* 1903, p.21. See also Holyoake, *Leeds* 1897, p.33.
122. Holyoake, *History of Co-operation*, pp.40–1.
123. Holyoake, *Co-operative Movement Today* 1903, pp.112–3.
124. *Co-operative News*, vol xviii 1887 p.1044. I owe this reference to Andrew Bibby.

125. Holyoake, *Derby* 1900, p. 128.
126. *Co-operative Congress Report*, held in Carlisle (Manchester: Co-operative Union, 1887) p.9.
127. McCabe, *Life and Letters*, vol.1 p.vi. See also Edward Owen Greening's affectionate *The Story of the Life of George Jacob Holyoake* (Manchester: Co-operative Union Ltd, 1917), and for another *movement* biography, important – like so many movement publications – for its form and presence as much as for the data it contains, see W.Henry Brown, *George Jacob Holyoake* (Manchester: Co-operative Printing Society,1906), Pioneer Biographies of Social Reformers no 1, and W.H.Brown, *Holyoake the Co-operator* (Manchester, Co-operative Printing Society, nd).
128. Holyoake, *Lectures and Debates: their terms condition and character* (privately printed, 1851), in the National Co-operative Archive.
129. Holyoake, *Bygones*, vol 1.p.263.
130. Holyoake, *Sixty Years*, 1 pp.246, see also pp.136–7.
131. W.H.Brown, *George Jacob Holyoake* (London and Leicester : C.W.Daniel and The Leicester Co-operative Printing Society Ltd nd but 1906) p.8.
132. Holyoake, *History of Co-operation*, p.616.
133. McCabe, *Life and Letters*, vol.1 p.294.
134. Holyoake, *Leeds* 1897 p.183.
135. In the *Reasoner* for June 3rd 1846 Holyoake discussed these matters in an article which he called 'Moral Mathematics' to which he returned in Holyoake, *Bygones*, vol.1, pp.19–20.
136. Holyoake, *Co-operative Movement Today* 1903 edition, p.142.
137. Holyoake, *History of Co-operation*, chap. xxvii, pp 397–406.
138. *Co-operative News*, vol.XVI, no.1 (Jan. 3 1885), pp.4–5.
139. Quoted in Andrew Bibby, *All Our Own Work: The co-operative pioneers of Hebden Bridge and their mill* (London: Merlin Press, 2015), p.119.
140. Holyoake, *Leeds* I897 p.191.
141. Holyoake, *Sixty Years* I, p.77.
142. Holyoake, *Co-operative Movement Today* 1903 edition, p.74.
143. Holyoake, *Co-operative Movement Today* 1903 edition, pp.160–1.
144. Holyoake, *Co-operative Movement Today* 1903 edition, p.20.
145. I got this from John Simkin, john@spartacus-educational.com Sept 1997 (updated Aug 2014).
146. Holyoake, *Co-operative Movement Today*, 1903 edition, pp.6–15.

147. For 'paramountcy', see Holyoake, *Bygones*, Chapters xxvii and xxviii and pp.57, 60, 65-91. The context is an acute, almost psychoanalytical account of Joseph Cowen of Newcastle. See also the use of the word 'depression' on p.60. For democrats as against those with a passion for ascendancy, see also Holyoake *History of Co-operation*, pp.300-01.
148. Holyoake, *Co-operative Movement Today*, 1903 edition, p.188.
149. Holyoake, *Rochdale Pioneers*, p.160.
150. Goss *Brief Life*, p.liv and *Bibliography* p.31.
151. Goss, *Brief Life*, pp.liv-lv.
152. Holyoake, *Co-operative Movement Today* 1903 edition, chap.vi pp.53-66. Another version of this in Holyoake, *Derby* 1900, pp.178-183, Chapter XVIII, 'Distinction between Store-keeping and Shop-keeping'.
153. Goss, *Bibliography*, p.18.
154. Holyoake, *Rochdale Pioneers*, p.21, 87.
155. Holyoake, *Leeds* 1897, p.43. McCabe, *Life and Letters*, vol.I, p.17.
156. A phrase Holyoake used with reference to Secularism in his *The Trial of Theism* (London: Holyoake and Co Bookseller and Publisher 147 Fleet St, 1858), p.174.
157. Holyoake, *Bygones*, vol.2, p.9.
158. Holyoake, *Bygones*, vol.2, p.114. McCabe, *Life and Letters*, vol.I, p.303.
159. Holyoake, *Rochdale Pioneers*, p.136.
160. Holyoake, *Co-operative Movement Today*, 1903 edition, pp.171-2.
161. Holyoake, *Rochdale Pioneers*, p.84.
162. Holyoake, *History of Co-operation*, 152-153, 218-219, 265, 547-551,603. The 'nimble eccentricity, quote is on p.216.
163. For example, J.E.M.Latham, *Search for a New Eden, James Pierrepont Greaves (1777-1842): The Sacred Socialist and His Followers* (London and Cranbury N.J., 1999); W. Hamish Fraser, *Alexander Campbell and the Search for Socialism* (Manchester: Holyoake Books, 1996); James Gregory, *Of Victorians and Vegetarians : The Vegetarian Movement in Nineteenth-century Britain* (London: I.B.Tauris, 2007).
164. Holyoake, *History of Co-operation*, p.153.
165. Holyoake, *History of Co-operation*, p.547.
166. Holyoake, *History of Co-operation*, pp.549-550.
167. Goss, *Brief Life*, pp.xv-xvi, and see p.liii for Quaker tolerance even of intolerant others.

168. Holyoake, *Co-operative Movement Today*, 1903 edition, p.10
169. Holyoake, *Co-operative Movement Today*, 1903 edition, p.138.
170. Holyoake, *Sixty Years*, p.11.
171. Holyoake, *Derby* 1900 chap. xv pp.154–161, which also focuses on the Midland Railway Institute.
172. Goss, *Brief Life*, p.xxxi.
173. Holyoake: *Sixty Years*, pp.98–9
174. Andrew Bibby, *All Our Own Work: the co-operative pioneers of Hebden Bridge and their mill* (London: Merlin, 2015), chapters 3 and 4, on 'Sharing the profits' and 'Governance' is the most considered recent treatment of this issue.
175. McCabe, *Life and Letters*, vol.1 p.176.
176. Holyoake *Bygones* II, p.115.
177. G.J.Holyoake, *Hostile and generous toleration (a new theory of toleration)*, (London: E.W Allen, 1886); Goss, *Bibliography*, p.45.
178. Goss, *Brief Life*, p.lxxvii.
179. Holyoake, *Co-operative Movement Today*, p.52. 'Good discernment' as a phrase is, perhaps inadvertently in Holyoake's case, characteristic of the Society of Friends.
180. The details are in Goss, *Bibliography*, pp.26–7.
181. McCabe, *Life and Letters*, vol.2, p.180. On p.266 of the same volume McCabe suggests that Holyoake 'thanked' T.H.Huxley for the term 'Agnostic' and 'resented the term Atheist, because most of those who would apply it to him understood it to involve a more or less dogmatic denial of the existence of a Supreme Being. Even in the forties, when he bore the name for a short time (during the editorship of the *Oracle*) he merely took it to express the fact that he was without such belief, not that he considered it could be disproved'.
182. Holyoake, 'Co-operation and Socialism' 1890, p.89.
183. Holyoake, *History of Co-operation*, p.300.
184. Goss, *Bibliography*, p.45.
185. G.J.Holyoake, *Deliberate liberalism: four instances of it* (London: John Heywood, 1886).
186. The first chapters of Holyoake, *Rochdale Pioneers* appeared in the *Daily News* in 1857, two years before Samuel Smiles published his *Self Help*.
187. Holyoake, *Derby* 1900, p.160.

188. Holyoake, *Derby* 1900, p.33.
189. Holyoake, *Sixty Years*, II, p.181
190. Holyoake *Bygones*, pp.264, 279-80; McCabe, *Life and Letters*, vol.2, p.9.
191. Holyoake, *Bygones*, II, pp.87-8, I, pp.31-2.
192. See Holyoake, *Bygones*, chaps. xxi -xxiii, pp.259-295 for the critical, unembarrassed disagreement which went with Holyoake's unashamed admiration for Gladstone, and for J.S.Mill, including for Mill's famous additional chapters on co-operatives and co-operation. See also Holyoake, *A New Defence of the Ballot in Consequence of Mr Mill's Objection to it*, the 4th edition of which is in the National Co-operative Archive (London: Book Store, 1868). Also in the NCA is a 29 -page tribute to Mill, G.J Holyoake, *John Stuart Mill: as some of the working classes knew him* (London: G.Trubner & Co., 1873).
193. Lee E. Grugel, *George Jacob Holyoake, A Study in the Evolution of a Victorian Radical* (Philadelphia: Porcupine Press, 1976), p.153. Holyoake was being careful not to offend Gladstone during the latter's last years, but not only that. He acknowledged his own thoughts concerning life after death while stating (perhaps as his main point) that 'my not being sure of it will not prevent it coming to me'. Keeping minds open, including his own, was always his priority: 'belief like toleration is the growth of wider information which I seek as far as I am able'.
194. See 'The 10th April of Spencer Walpole', in Royden Harrison, *Before the Socialists: studies in Labour and Politics 1861-1881* (London: Routledge, 1964). See also Royden Harrison, 'The British Working Class and the General Election of 1868', in *International Review of Social History*, VI (1961).
195. McCabe, *Life and Letters*, vol.2, p.164.
196. Holyoake, *Rochdale Pioneers*, p.135
197. Holyoake, *Anti-Boycott Papers* (Manchester: Co-operative Union, 1903) paper V p.7.
198. Holyoake, *Bygones*, vol.2 chapter xxx, pp.92-105.
199. Holyoake, *The Co-operative Movement Today*, 1903 edition, p.184.
200. Holyoake, *Rochdale Pioneers*, p.113.
201. Holyoake *Bygones* vol.1, p.260.
202. Goss, *Bibliography*, p.39.
203. A view shared by Raymond Williams, made explicit in his 'Conclusion' to *Culture and Society, 1780 to 1950* (London: Chatto & Windus, 1958).

204. Holyoake, *The Co-operative Movement Today*, 1903 edition, p.86.
205. Holyoake, *The Trial of Theism*, p.174. Holyoake liked to compare Secularist Societies with the local Athenaeums which existed in many towns in Victorian Britain.
206. Holyoake, *Rochdale Pioneers*, p.21; *Sixty Years*, p.579.
207. Holyoake, *Leeds* 1897, p.4.
208. Holyoake, *History of Co-operation*, pp.615-6.
209. For the later Marx on co-operation, 'the co-operative factories of the labourers themselves'and an emergent or immanent 'associated mode of production' within capitalism, see Chapter 27 of *Capital* volume 3, 'The Role of Credit in Capitalist Production'. In Chapter 23 Marx complained of how 'the vulgus is unable to conceive the forms developed in the lap of capitalist production separate and free from their antithetical capitalist character'.
210. E.P. Thompson's phrase in the much quoted Preface to *The Making of the English Working Class* (London: Gollancz, 1963).
211. Raymond Williams, *Keywords: a vocabulary of culture and society* (London:, Flamingo paperback edition, 1983), pp.318-320. E.J Hobsbawm and T.O.Ranger, eds., *The Invention of Tradition* (Cambridge: Cambridge University Press, 1983).
212. Quoted by John Burnside, *Gift Songs* (London: Cape, 2007), p.67, reference not cited.
213. Holyoake, *Co-operative Movement Today*, 1903 edition, pp.1-6. See also Holyoake, *The Spirit of Bonner in the Disciples of Jesus: or the cruelty and intolerance of Christianity*, (Hetherington, 1843), the 2nd edition of which is in the NCA.
214. Hans Magnus Enzensberger introducing his 'Summer Poem' (1964): 'Its formal principle is that of openness. One can regard poems as either closed and sealed, as impermeable structures, or as net-like constructions with which new experiences can be caught again and again – even when the writing of the text is finished'. Hans Magnus Enzensberger, *Selected Poems* (Harmondsworth: Penguin, 1968) p.89.
215. Karen Armstrong, *Fields of Blood: Religion and the History of Violence* (London: Bodley Head, 2014).
216. Holyoake, *The Trial of Theism* (London: Holyoake and Co, Bookseller and Publisher 147 Fleet St), p.176.
217. Stephen Yeo, 'A New Life: the Religion of Socialism in Britain 1883 – 1896', in *History Workshop Journal*, 4 (1977), pp.5-56

218. Kevin Cahill, *Who Owns Britain?* (London: Canongate Books, 2002) James Meek, *Private Island: Why Britain Belongs to Someone Else* (London: Verso, 2014).

219. Robert D. Putnam, *Bowling Alone: The Collapse and Revival of American Community* (New York: Simon & Schuster, 2001); in 2013 in Islington, 'The Sunday Assembly' began as 'an atheist congregation to 'celebrate life without God'. By September 2014 the Assembly had 28 groups across the world, and at that date was launching another 33 groups. Its CEO and co-founder (Sanderson Jones) did not expect it to become a movement, let alone a global one 'but with new people and new ideas, we discovered how to evolve this gathering into an international movement of people who want to live better, help often and wonder more', *Evening Standard*, Sept 18th 2014, p.41; see also Action for Happiness, set up by Richard Layard, Geoff Mulgan and Anthony Seldon in 2013, 'We've now got 30,000 members and 90,000 followers. Its about seeing how we can develop real communities and perform some of the function in their lives that, say, the church used to perform', see *The Independent*, July 14th 2014, p.19.

220. Lines from 'Song for the Rainy Season', a poem by Elizabeth Bishop (1911–1979).

221. *The Proceedings of the Third Co-operative Congress* (London: William Strange, 1832), pp.100, 103.

222. Robin Murray, 'A different way of doing things: the potential of co-ops to form the basis of an alternative economy', in *Red Pepper* (May 2012); see also Venu Madhav Govindu, Deepak Malghan, 'Building a Creative Freedom: J.C.Kumarappa and his Economic Philosophy', in *Economic and Political Weekly* (September 2005).

223. Macpherson, *Background* 1996, p.7 of 16.

224. Macpherson, *Background* 1996, p.11 of 16.

225. In the 1906 edition of the *History of Co-operation* the period from 1876 to 1904 was called 'the modern' phase of co-operation. In earlier editions of the *History* there had only been 'the enthusiastic' or 'pioneer' period followed by the 'constructive' period.

226. In 1900 the CWS had 1,249,091 members in shareholding societies; a total capital of £3,187,945; sales of £16,043,889; and a dividend on sales to members of 4d in the £. For the scale and ambition of the CWS see John F. Wilson, Anthony Webster and Rachael Vorberg-Rugh, *Building Co-operation: A Business History of The Co-operative Group, 1863–2013* (Oxford: Oxford University Press, 2013) and, in a different register,

Stephen Yeo, *Who Was J.T.W.Mitchell* (Manchester: CWS Membership Services, 1995).

227. For global reviews of co-operatives and peace see Ian MacPherson ed. *Co-operatives and the Pursuit of Peace* (Victoria, BC: British Columbia Institute for Co-operative Studies, 2007) and Yehudah Paz and Ian MacPherson eds. *Concern for Community: the relevance of co-operatives to peace* (Victoria, BC: BCICS, 2015). The latter was done as an e-book in December 2015.

228. Greening, *Holyoake* 1917, p.30.

229. G.J.Holyoake, *Organisation: not of arms – but ideas* (London: J. Watson, 1853).

230. Holyoake, *The Co-operative Movement Today*, 1903 edition, pp.180–1.

231. Robert Beevers, *The Garden City Utopia : a critical biography of Ebenezer Howard* (London: Macmillan,1988), pp.79–80.

232. Holyoake, *The Co-operative Movement Today*, 1903 edition, p.188.

233. Holyoake, *The Co-operative Movement Today*, 1903 edition, p.189.

234. Holyoake, *Sixty Years*, II, p60.

235. Report of Coming of Age celebrations of the Hebden Bridge Fustian Manufacturers Co-operative Society Ltd Sept 23rd and 26th 1891 reprinted in booklet form from *Co-operative News* and *Todmorden and District News and Todmorden Advertiser*, copy in the National Co-operative Archive. I owe this reference to Andrew Bibby.

236. Holyoake, *Sixty Years* II, p.185.

237. Holyoake, *History of Co-operation*, p.609

238. Holyoake, *Bygones* vol.1, p.77. For the Christian Socialists of the period 1848 to 1854 see John Saville ed. *Democracy and the Labour Movement: Essays in honour of Dona Torr* (London: Lawrence and Wishart,1954).

239. Holyoake, *Bygones*, vol.I, pp.76–8.

240. Holyoake's own description of the part he played is in Holyoake, *Bygones*, vol.1. pp.76–8. A detailed, modern account of these years, seen through eyes rather different from Holyoake's, is in Royden Harrison, *Before the Socialists : Studies in Labour and Politics 1861–1881* (London: Routledge and Kegan Paul, 1965).

241. Holyoake *Bygones* vol.I, p.78.

242. See Alex Butterworth, *The World That Never Was: a true story of dreamers, schemers, anarchists and secret agents* (London: Vintage, 2011).

243. Holyoake, *Self Help a hundred years ago*, p.v.

244. Holyoake, *History of Co-operation*, pp.301-2.
245. Holyoake *Rochdale Pioneers*, 10th edition 1907, pp.111-112
246. Holyoake, *Derby* 1897, pp.132-3.
247. Holyoake, *Sixty Years*, II pp.256-7.
248. Holyoake, *Derby* 1897, pp.132-3.
249. Holyoake, *Bygones* vol.I, pp.84-97.
250. Holyoake *Bygones* vol.I, p.96.
251. Holyoake, *Co-operative Movement Today*, 1903, p.71.
252. *Co-operative Wholesale Society Annual* (Manchester: 1901), pp.231-243.
253. Holyoake, *Against Clandestine Commissions: mainly in the interest of co-operative societies* (London: Gay and Bird, 1899).
254. Holyoake, *Sixty Years*, II, p.182; Holyoake, *A New Defence of the Ballot in Consequence of Mr Mill's Objections to it* (London: Book Store, 1868).
255. Holyoake, *The Principles of Secularism Illustrated* (London: Austen & Co 17 Johnson Court, Fleet St, 1871), p.17.
256. Holyoake, *The Trial of Theism* (London: Holyoake & co Bookseller and Publisher 147 Fleet St), p.175.
257. I take these phrases from Ian MacPherson's 1996, *Background Paper*, p.3 of 16. 'The Statement (i.e. the 1995 *Statement of Co-operative Identity*) implicitly recognised that the international movement has a unique opportunity to assist in the harmonization of interests among groups of people organized as consumers of goods and services, as savers and investors, as producers, and as workers. By providing a common framework, the Statement should foster understanding, joint activities and expanded horizons for all kinds of co-operative endeavour'. MacPherson points out (p.10 of 16) that 'since its earliest years, the co-operative movement has sought to bring together people of different classes; indeed that is what distinguished it from some other nineteenth century ideologies'
258. Holyoake, *Rochdale Pioneers* 10th edition, 1907, p.181
259. Holyoake, *Sixty Years*, II, p.76.
260. Goss, *Brief Life* p.lvii.
261. Holyoake, *Leeds* 1897,. 105.
262. Holyoake, *Co-operative Movement Today*, 1903 edition, chap. ix, pp 78-87.
263. Holyoake, *Co-operative Movement Today*, 1903 edition, p.86.
264. Holyoake, *Leeds* p.141. The map which went with this book has been

lost (put up on the wall?) in some of the copies I have seen.
265. Holyoake, *Derby* 1900, pp.178-82.
266. Holyoake, *Co-operative Movement Today*, 1903, pp.121-2.
267. In keeping with the language of 'Industrial and Provident Society' legislation, as opposed to Company legislation, it is interesting that Holyoake could sometimes refer to Co-operation as 'Industry'.
268. Holyoake, *Sixty Years*, vol.2, p.184.
269. Holyoake, *1846 Lectures*, p 65.
270. Holyoake, *A Logic of Facts: or plain hints on reasoning* (London: Watson, 3,Queens Head Terrace, 1848), p.viii.
271. Holyoake, *Sixty Years*, vol.1, p.136.
272. Holyoake, 'Co-operation and Socialism' 1890, p.97. For a direct assault on the Positivists, see Holyoake, 'State Socialism' 1879, pp.1116-7.
273. Holyoake, *Sixty Years*, vol.1, p.136
274. Holyoake, *Sixty Years*, vol.1, p.133
275. For this period see Gregory Claeys, *Citizens and States: politics and anti-politics in early British socialism* (Cambridge, Cambridge University Press, 1989); and, in an essay which owes a great deal to Claeys' abundant works, Stephen Yeo 'Towards Co-operative Politics: using early to generate late socialism', in *Journal of Co-operative Studies*, 42.3 (2009).
276. McCabe, *Life and Letters*, Chapter xxiii, 'Correspondence with Gladstone and Chamberlain', pp.161-183.
277. From the same correspondence.
278. Holyoake, *The Co-operative Movement Today*, p.59.
279. Holyoake, 'State Socialism' 1879, p.1116.
280. Goss, *Bibliography*, p.64.
281. G.J. Holyoake, *Anti-Boycott Papers* (Manchester: Co-operative Union, 1903). These can be consulted in the NCA. There were 10 distinct 'papers', from 6 to 12 pages long, published together with extra, and equally- mobilizing items which include 10 pages on 'Co-operation from the Standpoint of a Parish Priest'.
282. For rich material on this theme during the 1890s, particularly in the thoughts of J.C.Gray and Robert Halstead, see Bibby (2015), chap.9 'Capital and Labour', pp.118-127. This connects directly with the 'New Life' socialism of the 1880s to 1890s, particularly through Tom Mann's enthusiasm for Co-operation at that time, see my 'A New Life: the

Religion of Socialism in Britain 1883–1896', in *History Workshop Journal*, 4 (1977), pp.5–56.

283. The title of a lecture he gave on April 9th 1848, on the eve of the last great Chartist meeting, to a large audience at the John St Institution, an old Owenite venue. The title paints a backdrop to the rest of his life's work. I owe this reference to Edward Royle, *Radical Politics 1790–1900: Religion and Unbelief* (London: Longman, 1971), in which Royle includes an extract from it.

284. McCabe, *Life and Letters*, vol.1, p.181.

285. Holyoake, *Sixty Years*, vol.II, p.62.

286. Holyoake, *Co-operative Movement Today*, 1903 edition, pp.149–155.

287. *Co-operative Congress Report* (Manchester: Co-operative Union Ltd., 1890) pp.12–15. This contribution to the 1890 Congress was part of a debate initiated by Margaret Llewellyn Davies. She was Secretary of the Co-operative Women's Guild and a socialist. Her paper at Congress was called 'The Relations between Co-operation and Socialistic Aspirations', arguing for the necessity of state coercion if competition was ever to be overcome. Holyoake's was a direct reply. For E.V Neale's carefully considered views on Socialism, se *The Co-operative News*, vol. IX, no. 24, June 15th 1878, 'What is Socialism?' and 'The Relation of Co-operation to Socialism', Parts 1 and 2, read at the Rochdale Working Men's Club and published in *The Co-operative News* vol.X, no. 10, March 8 1879 and no. 11, March 15th 1879. In 1878 Neale's distinction was between 'Social Socialism' and 'Political Socialism', approving of the former, not of the latter. For Holyoake on 'State Socialism', see *The Nineteenth Century: a monthly review*, June 1879, pp.1114–1120.

288. Holyoake, *Sixty Years*, II, p.184. The letter was written for *The Times, Daily News* and *Echo* in August 1871

289. Holyoake, *Sixty Years,* II, p.257.

290. Holyoake, *Sixty Years* II, pp.182–3.

291. The *Jubilee History of the Denholme Industrial Co-operative Society Ltd 1880–1930* was published in Manchester and printed at the CWS's Printing Works, Longsight. At no point is it explicit that the author was Mr H.Whalley, President 1917–1930, although it seems clear that he had a, or perhaps the major role in it. He initialled the Preface: 'from the mass of details extracted (from the minute books) the following pages have been compiled, and are now presented in the hope that they will act as a stimulus to all who are left to carry on the work'. The quotation I have used is from the penultimate page, p.77.

292. *The Co-operative Movement Today*, 1903 edition, epigraph page.
293. Holyoake, *Leeds*, 1897.
294. Holyoake, *Rochdale Pioneers*, p.146-7.
295. Holyoake, *Co-operative Movement Today*, p.53.
296. Holyoake, 'State Socialism', June 1879, p.1114.
297. Holyoake, *Rochdale Pioneers*, 10th edition, 1907, pp.7-8.
298. Holyoake, Co-*operative Movement Today*, 1903 edition, pp.11 and 7.
299. Holyoake, *Derby* 1900, p.183.
300. McCabe, *Life and Letters*, vol.1, p.166. See Holyoake, *Anti- Boycott papers* (Manchester: Co-operative Union, 1903), paper III p.5 and paper X p.8 for co-operation firmly seen, by then, as 'a new industrial system'.
301. McCabe, *Life and Letters* vol.2., p.276.
302. Holyoake, *Co-operative Movement Today*, 1903 edition, p.58.
303. Holyoake, *Leeds* 1897, p.15
304. E. Hobsbawm and T.Ranger eds., *The Invention of Tradition* (Cambridge; Cambridge University Press, 1983); and E. Hobsbawm, using tradition in a less deliberate sense, 'Rival traditions in the British and French labour movements' in *Labouring Men* (London: Weidenfeld and Nicholson, 1964).
305. Holyoake, *The Co-operative Movement Today*, 1903 edition, p.15.
306. Holyoake, *Self Help A Hundred Years Ago*, pp.iii-vii, 1, 200-01.
307. MacIntyre left the Left towards the end of the 1960s, but not for the Right. His life work is voluminous – and radical in every sense of the word, arriving at a destination: 'revolutionary Aristotelian', Thomist Catholicism. Famously waiting (from the final page of *After Virtue* – 1981– onwards) for a combination of St Benedict and Leon Trotsky to come together, such a stance has kept him in dialogue with radicals across an astonishing range of social-scientific, literary and ethical disciplines. At different times a Marxist, a Trotskyite, a Christian, someone who described himself as a believer neither in Marx or God, and now a Thomist Aristotelian Catholic, he has a body of revolutionary Aristotelian followers of whose interpretations of his work he seems, for the most part, to approve. The affinities between his work and the co-operative movement are entirely in my head, not his. In ways which have largely gone unnoticed on the non-philosophical Left, where he was until the excesses of the student movement in the late 1960s, MacIntyre is interested in what 'plain people' do (his phrase, and Walt Whitman's) to sustain associative, civil, ethical, mutual, productive

and communal (not 'communitarian') practices and to resist and oppose dominant states and markets and their ideologies.
308. MacIntyre, *Dependent*, 2009, pp.129-131.
309. MacIntye, *Dependent*, 2009 p.145.
310. MacIntyre's work extends a long way beyond my own disciplinary competence. To write this book, I have used Kelvin Knight, *The MacIntyre Reader* (Cambridge: Polity Press 1998), including Part III 'Establishing a Tradition of Practical Rationality' in order to get into MacIntyre's *Three Rival Versions of Moral Enquiry: Encyclopedia, Genealogy, and Tradition* (Indiana: University of Notre Dame Press, 1990); John Horton and Susan Mendus, *After MacIntyre: Critical Perspectives on the Work of Alasdair MacIntyre* (Cambridge: Polity Press, 1994), particularly Andrew Mason, 'MacIntyre on Liberalism and its Critics: Tradition, Incommensurability and Disagreement' and MacIntyre, 'A Partial Response to my Critics'; MacIntyre, *Whose Justice? Which Rationality?* (Indiana: University of Notre Dame Press, 1988), particularly chapters XVII, XVII ('The Rationality of Traditions) and XIX. As in my work on Durkheim and co-operation/co-operatives, my impulse has been to find wider philosophical/moral settings (in Holyoake's sense more of an 'outside') in which the co-operative movement might be able to live, work and have more of a philosophical (independent, autonomous, open and voluntary) presence. From conversations with Ian Macpherson during the last twenty years of his life I know that he shared this impulse and would have helped me to follow it through better.
311. S. Mulhall and A. Swift, *Liberals and Communitarians* (Oxford: Blackwell, 1992), p.90.
312. I broached the matter of wider intellectual contexts for a specifically co-operative tradition in 'The identity of co-operative and mutual enterprises and the political sociology of Emile Durkheim: an introduction' in Lawrence Black and Nicole Robertson, *Consumerism and the Co-operative movement in modern British history* (Manchester: Manchester University Press, 2009), pp.86–107; and in 'Theorizing Co-operative Studies: Obstacles and Opportunities for Twenty-First Century Co-operative and Mutual Enterprises' in Ian Macpherson, and Erin Mclaughlin-Jenkins eds., *Integrating Diversities within a complex heritage. Essays in the Field of Co-operative Studies* (University of Victoria: New Rochdale Press, 2008), pp.345–390.
313. Holyoake, *Co-operative Movement Today*, 1903 edition, p.21.

314. A definitive introduction to this distinction is in Steven Lukes, *Emile Durkheim: His Life and Work* (London: Allen Lane, 1973) particularly pp.147–167, with, on page 158, a useful one-page tabulation of the ideal types, organic and mechanical. The vision is far-reaching, well expressed by A. Giddens in his 'Introduction' to *Durkheim on Politics and the State* (Stanford, CA: Stanford University Press, 1986), p.12: 'Labour is divided spontaneously only if society is constituted in such a way that *social inequalities exactly express natural inequalities*' (my emphasis).

315. For the world-changing implications of the Protestant inheritance see Michael Walzer, *The Revolution of the Saints: a study in the origin of radical politics* (Harvard: Harvard University Press, 1965).

316. Holyoake, *Sixty Years* p.33.

317. It was in his entry on Holyoake in the *DNB* (Oxford: Oxford University Press, 2004) that Royle identified *The Reasoner* as 'Holyoake's greatest achievement'. I differ from Royle's judgement, also in the *DNB*, that 'for Holyoake the sole principle was individual freedom of thought and expression without interference from state, church or society'. Such a way of putting his undoubted commitment to 'freedom from' is to steer Holyoake too close to what he meant by 'stationary' as opposed to 'deliberate' Liberalism and too far away from 'freedom to', and eventually for everyone. Royle's way of putting it makes Holyoake too easy to digest in our age of 'neo' liberalisms. He had a lifelong interest in values and principles and for the organisational (associational) connections between them, especially of the kind which could be shown to produce new 'circumstances', or new 'arrangements' of human 'powers' by and for a whole 'people'.

318. Alasdair MacIntyre, *Whose Justice? Which Rationality?* (Indiana: University of Notre Dame Press, 1988), Chapter XVII, pp.349–369, 'The Rationality of Traditions'.

319. As in Pat Conaty and David Bollier, *Toward an Open Co-operativism: a New Social Economy based on Open Platforms, Co-operative models and the Commons*, cited above.

320. Alasdair MacIntyre, *God, philosophy, universities: A Selective History of the Catholic Philosophical Tradition* (London: Rowman and Littlefield, and Continuum, 2009).

321. R. Sennett, *Together: the rituals, pleasures and politics of co-operation* (London: Allen Lane, 2012).

322. Holyoake, *Sixty Years*, II, p.170. This was in 1870–71, in pioneering work Holyoake did for the Foreign Office, towards international labour

statistics or Blue Books. He was vexed that Lord Clarendon changed 'my phrase "*purchasing* power of money" into "the *purchase* power of money". "Purchasing power" was a phrase new to the Foreign Office, nor was I aware that it had been used in this financial sense before I employed it. It seemed a fair form of the participle. The term afterwards came into general use, and is quite common now.'

323. Holyoake, *Rochdale Pioneers*, p.184.
324. Johnston Birchall, *Finance in an Age of Austerity: The Power of Customer Owned Banks* (Cheltenham: Edward Elgar, 2013). Chapters 2 'The Evolution of Cooperative Banks' and 5 'The Evolution of Banks Owned by Other Types of Cooperative'.
325. Holyoake in 1892, quoted in *Rochdale Pioneers*, 10th edition, 1907, p.184.
326. Holyoake, *Rochdale Pioneers*, 10th edition, 1907, p.46.
327. McCabe, *Life and Letters* vol.1, p.296.
328. Holyoake, *History of Co-operation*, pp.307-8 and p.300
329. Adam Brandenburger and Barry Nalebuff, *Coopetition: A Revolution Mindset That Combines Competition and Cooperation* (New York: Currency/Doubleday, 1996).
330. Holyoake, *History of Co-operation*, p.xiv.
331. Greening, *Holyoake*, p.17.
332. Goss, *Brief Life*, p.xlviii.
333. Greening, *Holyoake*, 1917, p18. Greening was referring to Holyoake's first, pamphlet-sized version of the *History*, written in 1857.
334. Holyoake, *Co-operative Movement Today*, 1903, pp.181-182.
335. Holyoake, *History of Co-operation*, pp.28-9
336. Holyoake, *History of Co-operation*, p.89.
337. Holyoake, *Co-operative Movement Today*, 1903, pp.188-9.
338. In Holyoake, *History of Co-operation* p.114, he has a footnote concerning this Labour Exchange story: 'the original correspondence on this subject and the statements and letters of Mr Bromley to Mr Owen are now in the possession of The Owen Memorial Committee of Manchester'.
339. Holyoake, *History of Co-operation*, pp.112-4.
340. Alasdair MacIntyre, *Whose Justice? Which Rationality?* (Notre Dame Indiana, Notre Dame Press, 1988).
341. Holyoake, *History of Co-operation*, p.307
342. Holyoake, *History of Co-operation*, p.307.

343. While at the Co-operative College as Principal, Mervyn Wilson, working with Gillian Lonergan produced a *Co-operative Principles Matrix* for teaching purposes, mapping the 1995 *Statement of Co-operative Identity* and the 1996 ICA *Clarification* onto the ICA 1934/7 *Definition* of co-operatives and the 1860 Pioneers' *Rules of Conduct*, revealing the echoes and equivalences. This is available from the Co-operative College.
344. Holyoake, *History of Co-operation*, pp.302-3.
345. There was then a break between this and the modern series of Co-operative Congresses which began in 1866 and continue to the present day.
346. *Proceedings of the Third Co-operative Congress held in London...on the 23rd of April 1832 and... on each of the six following days Sunday excepted* (London: William Strange, 1832). It is from these Proceedings that my quotations here are drawn. I want to thank Gillian Lonergan and Mervyn Wilson for drawing attention to the title page and particularly to pp.100-103.
347. G.J.Holyoake, *Hostile and generous toleration (a new theory of toleration)* (London: E. W. Allen, 1886). Goss, *Bibliography*, p.45 describes this pamphlet as an 'appeal for that which not only asserts a fair play, but takes care that rival opinion is not killed by foul play'.
348. They included: trading in 'articles of ordinary consumption' for the use of members and for the purpose of accumulation of capital towards 'community' (in this case, 'community in land'); the 'mutual employment of members'; 'the establishment of schools for the education of children, and of libraries and reading-rooms for adults'; the importance of the indivisibility of capital; and no taking or giving of credit. *Proceedings of the Third Co-operative Congress* ... pp.102-3
349. Holyoake, *Rochdale Pioneers*, 10th edition, 1907, pp.47-55.
350. MacPherson, *Background* 1996, p.1 of 16.
351. MacPherson, *Background* 1996, p.16 of 16.
352. Holyoake, *Rochdale Pioneers* 10th edition 1907, p.51.
353. The story is recorded in chapter xxiv of Holyoake, *Rochdale Pioneers* 10th edition 1907, from which the quotations here are drawn. The chapter is called 'Contests for Principle'. Secularists, Unitarians and 'Churchmen' were in favour of 'the Recognition of Labour to participate in Profit' 'Against the principle were a united party from the Milton Church (Independents), after them the Methodists, and a number from other sects ranked on the same side'. 'What I added', wrote Holyoake (in a note to p.162) 'was that new societies seeking members who would

vote for Labour, knew what sects to visit'.
354. Holyoake, *Rochdale Pioneers* 10th edition, 1907, p.162.
355. Holyoake, *Co-operative Movement Today*, 1903 edition, p.92.
356. Holyoake, *Co-operative Movement Today*, 1903 edition, pp.92, 174–9.
357. Holyoake, *Derby* 1900,pp.183–4.
358. Holyoake, *Leeds* 1897, chap, xx, pp.17–20.
359. Holyoake, *History of Co-operation*, p.87.
360. Goss, *Brief Life*, pp.xviii-xix.
361. Goss, *Brief Life*, pp.xiv-xv.
362. Quoted from Holyoake, Letterbook Jan.19th 1840, in the Bishopsgate Institute, by L.F. Grugel, *George Jacob Holyoake: a study in the evolution of a Victorian radical* (Philadelphia, Porcupine Press, 1976) p.10.
363. Holyoake, *Sixty Years*, II, p.163.
364. Goss, *Bibliography*, p.26.
365. George William Foote, *Secularism re-stated: with a review of the several expositions of Charles Bradlaugh and George Jacob Holyoake* (London: W.J.Ramsey, 1874), as glossed by Goss, *Bibliography*, p.98.
366. G.J.Holyoake, *Secularism a religion which gives heaven no trouble* (London: Watts and Co., 1882).
367. Andrew Bibby, *All Our Own Work: the co-operative pioneers of Hebden Bridge and their mill* (London: Merlin Press, 2015), p.103. Bibby's is the most recent and accessible as well as the best analysis of this debate so far. I owe all the references to Hebden Bridge and some of the references to *Co-operative News* concerning this debate to Bibby's work.
368. A learned co-operator and historian (and author of a brief study of Holyoake), W.H.Brown, modestly adding 'so far as I have been able to trace', thought that the first usage of the 'co-operative commonwealth' within the movement was an address by Dr Garth Wilkinson to the members of the St John's Wood (London) Co-operative Society in 1866; see *The Co-operative Manager* (National Co-operative Managers' Association, 1937), p.60. For this reference, see Keith Harding, 'The "Co-operative Commonwealth": Ireland, Larkin, and the *Daily Herald*', in Stephen Yeo ed., *New Views of Co-operation* (London: Routledge, 1988), pp.88–107. In Gregory Claeys, *Citizens and Saints: Politics and anti-politics in early British socialism* (Cambridge: Cambridge University Press, 1989), p.281, n.67, there is a possible reference to the use of the co-operative commonwealth during the 1850s, but it is not entirely clear that this is so.

369. *Co-operative News*, vol.xxi (1890), p.564.
370. The Mitchell quotations are from the Reports of Co-*operative Congress* (1887) p.7 and (1893), p.132, cited in Stephen Yeo, *Who Was J. T. W. Mitchell?* (Manchester: CWS Membership Services, 1995).
371. *Co-operative Congress Report* (1887), p.7.
372. Royal Commission on Labour. Mitchell's Evidence was given on October 25th 1893; see *Evidence before RC on Labour 1893–4* XXXIX pt.1, Questions 1–405., particularly Questions 372–3 and 293.
373. Joseph Greenwood of the Hebden Bridge Society used 'self-employment' in a co-operative (worker, producer or bonus to labour) setting (rather than in its modern, small-capitalist setting) in *A Brief Sketch of Twenty-one Years' Work in Co-operative Production* (Hebden Bridge: The Hebden Bridge Fustian Manufacturing Society, 1891, revised in 1896). I owe this reference to Andrew Bibby.
374. The best treatment of 'Working-class Limiteds' that I know, particularly in the coal-mining industry, is in G.D.H. Cole, *A Century of Co-operation* (Manchester: G. Allen and Unwin for The Co-operative Union, 1945).
375. For Lewis's in this context by a (then) labour historian, see Asa Briggs, *Friends of the People. The Centenary History of Lewis's* (London:B.T.Batsford, 1956).
376. Benjamin Jones, *Co-operative Production*, pp.248–251. This discussion can also be followed in *Co-operative News*, vol.xv, 1884, pp.368–9 and 370–1.
377. Stephen Yeo, 'Co-operation, Mutuality, and the Democratic Deficit or Re-membering Democracy' and 'Theorizing Co-operative Studies: obstacles and opportunities for twenty-first century Co-operative and Mutual Enterprises', in Ian Macpherson and Erin Mclaughlin eds., *Integrating Diversities within a Complex Heritage: essays in the field of Co-operative Studies* (British Columbia Institute for Co-operative Studies, University of Victoria, Canada, New Rochdale Press: 2008), pp.223–276 and 345–389; and Stephen Yeo, *Co-operative and Mutual Enterprises in Britain: Ideas from a useable past for a modern future* (London School of Economics, Centre for Civil Society, Report Series, no.4: 2002).
378. A. Chandler, *Scale and Scope: The Dynamics of Industrial Capitalism* (Cambridge Mass: Harvard University Press, 1990) for, as it were, 'Competition's' view on this, including a critique of the CWS's preferences, and J.F.Wilson, A.Webster and R.Vorberg-Rugh, *Building Co-operation* (Oxford: Oxford University Press, 2013), pp.95–6 for a more Co-operative take on the same, federal choices.

379. Bibby (2015), pp.106-7. The proposal was to restructure co-operative production in Britain so that each manufacturing works would be independently constituted but federated through the CWS which would hold shares in each. The CWS would not run the business from the centre. This is a great historical might-have-been.

380. For which see Jim Lamb and Steve Warren, *The People's Store: A Guide to the North Eastern Co-op's Family Tree* produced to mark the retirement of David Skinner, a Director from 1974 to 1996, a special limited hardback edition of which is in the NCA (privately published by the Society); and J.F.Wilson, A.Webster and R.Vorberg-Rugh, *Building Co-operation* (Oxford: Oxford University Press, 2013), pp.306-7.

381. 'Realising' rather than 'abolishing' contradictions is a nice distinction made by Marx in volume one of *Capital*.

382. Beatrice Webb put the language of 'federalists' versus 'individualists' into common currency; see Bibby (2015), pp.111-112. My *Who was J. T. W. Mitchell?* is full of more denigratory language.

383. *Co-operative News*, vol.xviii (1887), p.1044.

384. Andrew Bibby, *All our Own Work: the co-operative pioneers of Hebden Bridge and their mill* (London: Merlin Press, 2015), p.113.

385. *Co-operative News*, vol xviii, 1887, p.1044.

386. Greening, *Holyoake* pp.22-24. His judgement is amplified in an interesting and very personal paragraph of the kind which could only be written by an admiring friend.

387. McCabe, *Life and Letters*, vol.2, p.178.

388. McCabe, *Life and Letters*, vol.2, p.149.

389. Holyoake, *Co-operative Movement Today*, 1903 edition, pp.187-8.

390. McCabe, *Life and Letters* vol.2, p.149, and p.264: 'the hundred interests in secular causes that he had once thought to bind up in one organisation were now entrusted to a hundred intent and specialised bodies'.

391. Holyoake, *History of Co-operation*, p.xv, 'Preface of 1875'.

392. Holyoake, 'Co-operation and Socialism', 1890, p.95.

393. Holyoake, *History of Co-operation*, 'Preface 1906', *p.xi*. This may have been the last piece Holyoake wrote, see W.H.Brown, *George Jacob Holyoake* (London and Leicester n.d, but 1906), pp.12-3.

394. Holyoake, *Rochdale Pioneers*, pp.112-3.

395. Holyoake, *Rochdale Pioneers* 10th edition, 1907, p.184.

396. Holyoake, *Sixty Years*, II, p.304.

397. Holyoake, *History of Co-operation*, p.658.
398. *Co-operative News*, vol xxxiii 1902 p.602. I owe this and subsequent references to *Co-operative News* to Andrew Bibby.
399. See *Labour Co-Partnership*, vol.1, 1894–5.
400. Goss, *Brief Life*, p.lxiv.
401. *Co-operative News*, vol.xviii (1887), p.1044.
402. *Co-operative News*, vol.xxv, no. 36 (1894), p.100.
403. *Co-operative News*, vol.xxvi, 1895 no., 24 June 15^{th,} p.605. And the *Report of the Co-operative Congress* (1895).
404. Andrew Bibby, *All our Own Work: the co-operative pioneers of Hebden Bridge and their mill* (London: Merlin Press, 2015), pp.123–4 traces the mutation of the Labour Association into the Labour Co-partnership Association (1901), the Industrial Co-partnership Association (1928), the Industrial Participation Association (1972), and the Involvement and Participation Association (1989) 'It continues to operate today, using the strap-line "raising performance through workplace engagement"'. The Holyoake quote is from Holyoake, *Rochdale Pioneers* 10th edition 1907, p.1. Greening, *Holyoake* 1917, pp.21–23 gives a good account of his own work for 'Industrial Partnerships' and for 'the friends of Co-partnership and Co-operation' from 1865 onwards.
405. Quoted by Andrew Bibby in *All our Own Work: the co-operative pioneers of Hebden Bridge and their mill* (London: Merlin Press, 2015), p.122.
406. Holyoake, *Rochdale Pioneers* 10th edition, 1907, pp.182–3.
407. Thomas Hughes and Edward Vansittart Neale, *Foundations: a study in the Ethics and Economics of the Co-operative Movement, prepared at the request of the Co-operative Congress held at Gloucester in April 1879, revised in 1915 by Stoddart, A. and Clayton, W.* (Manchester: The Co-operative Union, 1915, 1st edition 1879). In subsequent Notes I refer to this as Hughes and Neale, *Foundations*.
408. Holyoake, *The Trial of Theism*, pp.173–174, headed 'The Secular sphere, subjects, and modes of action' includes this idea about local Athenaeums, of which there was an active example in late nineteenth century Reading.
409. Stephen Yeo, *Religion and Voluntary Organisations in Crisis* (London: Croom Helm, 1976). All references to the Reading Industrial Co-operative Society (and to the Reading Athenaeum) are collected and classified in the Index, pp.418–9; and my 'A New Life: The Religion of Socialism in Britain 1883–1896', in *History Workshop; a journal of socialist*

historians, Issue 4, Autumn 1977, pp.5-56.

410. For Tom Mann, see my 'A New Life', in the Note preceding this one, and Percy Redfern, *Journey Towards Understanding* (London: Allen and Unwin, 1946). Redfern also wrote the first full Histories of the CWS, interesting because of his own earlier 'journey' and because of his critical commitment to the Society. See *The Story of the CWS* (Manchester: CWS, 1913) and *The New History of the CWS* (London: J. M. Dent and Sons, and the CWS).

411. Holyoake, *Sixty Years*, II, pp.290-4.

412. This deserves a separate book. For decades now there have been calls for socialists to dig among their moral and ethical roots. These go back to E.P. Thompson's view in 1960 (quoted among my epigraphs to this book) in a collection of essays which Thompson edited and to which Alasdair MacIntyre contributed, that it would be 'foolish... to underestimate the long and tenacious revolutionary tradition of the British commoner .... (which) has expressed itself most naturally in the language of moral revolt', E.P.Thompson, 'Revolution', *Out of Apathy* (London: New Left Books, Stevens and Sons, 1959), p.308. MacIntyre's challenge, in the same book (p.196), was that 'the academic' nowadays, 'does not seek to be in any sense a prophet of hope; indeed the very notion seems to him pretentious and vulgar; see his 'Breaking the Chains of Reason', pp.195-240. More recently, Simon Critchley, *The Faith of the Faithless: Experiments in Political Theology* (London: Verso, 2012) (reviewed in *Saturday Guardian,* 4th February 2012 by Stuart Kelly) wrote that 'rather than seeing modernity in terms of a process of secularisation I will claim that the history of political forms can best be viewed as a series of metamorphoses of sacralisation'. Oscar Wilde, Kelly wrote in his review of Critchley, dreamed of a 'confraternity of the Faithless...where on an altar, on which no taper burned, a priest, in whose heart peace had no dwelling, might celebrate with unblessed bread and a chalice empty of wine'. Kelly's question is : 'how can those who cannot (his emphasis) "believe" reclaim from the vestiges of religion the moral authority and political radicalism it once had?'. '"Everything to be true must become a religion"', said Wilde. How could secular societies find a binding mechanism that effectively replaced traditional forms of unity? Alain de Botton is in this territory too, in his *Religion for Atheists* (2011), as is Terry Eagleton's recent work.

413. G.J.Holyoake, *The uselessness of prayer* (London: Holyoake and Co., 1860).

414. My own take on 'religions' is an open, even a loose one. They are

chosen rather than proven (in any scientific sense), and may be understood as inherited, invented or imposed sets of beliefs which attach to symbolic as well as to practical ways of making, doing and meeting here and now, and/or at some other time and place. 'Religions' may be understood as invented or received (from wherever or whoever) sets of beliefs, symbolic practices and imposed (as well as chosen) ways of living, often linked to forms of association which – to varying degrees – acquire a sacred character for their adherents. The force of 'invented or received' in this description of 'religions' is to allow for *varieties* of belief and forms of association within the categories 'religion' and 'religious', as opposed to limiting them, say, to 'supernatural' – or, for that matter to experientially proven – beliefs. Tom Holland takes an even looser view of 'religions'. Thinking about the Isis death cult and the religious roots of Islamic State he recently wrote that: 'Religions are not abstract entities that have some Platonic essence: they are essentially " the spectrum of those at a given time who choose to interact with a corpus of traditions and texts, and emphasise what they choose to emphasise"' - quoted in *New Statesman*, 12 March 2015, p.5. See also his, 'We must not deny the religious roots of Islamic State' in *New Statesman,* 17 March 2015. Another very 'open' approach to 'religion' is that of the anthropologist Bruno Latour. 'Religion' is, for Latour, a 'mode of existence', alongside other such modes such as law, and morality. See his *An Inquiry into Modes of Existence: an anthropolgy of the moderns* translated by Catherine Porter (Cambridge Mass.: Harvard University Press, 2013). In a review of this work (*Times Literary Supplement,* 10 January 2014) Jonathan Rée explains these 'modes of existence' as attempts to provide a vocabulary for framing even-handed descriptions of different kinds of society, serving, for Latour, as the basis for a 'symmetrical anthropology' freed from any bias towards the 'moderns'. As one such mode, Latour sees 'religion as essentially a thesaurus of "words of love" – words that can <u>summon us out of apathy, inspiring resilience in the face of discouragement</u>' (my underlining of Rée's words).

415. See Peter L. Berger, 'Some Second Thoughts on Substantive versus Functional Definitions of Religion', in *Journal for the Scientific Study of Religion,* vol.13, no. 2, June 1974, pp.125–133.

416. See J.E.M Latham, *Search for a New Eden, James Pierrepont Greaves (1777–1842): The Sacred Socialist and His Followers* (London: Associated Presses, 1999); and W. Hamish Fraser, *Alexander Campbell and the Search for Socialism* (Manchester: Holyoake Books, 1996).

417. 'Today no one could ask why religion should be taken seriously. Those who used to dismiss religion are terrified by the intensity of its revival', John Gray 'Lambs to the slaughter', in *New Statesman* 26 Sept.-2 October 2014 pp.62-65, reviewing Karen Armstrong, *Fields of Blood: Religion and the History of Violence* (London Bodley Head 2014). See also Michael Walzer, *The Paradox of Liberation: Secular revolutions and religious counterrevolutions* (New Haven and London: Yale University Press 2014 or 2015). And, for a box of fireworks, open Slavoj Zizek, *Living in the End Times* (London: Verso, 2010).

418. See Gregor McLennan, 'Mr Love and Justice', a review essay on Terry Eagleton's *Reason Faith and Revolution* (Yale: New Haven 2009) in *New Left Review* 64, July- August 2010, pp.139-149.

419. John Gray, *Journal*, in *The Guardian* Tuesday March 3rd 2015 pp.30-31. 'There is no sign anywhere of religion fading away.... The resurgence of religion is a worldwide development'. This essay by Gray seeks to connect 'the new atheism' and atheism as an 'organized movement' with 'an alternative belief system - typically, a set of ideas that serves to show the modern west is the high point of human development.'

420. The title of a seminal essay by Max Weber, in Hans Gerth and C. Wright Mills, eds., *From Max Weber: essays in sociology* (London: Routledge and Kegan Paul, 1948); see also Roland Robertson, 'The Development and Implications of the Classical Sociological Perspective on Religion and Revolution', and the case studies in Bruce Lincoln ed. *Religion, Rebellion, Revolution: an interdisciplinary and cross-cultural collection of essays* (London: Macmillan, 1985).

421. Peter Berger, *The Social Reality of Religion* (London: Longman 1969). For the porous boundaries between the religious and the secular see David Martin, *Religion and Power: no logos without mythos* (Aldershot: Ashgate, 2014), and Karen Armstrong *Fields of Blood, Religion and the history of violence* (London: Bodley Head, 2013), and Jonathan Benthall 'Poplars in the marsh', a review of both these books in the *Times Literary Supplement* December 12th 2014, pp.7-9. And Edward Walker, *Treasure Beneath the Hearth, Myth, Gospel and Spirituality Today* (Winchester, UK, and Washington USA: Christian Alternative Books, 2015), pp.12, 17, 53, 92.

422. John Bossy, 'Some Elementary Forms of Durkheim', in *Past and Present* no. 95(1), 1982, pp.3-18. The quotations from Durkheim are taken by Bossy from *Elementary Forms of the Religious Life* (1915), translated by J. W. Swain (London, 1915), 2nd edition with Introduction by R. Nisbet (London: 1976) p.225, and from Steven Lukes, *Emile Durkheim, his Life and Work* (New York: Harper and Row, 1973) p.233. Durkheim

'appeared to believe that a secular religion is possible – in other words that people can gain the benefits of religion while regarding it as a social construction, but no such faith has yet emerged.' M Prowse, 'Emile Durkheim', *Prospect* (February 2005), p.55.

423. See Peter Berger 'The desecularization of the world, a global overview', in P.L Berger, *The Desecularization of the World*, (Washington, DC, Ethics and Public Policy Centre 1999). My own interest in this began with David Martin's work in the 1960s, for instance *The Religious and the Secular: studies in secularization* (London: Routledge and Kegan Paul, 1969), and with Alasdair MacIntyre, *Secularisation and Moral Change* (Oxford: Oxford University Press, 1967). More recently, see Callum G. Brown, *The Death of Christian Britain: Understanding Secularisation 1800–1900* (London and New York: Routledge, 2001, 2nd edition, 2009). In the words of a reviewer (Jeremy Morris) in the *Historical Journal*, Brown has 'simultaneously rejected more strenuously than ever before the long tradition of British historiography that sought to apply the concept of secularization to the late nineteenth and early twentieth centuries and at once reapplied the concept exclusively and dramatically to the last forty years'. But see also D. Nash 'Reconnecting religion with social and cultural history: secularization's failure as a master narrative', in *Cultural and Social History*, vol.1, 2004, pp.302-335; and H. Mcleod, *Secularisation in Western Europe 1848-1914* (Basingstoke: Macmillan, 2000). David Martin has revisited his *A General Theory of Secularisation* (Oxford: Basil Blackwell, 1978) in *On Secularisation: towards a revised general theory* (Aldershot: Ashgate, 2005).

424. See the works of Karen Armstrong, for example, *The Case for God: what religion really means* (London: Vintage Books edition, 2010).

425. Hughes and Neale, *Foundations*, 1915 edition, pp.87, 24.

426. Earl Grey, *What Co-operation will do for the People* (1898) pp.4-5, 8, quoted in Andrew Bibby, *All Our Own Work* (2015), p.122.

427. Tithes were an issue for Holyoake from his childhood days in Birmingham when they hit his own family hard,and then in his business in Fleet St London; see Holyoake, *Sixty Years*, I, pp.251-253.

428. See Alasdair MacIntyre, 'The Essential Contestability of Some Social Concepts', in *Ethics*, vol.84, no. 1 (October 1973), pp.1-9. And Raymond Williams, *Keywords, a vocabulary of culture and society* (London: Fontana, 1976) 'Introduction', p.15.

429. For Weber on 'theodicy' see Richard Swedberg, Ola Agevall, *The Max Weber Dictionary: Key Words and Central Concepts* (Stanford: Stanford

University Press, 2005), p.274.
430. For this and the immediately preceding quotation, see Goss, *Brief Life*, pp.xl-xli.
431. Holyoake, *Sixty Years*, II, pp.290-4.
432. Holyoake, *Sixty Years*, I, pp.139-140.
433. Holyoake, *Sixty Years*, II, p.294, n.1 For another liberal, progressive-nonconformist appreciation of Holyoake see Dr John Clifford, *George Jacob Holyoake: full and revised report of a sermon delivered by Dr John Clifford MA on Sunday Evening, Feb 4th, 1906* (London: T. Fisher Unwin, 1906). Clifford also delivered an *Address... on the occasion of the Unveiling of the Memorial to George Jacob Holyoake in Highgate Cemetery, London, on November 9th 1907* (Manchester: Cooperative Union Ltd, 1907).
434. McCabe, *Life and Letters*, I, pp.209-211, 228-236.
435. Holyoake, *Bygones* I, 206-7.
436. Holyoake, *Sixty Years*, II, p.292.
437. Holyoake, *Sixty Years*, II, p.290.
438. Holyoake, *Sixty Years*, II, p.290.
439. MacPherson, *Background 1996*, pp.6 and 11.
440. Holyoake, *Sixty Years*, II, pp.290-2.
441. Holyoake's argument with Bradlaugh is described succinctly in *Sixty Years*, II, pp.293-4.
442. Holyoake, *Sixty Years*, II, pp.290-4.
443. Goss, *Brief Life*, p.xxiv
444. Holyoake, *Sixty Years*, I, p.141.
445. Goss, *Brief Life*, p.xxix. In Goss's opinion, for Holyoake 'the secular was sacred'.
446. Goss, *Brief Life*, p lv
447. G.J.Holyoake (writing under the pseudonym, 'A London Zulu'), *Cumming wrong: Colenso right: a reply to the Rev. Dr Cumming's "Moses right, Colenso wrong"*. Holyoake suggests that 'the form of religion which alone can be received by those whom Christians desire to convert (is) that which recognizes the natural powers of man, and insists on morality as its essence, rather than on creeds and articles', Goss, *Bibliography*, p.32.
448. Holyoake, *Sixty Years*, II, pp.202-4.
449. Holyoake, *Sixty Years*, I, p.206.

450. Holyoake, *Sixty Years*, II, pp.202-4.
451. For 'the co-operative mind', see Holyoake, *The Co-operative Movement Today* 1903 edition, p.21.
452. Holyoake, *Sixty Years*, I, p.184.
453. Goss, *Brief Life*, p.xxxi.
454. Holyoake, *Co-operative Movement Today*, 1903 edition, chap. xxiv, pp.179-192.
455. Holyoake, *Leeds* 1897,p.33
456. *Proceedings of the Third Co-operative Congress held in London... on the 23rd of April 1832, reported and edited by order of the Congress by William Carpenter* (London: William Strange, 1832), p.100.
457. Holyoake, *Leeds* 1897, p.33
458. Holyoake, *Derby* 1903, p.128.
459. Holyoake, *Sixty Years*, I, pp.138-140.
460. Holyoake, *Sixty Years*, I, pp.138-140.
461. In his 1892 Introduction to the English edition of his *Socialism: Utopian and Scientific'*, Engels wrote (in English) of the possibly 'dangerous' Salvation Army 'which revives the propaganda of early Christianity, appeals to the poor as the elect, fights capitalism in a religious way, and thus fosters an element of early Christian class antagonism, which one day may become troublesome to the well-to-do people who now find the ready money for it', see Marx, Engels, Lenin, *On Historical Materialism* (USSR: Progress Publishers, 1972), p.250.
462. Most notably by Ted Royle. See the earlier references in my Bibliography. Perhaps it was a sense of an unwelcome family resemblance between the 'religious' and the 'secular' or the porousness of the relationship between them which made the latter so threatening to the former. See Bruce Lincoln, 'Notes toward a Theory of Religion and Revolution', in *Religion, Rebellion, Revolution: an interdisciplinary and cross-cultural collection of essays* (Basingstoke: Macmillan Press, 1985), pp.266- 292, especially n. 11 on p.285. For the 'religiosity' of secularism see Susan Budd, 'The Loss of Faith: Reasons for Unbelief among Members of the Secular Movement in England, 1850-1950, *Past and Present*, 36 (1967).
463. Christopher Dawson, *The Gods of Revolution* (New York: Minerva, 1975), p.83. For further Robespierre references in this context see Bruce Lincoln's essay in the immediately preceding note, at his n.42, on p.289.
464. Karen Armstrong, *Fields of Blood: Religion and the History of Violence* (London: Bodley Head, 2014).

465. Holyoake, *Co-operative Movement Today*, 1903 edition, p.78.
466. Peter Gurney, 'The Middle Class Embrace: language, representation and the contest over Co-operative form in Britain 1860- 1914 ', in *Victorian Studies* 37/2 (1994), pp.253–286. See also my entry on 'co-operative association' in Tom Bottomore ed., *A Dictionary of Marxist Thought* (Oxford: Blackwell, 1983) pp.95–6, for Marx's openness to an 'associated mode of production. '
467. With the possible exceptions of Denmark and Sweden.
468. Goss, *Brief Life*, pp.li-ii.
469. Holyoake, *Sixty Years* I, pp.245–253, 'Perturbation in Whitehaven'.
470. Holyoake, *Bygones*, vol.2, p.115
471. Holyoake, *The Trial of Theism*, p.132.
472. Holyoake, *Sixty Years*, II, pp.142–148
473. Holyoake, *Sixty Years*, I, p.244.
474. See also V.A Demant, *Religion and the Decline of Capitalism* (London: Faber and Faber, 1952). Like R.H Tawney's *Religion and the Rise of Capitalism*, Demant's book derived from his Scott Holland Lectures, in Demant's case delivered in 1949.
475. Among recent experts, Birchall has warned against inflated claims for what he prefers to call, quite simply, 'member-owned businesses'; see Johnston Birchall, *People-Centred Businesses: Co-operatives, Mutuals and the Idea of Membership* (Palgrave Macmillan, Basingstoke and New York, 2011), p.210: 'there have often been theorists who, on discovering the idea of a member-based economy become excited about its potential to cure many ills. They see it is a replacement for capitalism …. We have to appreciate the potential of members-ownership but not put more weight on it than it can bear'.
476. See an interview with George Lakoff by Zoe Williams in *The Guardian* in Feb. 2014, see Http://www.theguardian.com/books/2014/feb/01/George-lakoff-interview. In 'Synergia' e mail exchanges, Yvon Poirier from Quebec in Canada warned the Synergia project to be careful about over-using the 'economy' and 'economic' language at the outset of the project. On 14.04 2014 she expressed a commitment to words like "life" or the Japanese 'Seikatsu' a concept similar to livelihood, or 'the conscious and non-submissive activity of ordinary people in shaping their lives'. The point is not to divide the spirit(ual) from matter or the material.
477. This sentence is from an encouraging reaction by Pat Connaty to an

earlier draft of this book. A fellow of the New Economics Foundation and a Research Associate of Co-ops UK, Connaty now thinks that 'cultivating the co-operative zeitgeist will be key....Gandhi called this the Swadeshi spirit'. He advocates a 'maximalist perspective', going along with Roberto Ungar's talks in London during November 2013, for which see http://www.nesta.org.uk/sites/default/files/professor unger social frontiers transcript.pdf. Connaty finds it 'impossible without a Gandhian model for winning heads, hearts and souls to transcend fear and the Grand Inquisitor barriers that just send everyone back to marginal improvement tinkering and efforts to repair a sinking economy ship running out of fossil fuels fast'. He also points to the more-than-fragments of a line of thought and action (a tradition?) which includes the work of Holyoake, but which is the subject for another, bigger book than mine. Tracking back from Gandhi (and Bhikhu Parekh's books on Gandhi's political philosophy, and the roots of soul force and truth force or Satygraha), Connaty would trace a line through Guild Socialism and G.D.H Cole; one of Cole's students, Geoffrey Ostergaard and his work on Co-operatives and his links with the Gandhi foundation; the work of E.F Schumacher who inspired the Gandhi Foundation as well as the New Economics Foundation, Schumacher College and the Soil Association; the Black Quaker leader in the USA, Bayard Rustin, who was Martin Luther King's mentor and went head to head with Malcolm X on how social and economic change in the USA could become transformative ... and many others. 'It is this soul force and truth force karma', writes Connaty, 'that is the massive gaping hole we need to fill again and this is needed very badly now.'

Index

America, 63
Aneskantavada, 168
Armstrong, Karen, 77
Association of All Classes of All Nations, 22, 25, 185
association
  by working people, 13, 36, 69-72
  importance to individuals, 78, 79, 90
  maxims of association, 33, 140-141
  of co-operatives, 45, 96, 99, 104, 150
  philosophy, 39, 138
associationism, 12, 19, 36
autonomy and independence, 89

Baernreither, J. M., 19
Barrington, Bishop, 106
Baume, Peter, 60-62, 165
Bellers, John, 62-63
Benjamin, Walter, 19
Berger, Peter, 161
Bernard, Sir Thomas, 106
Bibby, Andrew, 148
Birmingham Political Union, 27
blasphemy trial, 26-27, 77
Blatchford, Robert, 159
bonus to labour, 46, 135-137, 141-157
Bradlaugh, Charles, 64, 169
Bright, John, 166
Brighton, 24
Bromley, Mr, 126-127
Burnley Co-operative Society, 95-98
Bury Co-operative Society, 58
Bygones Worth Remembering (GJH), 87

Campbell, Alexander, 11
capital, 9, 37, 81-86, 92
capital and co-operation, 115, 122
capital and labour, 47, 145, 151-157
character, 12-13, 37-38, 45, 67
charity, 40
Chartists, 84, 86, 87
cheese, 123

Chesterton, G. K., 75
children's books, 23
Christian Socialists, 49, 64, 84, 101, 115, 162-163
Civil Service Supply Associations, 95
class ideology, 32, 46
Cobden, Richard, 94
Code of the ... Society of Secularists (GJH), 140
communism, 73, 74, 76, 93
competition and co-operation, 15, 54
conflict, 81-86
Cooper, William, 27-28, 49, 135-137
co-operation
  ancient concept, 66, 119
  and capital, 115, 122
  and competition, 15, 54
  between co-operatives, 100
  character, 67, 68
  definition, 130
  moral tradition, 35-36, 74-80
  system, 103-104
Co-operative College, 29
Co-operative Commonwealth, 132
Co-operative Congress
  commissioning work, 76, 162
  GJH involvement, 27-28, 30, 41, 63, 154-156
  Owenite, 78, 130-132, 173-174
  reports, 41-42
  Rochdale, 115, 135, 156
  speeches, 100, 144, 154-156
Co-operative Group, 116, 147
co-operative ideas, 34
Co-operative Miscellany, 129
co-operative movement state within a state, 8, 99-105, 116
Co-operative Movement Today (GJH), 52, 75, 81, 100, 138
Co-operative News, 41, 52, 146, 154
co-operative principles, 118, 129, 131, 132-134, 138, 141-157

241

Co-operative Union
Holyoake House, 53, 54, 56
leaders, 12, 44, 101, 154-155
national federation, 9, 154-155
publications, 41-42, 120, 162-163
co-operative values, 109, 133
Co-operative Wholesale Society
bonus to labour, 135, 143-147, 155
branding, 95-96, 98
leaders, 11, 64, 101, 144-145, 154
scale, 42, 43, 81, 100, 147, 153
co-operatives
and state, 116
bonus to labour, 46, 135-137, 141-157
civic rivalry, 101
committees, 58
communities and tradition, 78-79, 105-113, 116-119
development, 42, 44-45, 68, 74, 75-77, 80, 93-94, 110, 115, 129-130, 174
dissent without separation, 59, 113, 141
dividend, 46, 115
education, 38, 52, 59-60, 69-70, 167
employers, 64, 90, 92, 103, 130, 135-137, 141-157
members, 64, 115-117, 131-132, 145-146, 158
models, 95
moral philosophy and ethics, 105-108, 134
music, 38
obstacles, 58, 95
political and religious neutrality, 80, 132, 135-137, 168, 172
pre-Rochdale, 106, 119, 129-130
production, 52, 123-124, 146-149, 154-155, 163
religion, 64, 157-182
self-help, 44, 85
social improvements, 51, 54, 67, 85, 93-94
stories used for inspiration, 120-128
truth and honesty, 64
vested interests, 64-65
Co-operatives UK, 9
co-partnership, 155
Counsellor, 135-137, 151, 164
Cromer, 181-182

Denholme Industrial Co-operative Society, 100
Derby Co-operative Society, 29-30, 37, 63, 92, 174

Earnshaw, Isaac, 142
Economical Society, London, 46
education
co-operative, 38, 52, 59-60, 69-70, 167
GJH's interest in, 23, 31-32, 139
Eliot, George, 10, 87
Ellis, John, 63
Engels, Friedrich, 74, 80
equity, 30, 36, 109, 152
ethical criticism, 32
explanation and persuasion, 55

Foote, G. W., 140
Foundations: a study in the ethics and economics of the co-operative movement (Hughes and Neale), vii, 76-77, 157, 162
Fox, George, 63-64
France, 42, 177
freethought, 34
French, Mr, 62
funeral orations, 49, 50

Gandhi, 79
Garden City Association, 82
Garibaldi, 81
gentlemen and workmen, 69-70, 90
Gladstone, William Ewert, 10, 16, 47, 68-69, 95, 117, 154
Godin, Jean-Baptiste, 16
Goss, Charles, 11, 165, 170
government, 25, 88-89, 99
Gray, J. C., 44, 52, 147, 155
Greaves, James Pierrepont, 60-61
Greening, Edward Owen, 16, 32, 48, 120, 149
Grey, Earl, 163
Grocers' Association, 95
Groves, Catherine (GJH's mother), 21
Gruyère cheese, 123

Halifax, 29
Ham Common Concordium, 60-61
Hebden Bridge Fustian Manufacturing

242

INDEX

Co-operative Society, 12, 41, 44, 64, 83, 148, 154
Hetherington, Henry, 49, 85
History of Co-operation (GJH), viii, 32, 34, 51, 60, 73, 118, 121, 138, 184
History of Co-operation in Halifax (GJH), 29
History of the Travelling Tax (GJH), 88
Hobson, J. A., 30
Holyoake, Austen (GJH's brother), 22-23
Holyoake, Eveline, (GJH's daughter), 23
Holyoake, George (GJH's father), 21-22, 63
Holyoake, George Jacob
activist and advocate, 12, 26-28, 30-32, 84, 111, 149-150, 167
avoidance of anger and violence, 51, 74, 83, 179-181
birth and childhood, 7, 21
character, 33
death and memorial, 8, 53, 54, 56, 81
debating style, 48, 51, 55, 59-60
descriptions of self, 15-16, 28, 66
education, 7, 8, 23, 31-32, 139
family, 21-24
financial situation, 23, 24
flexibility, 13, 15
'Grand Old Man', 42, 44
historian and promotor of co-operation, 28-30, 45, 120
humour and irreverence, 15, 51, 60
journalism, editing and publishing, 18, 22-23, 28-30, 104, 139-140
language creative use, 12, 36-38, 74, 114-119
language new terms, 55, 65-66, 114-115, 165
language preferences, 47, 129
legacy, 8, 9, 183-185
mathematics, 31, 139, 169
on co-operation, 30, 66, 96, 112, 118
Owenite, 22, 25, 45
parliamentary candidate, 28
politics, 13, 26, 28, 32, 67-69, 87, 93, 149
relationship with International Co-operative Alliance, 153
relationship with Rochdale Society, 135-137, 151

religion and belief, 48, 49, 64-66, 77, 88, 132, 135-140, 157-182
shoe brand, 96, 98
social and political reform, 86-99, 111
socialist missionary, 94, 139, 170
speeches, 27-28, 48, 49, 50, 148, 179, 181-182
stature and voice, 48
storytelling examples, 60-61, 119-128, 151-152, 181-182
storytelling parable and fable, 10-12, 18-19, 25, 114, 160, 164
trial for blasphemy, 26-27, 77
war and conflict, 81-86, 88-89, 94, 177-178
whitesmith, 7, 21-22
writing style, 10, 11-15, 18, 25, 34, 37, 114
Holyoake House, Manchester, 53, 54, 56
Holyoake, Madeline (GJH's daughter), 23
Holyoake, Malthus (GJH's son), 23
Holyoake, Manfred (GJH's son), 23
Holyoake, Maximilian Robespierre (GJH's son), 23
Howard, Abraham, 135-137, 151
Howard, Ebenezer, 82
Hughes, Hugh Price, 166
Hughes, Thomas, vii, 38, 76, 84, 144, 148, 156, 157, 162

imperialism, 55, 57
independence and autonomy, 89
Ingersoll, Robert Green, 32
International Co-operative Alliance, 153

jingoism, 55
Jones, Benjamin, 146
Jubilee History of the Derby Co-operative Provident Society (GJH), 29-30, 37, 63, 92, 174

labour
and capital, 47, 145, 151-157
bonus to labour, 46, 135-137, 145
divisions of, 57
position of, 7, 8, 37, 46, 47
wages, 46
Labour Association, 153

243

Labour Exchanges, 125-128
Labour Leader, 24, 159
Labour Party, 12, 159
language
creative use, 12, 36-38, 74, 114-119
new terms, 55, 65-66, 114-115, 165
preferences, 47, 129
Leader, The, 104
Leeds Co-operative Society, 54, 59, 91-92, 100, 105, 138, 142, 173, 174
Legacoop, 29
Lewes, George Henry, 10
Liberal Party, 13
liberalism, 67-69
Livesey, Thomas, 49
London
co-operation, 38, 78, 95, 123-124, 130
organizations, 22, 31, 46, 126
Ludlow, J. M., 157

MacIntyre, Alasdair, 106, 107-108, 110-113, 129, 164
MacPherson, Ian, 35, 79-80, 109-110, 133-134
Manchester Congress of the Universal Community Society of Rational Religionists, 170
Manchester Unity of Oddfellows, 38, 39-40, 76, 171
Mann, Tom, 144-145
Marriott, Reverend, 173-174
Martin, Emma, 49
Marx, Karl, 74, 85, 159
masters and employees, 103
Maurice, F. D., 49
Mayhew, Henry, 30
Mazzini, Guiseppe, 10, 13, 157, 166
McCabe, Joseph, 13, 15, 149, 150
McLennan, Gregor, 161
Mechanics Institute, Birmingham, 8, 22, 138
Mercer, T. W., 12
Mill, John Stuart, 68, 117
Mitchell, J. T. W., 11, 101, 144-145, 154
Moral Errors which Endanger the Permanence of Co-operative Societies (GJH), 58
morality

and religion, 27, 140, 165, 170
co-operation, vii, 12-13, 35, 58, 59, 70, 87, 120
economy, 9, 47
GJH, 8, 10, 39-40, 55, 57-59, 68, 180-181
tradition, 74-76, 90, 96, 105-113, 140, 183-184
Morris, William, 52, 59, 159
Movement, The, 22, 96
music, 38
mutuality, 81

National Charter Association, 27
Neale, Edward Vansittart, vii, 38, 76, 101, 148, 157, 162
New View of Society (Owen), 36
Newcastle, 124-125
Newman, F. W., 169
Northern Star, 57

oath-taking, 68
O'Connor, Feargus, 57
Oddfellows, 38, 39-40, 76, 171
Oracle of Reason, 22, 170
Origin and Nature of Secularism (GJH), 69
Owen, Robert
co-operation, 16, 67, 78, 130-132, 173-174
ideas, 12-13, 65, 86, 103, 104, 110
Labour Exchanges, 125-128
memorial, 49
Owenites, 22, 38, 94, 103
religion, 62, 64, 131, 160
Oxford, Bishop of, 171

Palmerston, 11
paramountcy, 57
Pare, William, 180
parliamentary elections, 15, 67, 86-90, 99
Pearson, Mary Jane (GJH's second wife), 24
people and the state, 25-26, 33-34, 83-84, 95, 103
persuasion and explanation, 55
Phillips, Commissioner, 179
Pitman, Isaac, 22
political and social reform, 86-99
poverty, 36, 67, 82, 106, 163
Principles of Secularism Briefly Explained

(GJH), 66, 139-140, 159
progression, 39-40
progress as human struggle, 93

Quakers, 62-64

Raiffeisen, Friedrich Wilhelm, 16
Rational Friendly Society, 41
Rationalist Press Association, 171
Reading Co-operative Society, 38, 158
Reasoner, The, 30, 39, 110, 113, 172
Redfern, Percy, 158
Reform League, 13, 27, 69
religion
co-operation, 64, 157-182
religious neutrality, 80, 132, 135-137, 168, 172
Robert Owen, 131, 160
toleration, 40, 48, 62-66, 77, 88, 132, 138-140
revolution, 81-86, 94, 96, 177
river, comparison with social movement, 72
Robespierre, 15, 176-177
Rochdale Pioneers
as legend and example, 49, 74, 95, 102, 104, 120, 122, 133, 151-152
duties of committee, 58
education, 59-60, 69-70
history, 13, 28-29, 45, 59, 70, 101, 115, 119-120, 134, 136, 151
relationship with GJH, 135-137, 151
Rosebery, Lord, 100
Royal Commission on Labour, 144-145
Rudiments of Public Speaking and Debate (GJH), 48
Rumford, Count, 106

Scottish Co-operative Wholesale Society, 146
Scotton, Amos, 29-30
sea, comparison with industrial world, 24-25, 72
secret ballot, 88-89
secularism
origins, 26, 65-66, 110
practice, 71, 77, 139-140, 157-158, 169
self-help

by working people, 32, 38, 55
legislation, 28
limitations, 68
through co-operatives, 44, 85, 96-97, 109
Self Help a Hundred Years Ago (GJH), 31-32, 105-106
Self Help by the People: the history of the Rochdale Pioneers (GJH), 13, 28-29, 45, 59, 70, 101, 115, 119-120, 134, 136, 151
Sennett, Richard, 119, 168
Sixty Years of an Agitator's Life (GJH), 15, 94, 165, 170, 175
Shaftesbury, Lord, 87
silk handkerchiefs, 123-124
Slavery, 116-117
Smiles, Samuel, 38, 67
Smithies, James, 49
social philosophy, 35
socialism, 73, 92-99, 111
solidarity, 59, 79-80, 108-110, 117
Southwell, Charles, 22
Spencer, Herbert, 68
state and the people, 25-26, 33-34, 83-84, 95, 103
state and co-operatives, 116
state reaction to activists, 83-84
Statement on the Co-operative Identity, 34, 59, 78, 114, 133, 158, 168
storytelling
examples, 60-61, 119-128, 151-152, 181-182
parable and fable, 10-12, 18-19, 25, 114, 160, 164
suffrage, 15, 67, 86-90, 99

Tawney, R. H., 183
Thompson, E. P., 184
tinsmith, 7, 21
toleration, 58, 65, 88, 132, 168, 171, 175
traditions, signs, 113-114
Travelling Tax Abolition Committee, 88
Trial of Theism (GJH), ix
truth
common, 141, 142, 152-153, 182
fundamental, 31, 39, 60, 68, 72, 131, 163, 175
in co-operatives, 64-65
necessary, 64-65, 129, 176, 181

245

whole, 142, 148, 168
Tyne Bridge, 124-125

union, 36, 89, 105, 117, 149, 156, 163
United Diversity Co-operative, 168
United Nations International Year of Co-operatives, 10
unity, 36, 38, 89, 117, 171-172
Uselessness of Prayer (GJH), 159
utopia, 36, 66, 80, 93, 107

violence, 51, 74, 81-86, 88-89, 94, 177-181
vote, 15, 67, 86-90, 99

Walpole, Spencer, 84
war, 81-86, 88-89, 94, 177-178
Webb, Beatrice, 142
Weber, Max, 37, 161, 164, 183
Whalley, H., 99-100
Whitehaven, 1790181
whitesmith, 7, 21
Williams, Eleanor (GJH's first wife), 23
Williams, Raymond, 75, 164
women, 15, 49
working people
and the state, 25-26, 33, 34, 83-84, 95, 103
association, 69-72
challenge to authority, 70, 117
radicalism, 16
workmen and gentlemen, 69-70, 90
world-making, 9, 66, 107
Wright, Daniel, 22